The Audition Room

The Audition Room
A Down To Earth Guide

Sharon Sorrentino

The Book Guild Ltd

Second Edition
First published in Great Britain in 2017 by
The Book Guild Ltd
9 Priory Business Park
Wistow Road, Kibworth
Leicestershire, LE8 0RX
Freephone: 0800 999 2982
www.bookguild.co.uk
Email: info@bookguild.co.uk
Twitter: @bookguild

First edition published by Calm Publishing in 2013

Copyright © 2017 Sharon Sorrentino

The right of Sharon Sorrentino to be identified as the author of this
work has been asserted by her in accordance with the
Copyright, Design and Patents Act 1988.

All rights reserved. No part of this publication may be
reproduced, transmitted, or stored in a retrieval system, in any form or by any means,
without permission in writing from the publisher, nor be otherwise circulated in
any form of binding or cover other than that in which it is published and without
a similar condition being imposed on the subsequent purchaser.

Typeset in Minion Pro

Printed and bound in the UK by TJ International, Padstow, Cornwall

ISBN 978 1911320 463

British Library Cataloguing in Publication Data.
A catalogue record for this book is available from the British Library.

CONTENTS

Introduction	vii
1. The Business of Show Business	1
2. Getting The Industry's Attention	33
3. Marketing Tools	61
4. The Casting Process	101
5. Preparing For The Audition	129
6. The Day of The Audition	154
7. Ready For My Close Up	181
8. Treading The Boards	209
9. Giving a Performance	240
10. Collaborative Work	271
Resources	307
Glossary	312
Author's Biography	314
Acknowledgments	315
Original Acknowledgments	319

INTRODUCTION

The aim of this book is to offer advice and tips to working actors and new graduates alike, on ways in which you can improve upon your position or get started on your chosen path. There is pragmatic guidance to aid you to get into the audition room itself then, once in those fateful auditions, how to make the most of your allotted time. The text is filled with practical and sage words of wisdom from a number of renowned industry professionals – actors, directors, casting directors, radio producers, voice artists, authors and acting coaches.

You need to acknowledge and accept the idea that 'the business' is just that, an enormous ever-revolving mechanical industry full of separate interlocking cogs. They keep on turning regardless of any particular individual, churning out production after production in all forms of media. Once you've grasped that, then you can begin to see yourself as a component part of it. Each section functions to bring together works of beauty or genius, every part is integral like the workings of a clock. You are an important piece of it but you have to keep on your toes because there are always another hundred actors, or more, stood behind you just as hungry for work, if not hungrier! And complacency can come back and bite you in the career. There's a precision to it all, which requires talent, professionalism, dedication, drive, passion, self-awareness and pragmatism. There is also luck and all the other variables that are out of your control, which will always play their part in your career, the hits and misses. Whilst you can't change those, you can make informed decisions and take control over the things it is in your power to impact upon.

Treat this book as a helpful insider within the audition room, someone who wants to help you with your chosen career. Each chapter builds upon the last but if you need tips on any particular thing you can always just flip forward to that section, just like you would ask a specific question of a helpful friend.

Good luck.

CHAPTER 1

THE BUSINESS OF SHOW BUSINESS

In this chapter we are going to look at the business side of the entertainment industry and what that means to you as an actor, creatively and financially, we'll look at:

- The monetary aspects you need to consider for the present and for the future.
- Breaking down some important myths and misconceptions about casting.
- Where and how to focus your attention.
- Your chosen career and objective goals.
- Aiding you to see where you are in the industry as a whole.
- Success, and an introduction to marketing.

THE BUSINESS OF SHOW

To put the economic side of the industry that you are a part of into context, here are some figures to mull over:

> 'From 1998 to 2010 the value of the worldwide entertainment industry grew from $449 billion (£285bn) to $745 billion (£474bn).'
>
> Mike Masnick, CEO of Floor64, USA

Mike Masnick made this statement in an interview for www.wired.co.uk in early 2012. You might ask yourself how this affects you personally as an actor? Well, our industry is turning a profit and more is being invested into production every minute, so you can share in that wealth. This big ol' pot of cash does not just stay within the industry, it adds to the GDP(1) of the country as a whole, as Dame Helen Alexander CBE said in an address in March 2010.

> 'By 2013, NESTA(2) expects there to be around 180,000 creative businesses in the UK, contributing as much as £85bn of added value to the economy – and 150,000 new jobs.'
>
> Dame Helen Alexander CBE, Chair of the Port of London Authority and Incisive Media, UK

So the industry is a really important part of the country's economy and you are a part of it. Though many working in it may feel there's no business like show business, there are plenty of other creative endeavours that consider their product, design and manufacture, an art form *and* they all need to be commercially viable. Let's tackle the idea that this business is primarily a 'Fine Art' now – fantastic creativity can certainly be achieved within it but that is not the primary function of the industry.

> 'It is a business.'
>
> Ann Mitchell, Actor and Director, UK

Is there much point in producing a theatrical show or film which feeds the soul and yet no one sees? For the artist possibly, but not for the backers. Those funding a project always want to envisage a great financial return – and why shouldn't they? – it is their money after all.

How important is it for actors to see themselves, or at least part of themselves, as a business? All the distinguished industry professionals interviewed said 'Very', that should tell us something. The financial side of 'the business' is a solid reality many actors ignore, but should in truth take their 'for my art' blinkers off and accept, Mark Bowden explains:

> 'We know acting's an art but actors also have a commercial responsibility to themselves and there's a lot they can learn from businesses in the way that businesses are able to create energy around them and also create some kind of wealth.'
>
> Mark Bowden, Author, UK

GET AN ACCOUNTANT; THEY'RE WORTH THEIR WEIGHT IN GOLD

So as an actor, what are you doing about the financial side of things?

- You have to register with the HMRC (Her Majesty's Revenue & Customs) as self employed within 3 months of earning monies which are not PAYE, or they can issue you with an unpleasant fine and they'll watch you for the smallest errors for years.
- HMRC will give you a unique tax reference number; it's a 10 digit number with a space in the middle. They used to be called 'Schedule D' numbers so if someone asks for your Schedule D that's just their old school way of speaking.

Most theatrical work, be it plays or musical theatre is paid by bankroll, you will receive payslips rather than having to invoice directly or via your agent. Most TV and film productions bankroll now too. If you look at a payslip you've received you will see how your fee is broken down into each financial obligation, National Insurance is often taken at source unless you are trading as a limited company which is now getting harder for individuals to do.

How are you going to pay your NI contributions?

- Class 2 is paid on profits of £5,965.00 or more. Class 4 percentages are 9% on profits between £8,060.00 and £42,385.00 and 2% on profits over £42,385.00.
- From 2015-2016 Class 2 will be paid along with Class 4 with your Self-Assessment. Both will be worked out at the end of the financial year by the HMRC or your accountant and you'll be advised as to what you owe.
- If you expect your profits to be less than £5,965.00 you may not have to pay Class 2 contributions. However, you may still want to as Class 2 goes towards your state benefits and pensions. Personally I'd suggest you do pay the voluntary amount as you never know if you may find you need those benefits.

As a self-employed individual, how are you going to work out if/what you can claim against your tax?

- Keep all your receipts for the financial year (6th April to the following 5th April) and separate them into categories not just date order.
- The dates for filing your tax returns are: for paper returns 31st October, for online returns 31st January, this is for the previous 6th April to current 5th April – i.e. tax year April 2015 – April 2016 paper return October 2016, online return January 2017.
- Get an accountant, there are plenty that specialise in looking after performers. Use one. I have included a selection in the Resources section at the end of the book.

For the couple of hundred quid you spend on an accountant they will save you a whole load of money. As long as you send everything they require in the way they specify *and* by the date they request, they will work their magic and file your tax return in time. You won't get fined and you'll most likely pay much less than if you had filed your own return. My experience of ringing up the Inland Revenue to ask them what I could claim elicited a response of 'Nothing' and that is absolutely not the case. You'd be surprised what you can claim for (e.g. bags and cases as presumably they're for when you're on tour and travelling to digs). What percentage of the total cost of this item can be claimed is also something the tax office like to keep to themselves. In your first year as self-employed you can claim the entire cost of new purchases for your office equipment, so if you need a new computer your first year is a great time to buy it.

How are you going to pay your tax bills?

- Put away a quarter of your earnings. Many of us in the industry have ignored this sage advice in the past and found it difficult when it came time to pay the taxman; they only accept pound sterling not an IOU. This way at the end of the financial year, you won't be scrambling around trying to find the coppers behind the cushions on your sofa, at least you will have saved towards your tax and NI… just something to think about.
- Check your payslips when you get them, don't ring up your agent in a temper the day before your tax return is due in if there has been an error.

HMRC calculate what you owe per tax year based on half of the current year's income (from your tax return) and a prediction for half of the following year. There are two payment dates per year, the 31st January and 31st July, at which you either pay, or receive a rebate if you paid too much the year before. The personal allowance of income that you do not have to pay tax on is £10,600.00 (2015-2016) monies earned above that are taxable.

EQUITY – THE ACTORS' UNION

Whilst you no longer *need* to be a member of Equity to work as an actor, you may still want to consider joining.

- Equity have minimum rates of pay for different mediums so there is something in print to protect you, as most theatre producers, television and film production companies adhere to Equity rates in the UK.
- Equity can provide advice if you feel an employer is taking advantage, or your working conditions are not appropriate, etc.
- They also offer a pension scheme, the only scheme which is designed for members of the performing arts and which participating production companies will contribute to.

WHETHER YOU RETIRE AS AN ACTOR OR NOT, YOU NEED A PENSION

How long will you earn a living from acting? What will you do when you turn 67?

If you're lucky enough to have been working as an actor for X amount of years continually and have been financially canny, you may be set up and fine for your retirement and old age, but most aren't in that fortunate position.

Why do you need to think about this now? When surely you'll be rich and famous by then – because the reality of being a jobbing actor is neither riches nor fame. Much as we know actors love to keep working, there are fewer roles for actors of a certain age (especially women). Retirement can feel like death, worse than death, you'd be alive but people would think you were dead because you weren't working and there's nothing worse than being thought of as dead or just plain forgotten. Richard Briers

CBE had a lovely way of putting it when he quoted Sir Laurence Olivier:

> "'Look at me, look at me, look at me, look at me, look at me, look at me" which was you know quite a frightening thing to say, but that's what it was about, it's "I want you to notice me, because otherwise I don't quite know what I'm here for."'
>
> Richard Briers CBE, Actor, UK

So coming back to the future, the annual allowance set by the Inland Revenue is £40,000.00 for the tax year 2015-2016. You would only get tax relief on £3,600.00 of that per year though. If you do not pay tax because you do not earn you can still pay a maximum of £3,600.00 gross into a personal(3) or stakeholder pension scheme(4).

There are many pension schemes out there, a financial advisor (and some theatrical accountants) can advise you on the best one or combination for you. The new 2015 legislation on employer pension auto-enrolment schemes means you could end up being enrolled into many different pension schemes. The thing with Equity's pension scheme is that it was designed with actors in mind, so if you like you can pay your contributions on an engagement only basis when you're working which means it stops automatically when you're not. You can also make additional payments monthly, or as and when you can, as long as each is £20.00 gross minimum. Actors like most in the entertainment industry work freelance primarily (rather than prolonged PAYE employment), though each production varies. It's never easy being freelance and having a sensible financial plan for the future is essential. Banks and building societies use actors in their commercials but often can't help you with mortgages/loans etc.

- Actors working on theatrical contracts or as regulars in

television series are in a better position than say a jobbing actor who has large gaps between his/her gigs. Theatrical contracts for musical theatre are typically 12 months, in which case you will have enough payslips from the bankroll to approach a bank or building society regarding your financial needs.
- If you are resting for months on end between gigs, unless you've already got lots of capital behind you it will be harder and in today's economic climate all financial institutions require more capital from you for their mortgages or loans.

Some people make other financial plans for the future, shares and investments or property. The chances are when you actually think about setting these up, that you're coming towards the end of a three month theatre tour with nothing else lined up yet. Most freelancers in the business (whichever side of it they are on) experience the monetary side of work-life as feast or famine. We enjoy the feasts and then regret the countless pairs of shoes/nights on the town we paid for when famine hits. Suddenly it's not just mums who go to Iceland. So think about the potential for famine and put some money aside – and don't dip into that quarter you're putting away for your tax…

HOW DOES CASTING WORK?

Now you're no longer singing 'There's no business like show business'… but you probably still have a lot of misconceptions about how casting works, it's time to clear some up.

- 'Casting Agents.' There is no such thing!

There are theatrical agents (or talent agents as they are called in the US) and casting directors, two distinctly different jobs.

Agents look after the actors on their books for all their acting work, getting meetings for them, negotiating deals, making sure their clients are protected contractually in each job, taking industry professionals to see them in shows, etc.

Casting directors cast theatre, film, television and commercials, some cross all those media, some specialise in a preferred medium. Casting directors do not have people on their 'books' – they do not manage actors. Something to be aware of when doing mail outs which we'll cover in chapter 3.

- The Producer is just the money person.

Well, yes but not solely: producers bring the money to any creative endeavour be that theatrical or for the screen; but they always have a say on everyone who is hired from the creatives to the actors and some producers are very creative.

- The writer's job finishes when the script is delivered, the cast can then 'improve' the dialogue.

Writers come up with the initial idea, write the script, continue re-writes up till and often after production has started. There are some productions which rehearse with a workshop process, whereby the director and actors breakdown scenes and improvise around the characters and situations. If that's not how the creative team are approaching the production, maybe remember that you wouldn't adlib Shakespeare or argue your character's motivations, so probably best not to on your episode of 'Doctors' unless you're asked to.

- Directors are all-powerful and are the ones to impress at all costs. And strangely – on the flip side it's sometimes assumed that directors will block an actor's great input because though it's a good idea it wasn't their own.

Directors bring the vision to the script and bring it to life, it's their interpretation you're working on. All the creatives, crew and cast involved are working to that vision and they are *all* important, including you. Any director worth his/her salt is not going to block a good idea, period; they want the end result to be brilliant. It reflects on them too.

- The Casting Couch… flirting with casting directors, directors and/or producers is a good idea and sure-fire way to get you a job.

It is not! It looks and smells desperate, which is exactly what it is and desperation is not attractive professionally or personally. Having a natural charm or flirty nature is not a problem, but 'give me the part and I'll show you a good time' too long held gaze *really* is. Don't prostitute yourself for an acting gig, it is humiliating and insulting to all parties involved.

When it comes to casting the piece, whichever medium it is it generally follows the same pattern which we will go into in further depth in chapter 4 and theatrically in chapter 8.

WHY DO YOU NEED AN AGENT?

After all they just take 12.5% of your hard earned cash and for what, what do they actually do all day?

Most working actors have agents; very few successfully manage their own careers for a whole plethora of reasons. You need an agent because they:

- Have good working relationships in place with casting directors and that's whom you need to be meeting to get your next gig.

- Negotiate as much as possible in your favour, they know contracts inside and out and boy can they argue!
- Bring casting directors, producers and directors to see their clients in theatre shows and to screenings. This not only cements their working relationships but also gives you the client an opportunity to be seen in person and meet them over a drink after the show to make a personal impression. They are usually very adept socially and are quite charming, on these evenings they are your 'wing man'.
- Work a lot harder for you than you will *ever* realise.
- Are sent the character breakdowns for West End, regional and touring theatre, TV, film, commercials and corporates(5). As an actor on your own you won't get a look in to most of that. Casting directors simply do not have time to deal with hundreds of unrepresented actors every day when they can deal with agents whom they know and trust.
- Validate you by association, because they wouldn't have you on their books if you weren't talented.

Some actors will have their acting and voiceover representation by separate agencies, some will also have a presenter's agent. All their acting work is looked after by the same agent and he/she is not sat with their feet up on their desk, cigar in mouth, counting their commission from your money, they're working hard to get you your next job. Actors in the US have managers too, but not in the UK.

SEEING YOURSELF AS A BUSINESS PROPOSITION

So, you are a small part of the industry. It can be difficult to see yourself as a positive business proposition and take a pragmatic view of your career. Tim Pigott-Smith has an inspired, practical way of looking at it:

'Sometimes I teach in Drama schools now... one of the things I say is "You have to imagine that you have two boxes and one is your career box and the other is your talent box... How do we square this particular circle? What do we do?" Actually the answer is: all you can do to take responsibility for yourself, is to do a little bit of work on each of those every day. Make a phone call about something, ring a friend who was a director... keep in touch with the business, do a few voice exercises, keep both boxes on the go. Objectifying who and what you are helps people think about what they have to do, which is promote themselves, a horrible thing.'

Tim Pigott-Smith, Actor and Director, UK

Tim's shrewd theory paints a realistic picture on the practical necessities of being a jobbing actor. Separating your talent and career so you can work on them as distinct realities, which are not a part of you, is really quite ingenious.

There are proactive measures you can take towards your career and talent in relatively short allotted time slots, which all things going well should work exponentially in your favour. A strict goal oriented approach like this is not right for everyone, but it can help focus you if you're a procrastinator at heart. I'm sure you can think of these yourself, but here are a few examples...

Your talent slot could include:

- An acting, voice, singing or dance class.
- Reading a play or a screenplay (which you're not working on currently) to broaden and improve your knowledge base.
- Going to the theatre to see other work is always good for actors, the same for watching film and TV – you internalize what you've seen and think about how your performance of that role would have differed, so it always informs you.
- Running scenes with an actor friend just to keep in practice.

- Alexander Technique to learn relaxation.
- A martial arts class.
- A foreign language class.
- Any sports in which you specialise rather than just doing for fun, including lifting weights (if you're body building or weapons training this is a specialised skill, just look at Arnold Schwarzenegger – if you can bear to).

Your career slot could include:

- Updating your CV and your Spotlight CV.
- Looking for jobs in trade papers, magazines and websites, i.e. Spotlight, The Stage, The Guardian (media section), Casting Networks, Casting Call Pro, Mandy.com, etc.
- Building up your social media network, Twitter, Facebook, online blogs, etc.
- Sending a charming email to an agent or a casting director, one which you have, titled, addressed and researched appropriately. I will come on to this more in chapter 3.
- Getting a director friend to tape you audition for screen work, for practice. This is not your talent – acting is your talent. Audition technique and being aware of how you are perceived on camera will help your career no end.
- Going to the gym and keeping fit. Being able to run on a treadmill is hardly a talent, certainly not one that would make you stand out from other jobbing actors, but a certain amount of fitness, stamina and physicality is usually expected – even from character actors. This doesn't mean you need to become Arnie or Jodie Marsh.
- Networking, we'll look at this in chapter 2.
- Going to the theatre, yes I did mention it for talent but it is twofold because this can expand your network as you'll always run into other actors, directors, agents, casting directors and producers.

- Keep a list of good dramatic and comedic monologues from the plays you read. You may be asked to prepare two contrasting monologues for theatre auditions, so this will cut the panic when you are asked to prepare this two days before your meeting.
- Taking part in a casting director led workshop, to demystify the casting process.
- Being an audition reader, or reading in the parts not yet cast for a TV production read through. This can be small parts and potentially feel that you weren't considered for the show, but the directors, producers, execs and possibly network representatives will be there and can see you.

Focus on both elements, many performers don't see the connection of what they do and don't do to both intrinsic components of their working life.

Should you need it, over the page is a template to keep track of what you're doing for each on a weekly basis, you may find you're already doing more than you realise.

THE AUDITION ROOM

TALENT BOX		CAREER BOX	
ACTIVITY	NOTES	TASK	OUTCOME
e.g. Acting/ Voice Class		e.g. Updating your CV and Spotlight CV	

We'll cover the various methods of promoting yourself mentioned above in chapter 3. Taking responsibility for yourself is a theme I touch on throughout this book, it is your career after all.

You're a business but you're also the human being behind it. Sometimes you need to leave work at work and just be yourself.

- Ensure you make time to do the things you enjoy personally, things that have nothing to do with acting. Time spent doing something just for you is also incredibly important; you are not just your career.

COMPETITION IS GETTING FIERCER

Something that troubles many in the industry is the multitude of drama school graduates every year and less screen/stage shows in production, reality TV takes up a huge proportion of TV scheduling and theatres can be dark (no shows on) for months. Competition is fierce. Does anyone tell students what it's really like out there in the big bad world? Back in the days when you had to be a member of Equity to get paid work competition was less, but it was incredibly hard to break into showbiz. The Catch 22 situation demanded an Equity card in order to get paid employment but required paid employment to qualify for your Equity card (unless your university awarded you one)… The playing field has opened up now that that Equity union stamp of approval is not needed. The long-term effect of this however has led to many more actors striving for the same jobs now, because that first stage filtering system which was once in place is no longer there. So the dream often holds little or no substance for many a young hopeful or indeed seasoned actor.

> 'I do go to drama schools and do various sessions with them and they always say "Oh yes we know there isn't much work out there, but we're going to be fine." And you think "Well how are you going to be fine? What is it that you're going to do that's going to work differently for you?" And a lot of the time you find they have no conception of the business really before they actually get into it and it's just a frightening and overwhelming place, unless they're lucky enough to get the help of a good agent, you know to guide them through.'
>
> Alison Chard, Casting Director, UK

Time and again acting fraternity stalwarts, directors and casting directors bemoan that there is no Repertory theatre anymore. Whilst the collective term for a group of actors is a 'whinge', they're not just whinging for whinging's sake here, they're in fact highlighting a very real concern.

> 'Because Rep has gone... (a lot of our theatrical knights now, served 5 or 6 years kind of apprenticeship at the RSC in their youth). And there is now a mindset that you come out of drama school and the thing to do is to go to Hollywood and make a movie without laying down the groundwork of theatre which every actor needs and without – if you like – learning your trade properly.'
>
> Alison Chard, Casting Director, UK

The hierarchical system of Rep was a great and deeply valued training ground for really learning and honing the craft for so many of our great actors. Learning on the job, alongside the older generation who passed down knowledge, the newbies soaked it all up. Rehearsing and playing several plays at once and keeping the performances fresh over time, starting out with the very small roles and gradually working their way up the ladder. Actors often wax lyrical about their Rep days for good reason.

> 'What people did then was go to Rep and I became an Acting Assistant Stage Manager at the Bristol Old Vic which was great... That's the way it worked, that's what you did and what you expected to do, spend a few years in Rep maybe and then work your way up the theatrical ladder.'
>
> Tim Pigott-Smith, Actor and Director, UK

> 'I wrote begging letters to various Rep companies and I got an audition and I got into Birmingham Rep and I stayed there for 3 years. And the natural progression from Birmingham if you had any aspirations to be a classical actor certainly was Stratford Upon Avon which is only 20 miles away.'
>
> Sir Derek Jacobi CBE, Actor, UK

We can't turn back time to the days of yore for our new graduates to join a Rep company and learn their trade. So for stage or screen work, think of on the job learning like a thespian's version of the Green Cross Code: Look, Listen and Learn. In a sense landing a role on an episode of a TV serial is akin to rep in many ways as there is the chance to watch and learn from the regulars in much the same ways; or understudying a more experienced actor in a stage play. Don't begrudge working your way up: with stage work it would be ensemble parts and covers (understudying); with screen work it would be small parts, 1 liners, short films, etc building up to supporting roles.

YOU'RE ONE SMALL PART OF A PRODUCTION... AN EXPENSIVE ONE

The rep system also had the huge advantage of clearly showing new actors how they fit within a production as a whole. Although this is done in training it's often with your acting peers taking the jobs of stage or floor managers, as they want to be actors too, that's a whole different ball game.

When you're in the working arena there are certain expected standards and protocols. Everyone in each field is a professional and has a job to do, a job as important as yours. How can you have a film without a camera operator or a grip? How can you have a stage play without a box office or follow spotter? So in terms of the work you do as an actor, sorry to say, you have to take your ego out of the equation. I say this not to chastise or patronise, but to highlight, because many a talented actor has lost opportunities because of ego and that's a great shame both professionally and personally.

> *'Remember when you're making a film that your performance is only part of it and often actors think that when they do a scene, that's it's all them. First… it's intercut with other things so you're never on screen all the time, so your performance is broken anyway. Secondly there's music, there's effects on top, there's camera movement, there's all sorts of things going on that build into the completeness and also your performance is about the whole film, not the one scene… don't make a big deal about the four lines.'*
>
> Robert Bierman, Director, UK and USA

There is always the dark omnipresence of the budget hovering with intent, be it on stage or set, 'time is' – to coin that dreadful 80's phrase – 'money'. Producing a show is a really expensive endeavour. An awful lot of money is spent on every production; most of it of course is not your salary or anything to do with you specifically.

Films often talk about the above the line and below the line costs: above the line are the creatives who drive the narrative and direction of the piece, this includes writers, director, producer and cast; below the line includes all the production and post production costs including staff. When looking at how much of the budget is above the line it varies from approximately 20-50% depending on if you have huge stars attached to a project. The rest of the budget is for the actual making of it.

> 'The biggest difference between television and film... is the budget, the money, when you're on a big film, we're talking 100 million plus type film... most people are looking up to about a minute and a half a day of screen time out of that day's shooting. So that's including the stuff that ends up on the digital cutting room floor, but that's what you're looking for in screen time. On television in the most expensive television filmed drama you're probably looking at least 4 to 6 minutes per day, which is still a lot more. And if you're looking at soap opera, you're looking at say 1 or 2 days at the most to film a half hour episode, so that's 13 minutes a day as opposed to your minute a day. What does that mean for the actor? Well it's good and bad, the good side is (a little bit more like theatre) you may have a rehearsal before hand, not for things like 'The Bill', but you may. You will then find that you will go in longer chunks, that there'll be less waiting around... if you're on a small budget thing because the lens doesn't have to be changed so much.'
>
> Mel Churcher, Acting and Dialect Coach, UK and USA

And, if you have questions ask in rehearsal, under no circumstances wait till filming has started...

> 'Never leave it till you're shooting, because shooting's the most expensive time possible, before shooting... is cheap

> *time and cheap time is great talk time, talk time on the floor is really expensive time wasting.'*
>
> Robert Bierman, Director, UK and USA

Much as you'd be wasting money by asking inopportune questions or holding up rehearsals or shooting, it also makes you look unprofessional. You *are* a professional, don't be scared to ask, just pick your moments wisely.

PROFESSIONALISM AT ALL TIMES REQUIRES SELF-DISCIPLINE

With so much competition, professionalism has become a factor almost as important as talent. There isn't time, money or patience to wait on cast who are for example: late to set; haven't learnt their lines (further holding up production); late to rehearsals/stage calls or rude to other members of cast and/or crew. This of course applies to everyone involved, not just actors. A lot of people want to be a part of the industry, so whether you're already a jobbing actor or just got your foot in the door, treat it with the respect it deserves. We all relish the opportunity to work with consummate professionals (on all sides of the business) who love and respect what they do and everyone involved. Self-discipline and the basics of professionalism are themes we'll keep returning to. Always be the three 'P's:

> *'Being polite, being punctual and… being prepared.'*
>
> Alison Chard, Casting Director, UK

Those 'P's have an integral part to play in your career as a whole. Alison put it in a wider context:

> *'You get schedules through late and scripts do change at the last minute and I'm afraid you are expected to roll*

with the punches really... If you expect these things to happen... take it in your stride then you're gonna give us your best. But if you kind of think "Oh God, they've changed the script again," "they've changed the time" or that kind of thing, it's going to throw you. And it will effect your next job, because directors are incredibly loyal people and if they've had a good experience with an actor and the actor's really pulled their fat out of the fire, then they're gonna turn to them when there's a similar situation. So even when you're working, you're auditioning for your next job really and I think that should be borne in mind as much as just the audition process itself really.'

Alison Chard, Casting Director, UK

We all learn through practice. The knowledge you build up from production to production, regardless of the medium, adds to your experience and broader understanding of who you are, your talent, the industry and your place within it.

'I do a lot of work on my own, I do a lot of thinking, I do a lot of research and I do a lot of putting myself into that world, so I think all that kind of work goes on subconsciously while you're carrying on with your life.'

Ann Mitchell, Actor and Director, UK

MAKING USE OF DIGITAL TECHNOLOGY TO IMPROVE PROFESSIONALISM

Everything seems to be going the way of the Internet these days personally and professionally. Gone are the days of faxing; calls are often backed up with an email as standard now. It all makes for a much more efficient process for casting, production and also for you the actor being constantly aware and available. A smart phone, tablet or some such device mean you can be check your emails for scripts as soon as you've spoken with your agent.

> 'Communication is so much better. Breakdowns can go out and suggestions can come back within the hour. Whereas it used to be when you put a breakdown out, you'd be lucky if it came out in 6 days time. So things have changed out of all recognition, the days of Lloyd, my postman, staggering up to the door with two sacks of mail for about three weeks has long gone – he's glad to know. But that's what it used to be like; you'd get sacks full of mail. Whereas now it's largely electronic and it can all be sorted into different lists and character lists and run off to the directors and the producers instantly, so it's much more focused… You no longer have to rely on bikes and couriers and again the scripts can go instantly to an actor who can decide whether they like the look of the part, or whether they want to come in. And it does give everybody a kind of foreknowledge of everything so it's a real help.'
>
> Alison Chard, Casting Director, UK

So be aware, have your gadget at the ready:

- For your phone calls and emails with attachments for you to prepare.
- Make sure you have voicemail and check regularly if you're somewhere your phone can't be on and in your pocket all day i.e. you're on set/stage, rehearsing or in a day job when resting.
- A pay as you go contract for your mobile phone with no voicemail and not returning your agent's call for 2 days often leads to actors missing very important meetings. It smacks of disinterest and a lack of professionalism, when actually more likely it's just a financial consideration that's not been given appropriate importance.

- Remember however, to turn off said gadget when you're in an audition or on set.

RESTING…

There will always be times for actors, like anyone who does freelance work, where they will be without paid employment in their chosen field for a time. What do you do? Well actors, perhaps even more than other creative fields other than Fine Artists, should always have a secondary trade. For most jobbing actors the harsh reality of life is just that – they will be using that second trade more often than they'd care to. Be it supply teaching, bricklaying, hairdressing, IT. It doesn't matter what, it just needs flexibility and an understanding boss. I temped in a bank on weekdays when I first came to London and was working on independent theatre and short films on weekends and evenings, we all did/do it. Ann Mitchell reflects that:

> 'Looking back on it now I would have done something different… I had to survive so in the periods of unemployment I worked, I worked; I worked as a receptionist, I worked as a telephonist, I worked as a waitress. I did anything that I could, anything that was offered to me. Now I think it's changed so much that what I would advise and try to guide people towards is having and developing other skills… So that you're in control of a part of your life… The state of the industry as it is, actors can no longer wait for the work.'
>
> Ann Mitchell, Actor and Director, UK

Remember though, it is meant to be your secondary trade; you can't let it become something you are tied to permanently. If you turn down acting work for 'the job' not only will that not fulfil you, but your feelings towards it can evolve to dissatisfaction or worse. Your agent may feel you're not all that committed if you are prioritising something else.

Even if you have been working on great projects and have had some acclaim from the industry, it doesn't mean that you will always have acting work.

How you cope with unemployment and what you do during those times is a part of the self-discipline and motivation that you need to make it in this business.

> *'I had a year where strangely enough, I'd worked at the Royal Shakespeare Company, the National, in the West End, I'd won a couple of awards… So I was very much on a high and I was looking like you know "This is an actor to watch." So everything was going really well and I think I became really quite blasé and thought "Well this is the actor's life, you just get offered work and you do it" basically. And I was finishing a play… and Peter Hall asked me to stay on at the National Theatre to do a series of plays and to play Laertes to Albert Finney's Hamlet, things like that. I didn't want to, so I turned him down and I was obviously tempting the fates because I didn't work for a year after that. And it was just after I'd had my most successful time and I had won these awards and stuff and it just stopped for a solid year!… I learnt a huge amount about myself during that year.'*
>
> Peter Egan, Actor and Director, UK

On a practical note, I mentioned it earlier and whilst not trying to teach you to suck eggs…

- Don't spend as though you are earning when you are not.
- Remember you may be resting for longer than anticipated.
- Don't use your tax money to continue the lifestyle, 'Keeping up Appearances' is an old BBC sitcom and should not be your life, unless you *are* Hyacinth Bucket.

- If you are working a 'day job' while resting make sure you are still working towards your career. Read those plays, scripts and books on the bus or train on your way to work instead of playing games on your phone.

THE SECRET TO MY SUCCESS?

There are varying schools of thought on whether success generates success… or not.

> 'No work breeds no work, work doesn't necessarily breed work. But no work for sure breeds no work.'
> Tim Pigott-Smith, Actor and Director, UK

Personal motivation and drive is essential for any successful career. If you are not sure where you are heading, make an exercise of it:

- Write down your aims and ambitions so they are clear to you. Having a game plan, a vision of where you'd like to be helps to solidify your strategies for getting there regardless of what may be occurring in your personal life.

> 'I think success breeds success, if you have a success when you're young; it's very likely that you're going to be asked again and so on. I think if life deals you some deadly blows, equally talented you may be, then of course that will affect you… That's why you can't rely on this profession to give you a sense of self, whether you're enormously successful strangely enough or not, you have to work on yourself and developing yourself is the best way you possibly can, without needing the constant approval of this industry.'
> Ann Mitchell, Actor and Director, UK

If work leads to more work, is that why the successful remain at the top? For many one particular incident will drive home the message 'always keep working'...

> *'I was sent over to LA to record Orson Wells saying "Carlsberg, probably the best lager in the world" and this was a dream come true job... What it taught me at the end of the day, even the greatest genius of film making has to earn a living and making films and being an actor, doesn't matter how great you are, if you're not earning a living, you're not doing the job. Seeing Orson Wells do this advert for Carlsberg showed me that it doesn't matter where you are in your career, you just have to keep working.'*
>
> Robert Bierman, Director UK and USA

Whether you're in work and going straight into another job or you're resting between gigs, take a critical look at your working patterns and analyse what they mean financially.

The 80/20 Principal is a theory by Financial Times writer Richard Koch which boils down to the idea that 80% of your wealth is usually generated from only 20% of the work that you actually do. Most of us seem to focus on the wrong percentage however and have not considered where our money comes from. This is crazy. Every other profession would look at it seriously. Would a business continually sell and back a product that made them no money while ignoring the most profitable part of their work? – not likely. Navel gazing, resting on laurels then buckling down to the 'perceived' un-enjoyable tasks is often how it's approached. Yes, yes, we know you're in it for 'the art' and actually so are the rest of us, we wouldn't be here if we didn't see it as our 'art'... but you still have to pay your rent.

> *'So if you want to make more money and be more successful in business you should concentrate on that 20%*

of the work that you do and create more of that 80% of income. If I'm for example making most of my money from adverts, yet the adverts that I record take up a tiny proportion of the amount of work that I do (I do two days on an advert yet I make £15,000 that might be a huge amount of my yearly income) why then am I sending out my CV to Shakespearean companies? It can't be because I want to make money, I should be trying to get more adverts if I want to make a lot of money.'

Mark Bowden, Author, UK

WORK HISTORY		FINANCIAL RENUMERATION	
E.G. COMMERCIAL	12 – 17 FEB 2016	£5,500.00 buyout UK	£5,500.00 for 5 days work
E.G. THEATRE	3 JUN – 31 AUG 2016	£450 per week	£5,850.00 For 3 months work
E.G. SHORT FILM	2 – 12 SEP 2016	Expenses only	10 DAYS, Oyster refund and lunch

On the previous page is a template with a couple of examples for you to work out your recent work history and the financial gain from that work, just to put the fees into perspective.

Also – and this is something that can get lost in all the talk of business strategy – people are usually inspired to become actors for reasons other than finance or fame. Influenced by specific ideas like a love of the perfection that can be achieved in screen acting or playing to a live audience and altering your performance nightly. Consider how to best utilise the acting work that brings the most revenue to allow you the freedom to pursue the medium which you find most artistically rewarding. You may long to do Shakespeare in regional theatre for the majority of your career, if you wish to survive financially doing this and perhaps want a family and need a mortgage, then a few corporates or lucrative adverts can bring you a great financial return for a short investment of your time. Of course I am not suggesting you make decisions solely on finance, always choose wisely, you want to be proud of all your work and you *can* say no to jobs.

There's a popular belief, that 90% of actors are unemployed 90% of the time. If that's true 10% are getting most of the work. What do that 10% do? There are too many variables to have hard and fast rules, however sometimes having an established history of well received roles means the work rolls in. John Hubbard makes that point, then mentions the elephant in the room…

> *'Because they have a name, they've done a body of work, they're getting the work basically, but it's not what the other percentage are doing is wrong at all, it is the totally unfair nature of the business that recently we've had this massive move to reality television and inevitably that has hurt drama, so there's less drama being produced… It's not just the others are all wrong but do remember… there's*

a big percentage of the people not working who are just not good enough. It is a refuge and you do meet people who you know there's nothing else they can do, or they're damaged in some way and it's a sort of outlet for them, but that doesn't make you a good actor.'

John Hubbard, Casting Director, UK

Sometimes lesser talented individuals seem to progress much higher than their more worthy counterparts, why is that?

Some people have more natural charisma and are incredibly driven even if they don't really have the goods to back it up. Their manner convinces people for a short while, conveniently for them usually when there's a job going. You can build up your own business charisma, there are specific things that you can do to help yourself, we'll look at the various aspects of this later in the book. How you are marketed is also an important part of this equation.

'It's not the best actor that succeeds commercially but often the best sold actor... Of course as an actor you've got to have the talent to back up this presentation, however the best sold actors don't have to be the best actors. You've simply got to be consistent; the image that you sell has got to be congruent with the goods that you provide.'

Mark Bowden, Author, UK

Marketing is an essential part of any business, not least for yourself if you consider you yourself as a business. Why would anyone use you if they don't know who you are and what you have to offer?

'I wish it was all about talent, but then talent is highly difficult to measure and is highly subjective. I suspect it's more about the negatives: bad promotions; people

promoting themselves badly or making mistakes in promotion, than the positives. I think unfortunately in this visual age, it's more down to image, which can be part of promotion. I would say it's probably... 6 to 4 to put numbers on it, promotion to talent. I would prefer it was the other way round.'

Simon Dunmore, Director and Author, UK

While it might feel a little artificial that the most successfully promoted people do well, try to consider it a little differently.

- Does the person who has not the spent time effectively promoting themselves look professional? Do they seem to understand the industry?
- Do they appear to take the time to apply themselves to communicating properly to the people who need to know their skill set very quickly?

If you have thought about these questions honestly, perhaps now you can see the problem of poor communication and promotion a little more from the casting and production side. Back up your talent with your promotion.

It is a business not a fine art, don't die for your art, enjoy it, make a living from it and feed your soul. There's a huge monetary pie out there, no reason you shouldn't be sat at the table eating from it.

SUMMARY

In conclusion what you can take from this chapter is that show business is just that – a business and needs to be regarded as such. Being an actor is your chosen career there's no shame in wanting to make money from it as well as creating your art. The financial realities of your career involve informing the tax office that you are self-employed, getting a pension and realistically an accountant unless you do actually enjoy those self-assessment forms…

We've covered some of the more common casting misconceptions and why being represented by an agent is a much more sensible approach to working than trying to represent yourself. We've seen how taking a pragmatic standpoint to your career and your talent as two separate entities can really aid your working life. Competition is fierce. Learning where you fit into the business, appreciating the difference in budget and how that effects television and film considerations, the application of the 3 'P's of professionalism are all key points to think about when looking at how best to improve on your standing. Success often begets success but every actor spends some of their time 'Resting', it's not something to be embarrassed about it's the nature of all freelance work. We've covered how time off can be used wisely. Looking practically at which gigs give you the best remuneration, in particular how applying the '80/20' theory will help you navigate the business elements of your career. The need for self-promotion in today's industry is very real and if you take the time to look at those who appear to be lucky and getting gig after gig, their marketing is actually quite evidently aiding their careers.

CHAPTER 2

GETTING THE INDUSTRY'S ATTENTION

In this chapter we will look at the ways in which you can increase your chances of being noticed by the industry and once you have their attention what to do to keep it. We'll look at:

- Choosing the right agent.
- Marketing.
- Seeing yourself as a product.
- Capitalising on your assets.
- Branding and its associations.
- Giving yourself the edge.
- Networking.
- Having an Internet presence.

CHOOSING THE RIGHT AGENT

We've established why you need an agent. Now we'll look at your choice of agency representation, as it is part of your marketing choice on all levels, ultimately it helps to get the rest of the industry's attention. A good working relationship with your agent is a partnership in your career. Having the right agent is of paramount importance. You should feel the following about your agent:

- You trust them and their judgement.
- You respect them and their knowledge.

- You feel confident in their existing working relationships with casting directors, directors, producers and production companies.
- That they are a respected agency.
- That they will always negotiate the best deal they can for you.

You should sense that your agent feels about you:

- They respect your talent.
- They believe you to be an intelligent and capable individual.
- They trust you.
- That they care about you.

You should not be scared of your agent. Whilst I'm not suggesting you become best friends, you should like them and feel they like you. This builds your professional relationship.

Research the agency:

- Look at their client list, if there's already someone very similar to you, or a handful if it's a very large agency, keep looking.
- Do you like their clients – do you think the pool of actors they represent are a talented group of people with whom you want to be associated?
- How long have they been agents? Are they established? Are they members of the PMA – Personal Managers Association?

If you are looking to sign with an agent because you are currently unrepresented or are looking to move, as you feel the relationship you have with your existing agent is not moving your career forward, take stock of the above points.

You need to consider which type of agency you want to be represented by. Don't just assume a large one is the right choice for you, as whilst they have great industry relationships, so do small established ones. A small/boutique agency will always try not to have clients who are too similar to each other. A large prominent agency may sign up a few actors at showcases who then fall by the wayside because they are one of so many; though they may be able to open more doors for you stateside. Would you like to be part of a co-operative agency and work a few days per month in the agency and have a more hands on approach to deal making? A reputable agency for your acting work will not ask for money to join their books, the agency makes its income from commission. With modelling agencies this is not always the case and there may be fees to join.

When you meet with an agent with a view to being taken on, you are evaluating them as much as they are you. Look to the checklist above. You should feel that they seem excited by what they can do for your career. Agents are creative individuals too and by the nature of looking after the people on their books they want the best for them.

Some points to remember about communication with your agent, always inform them:

- If you arrange any other work, or personal commitments so they have your up-to-date availability.
- If you move house, change your mobile number or email address – in particular, don't just assume if you email from a new address it will be noted.
- If you're booking a holiday but would postpone or cancel it for work – and make sure you have had that discussion with whomever you're travelling with.

How often should you call your agent?

- When you actually need to, NOT every day or weekly. It is counter productive, they could be working for you.

DON'T BE PASSED BY

Nowadays it's just too easy to be passed by as a jobbing actor. There are countless performers out there with various skills available, asking to be hired. Often it's because an actor stands right next to an opportunity whispering 'Pick me' – choosing not to actively promote themselves – in other words not saying 'Pick me!' loud enough to be heard (figuratively speaking of course). Many actors lack self-confidence about their talent and in themselves, their insecurities cause them to project those fears. A belief that people will see that the person they have bought into is somehow lacking and not all they were advertised as. Those actors believe that:

> '... *they're a fraud and they're worried that people will find out that they're a fraud so what they do is they undersell themselves. They undersell themselves via their marketing tools: their photographs, their CV, their covering letters, so that when they get into an audition if they manage to get in, they can also undersell themselves there as well. So what they don't want is for the person interviewing them to ever say 'You are nothing like you have represented yourself, you're a fraud' so they constantly, constantly undersell.'*
>
> Mark Bowden, Author, UK

You can't afford to think like this. As an actor you have to take stock of your skills, strengths and weaknesses, your assets and everything you have going for you. Think about these attributes in a positive light because in many cases you have the goods, you just don't quite believe it.

And *you* must believe it before anyone else can. In this competitive industry, you have to market yourself and go get 'em. It is not possible to just hope for the best. No one likes to have a brash individual in their face banging on about how great they are (and I am not advocating that) but a continual subtle approach will help your career no end. Internet Marketing expert Duran Inci explains why you need marketing:

> 'What does marketing do to help make money for a business? That's simple – it exposes people to your product and your brand. How many songs do you know just because you heard them on a Mac commercial?... We need marketing to be seen, to be found, to create an interaction that will lead to the ultimate desired goal.'
>
> Duran Inci, Internet Marketing Expert, USA

THE DIRTY 'M' WORD – MARKETING

So what is marketing? We are all told we have to market ourselves but what can this mean in the context of an actor, after all you're not product or a service… are you? Well, actually you are. As an actor you're selling your skills in performance, in presence, in bringing a character to life, but there's no tangible physical item; you're not a painter, shoe designer or candlestick maker. The product or service that is being bought is essentially you. This can materialize as your ability to inhabit a role, your comedic timing, your mastery of language and Shakespearean text, your combat or equestrian skills, your ability to speak another language fluently, your dance background, your singing and vocal range, as well as your dark brooding looks or characterful face.

> 'Marketing is the magic fairy dust you apply to a business to get your delicious offerings found by the people who want them, who in turn reward you handsomely with money.'
>
> Ameena Falchetto, Marketing Consultant, UK, France & UAE

Many actors are resistant to the idea of marketing. Unfortunately self-promotion is increasingly a real necessity for jobbing actors. You may well find you work less (even if you have an amazing agent) if you don't become adept at some part of it at least. Many people find it difficult to promote themselves, because selling yourself is actually a very hard thing to do regardless of your talent.

Tim Pigott-Smith's box analogy from chapter 1, is extremely helpful in this regard. If you view your career box as your business, your talent box more like product development. All marketing activities that you conduct are fulfilling the requirements of your career box.

Marketing for any business is all the activities whose purpose is to sell a product/service. There are many different aspects of marketing and these can all be applied to how you deal with your self-promotion.

Imagine the following list including yourself:

- Development of a strategic marketing plan – who do you plan to target, in what order and how will this maintain your image? This is the most complex part of any promotional activity.
- Distribution of product – how will you get yourself or your promotional items to the identified people you are contacting?
- Staff training – how will you convince others such as your agent, to see you in the way that you wish to be seen?
- Product improvements – what are you doing about your talent box?
- Face-to-face marketing – how you maintain your brand image when you meet others.
- Public Relations – how can you ensure only stories and images that are appropriate to your brand image are widely available?

- Digital presence – are you maintaining an up-to-date log of your work on digital platforms, i.e. Spotlight and IMDB?
- Networking – have you developed a good networking persona and are you aware of the rules of networking both face-to-face and digitally, i.e. you're being charming and not a nuisance?
- Advertising – while most people think of advertising as marketing, in reality the closest you will need to come to classical advertising is direct mail (a letter to the person/company you are approaching).

'The best piece of marketing was actually a kind of face-to-face marketing really. I did a session at the Actors' Centre and there was an actor that I hadn't met before and he was so focused, committed, articulate, knew where he wanted to go, and it wasn't an outrageous place that he wanted to go. And he spoke really I thought quite intelligently about him and his place in the industry and I then subsequently got him in.'

Alison Chard, Casting Director, UK

SELLING YOURSELF – THE SIZZLE NOT THE STEAK

Have you ever gone into a shop for one item and subsequently purchased a different one (or many accessories) because you liked the sales person? Not because they were handsome or pretty, but because they seemed friendly, knowledgeable, trustworthy and attentive to your needs. Basically you 'bought' the sales person – you could have purchased exactly the same item(s) at any number of places. In retail and sales, people are trained to sell the product, the company *and themselves*, they become ambassadors for the company. They put you at ease, they tell you what they need to impart all whilst making it personal;

they've tried it too/they've got it at home/they bought it for their mum, etc. People buy more from sales people they feel are both well-informed and honest.

If you're in a commercial for a particular product, whether you're the face of it, the voice or both, in many respects you're actually selling yourself not the product. If the set up of the advert is a romantic dinner, as an audience we are buying whichever sauce it is because we've bought into the story, the idea and the hope. We imagine that the sexy, tall, dark and handsome guy will be cooking the meal for us, or the beautiful lady sat at the table watching, coquettishly drinking her wine and smiling is in fact smiling at us. I hate coffee but I'd drink it if it actually came with George Clooney...

> *'It's not the best actor that succeeds commercially but often the best sold actor. In a sense you're selling 'Sizzle' and not the steak and you've got to create some sort of excitement around yourself. It was interesting, I was watching the Golden Globes and there they all were on the red carpet and if you looked up into the air just above you; you could see that they were flashing strobe lights around these actors to give the impression that there was paparazzi around them, that they were being photographed. But of course they weren't or there were only a few cameras there, but even big Hollywood names need some kind of excitement around them.'*
>
> Mark Bowden, Author, UK

The same principle applies across your career as to the product in a commercial. You're making yourself the desirable, sought after, someone special. You must get behind the idea of selling yourself. You need to identify those attributes about you that make people want to see more. M&S use Matthew MacFadyen, he's got a soft, comforting voice but he's also played Mr Darcy and a British spy, so M&S is at once safe and alluring and the more considered choice, three hits.

> 'You're a product you know and you've got to market yourself, you've got to think now "How do I publicise myself, how do I get into the TV casting directors in London? How do I use my picture, how do I use my CV, how do I get information about what's going on? Maybe I'll call Pinewood and try and make friends with somebody there, find out what's going on, tell my agent." So advertising is very relevant to being an actor; because if you're completely unknown, if you're an unknown product, you have to advertise or use public relations or use communication to tell people about yourself.'
>
> John Hubbard, Casting Director, UK

CAPITALISING ON YOUR ASSETS

Always make the most of your assets, because everyone else is making the most of theirs. Tim Pigott-Smith has a few wise words for the more self-deprecating among us:

> 'Any kind of false modesty is gonna work against your career. You've just got to be realistic about it.'
>
> Tim Pigott-Smith, Actor and Director, UK

If you want to succeed you must be proud of your achievements. Look at your skill set, attributes and accomplishments:

- Have you already had some success in a particular theatre run, film or TV show? Did you appear in an award winning production?
- Are you an expert in some field, be it intellectually or practically?

- Have you traded on your looks before, have you modelled?
- Do you speak other languages, fluently or conversationally? Just pronouncing the menu well or pulling a good 'De Niro' face doesn't count. Real proficiency in other languages can bring in a lot of lucrative commercial and corporate work. It also opens up more roles to you both here and abroad.
- What other skills do you have within the arts? Are you already moonlighting as an after dinner speaker, presenter or puppeteer?

Don't hide these talents under a bushel, use them to your advantage, be it on your CV, or face-to-face in auditions, or when networking.

> *'Much too late in my life [I realised:] it is a business, it is a business and I had no idea. If I'd have known when I was younger, it would have altered the way I conducted myself, the way I presented myself. I would have made sure that I capitalised on my assets: I would have made sure that as a good looking, young woman… (and this sounds very mundane) that I was seen in the right places; that I would have had an image that was pleasing, etc.'*
>
> Ann Mitchell, Actor and Director, UK

BRANDING

> *'A brand is simply an organization, or a product, or a service with a personality. So why all the fuss?'*
> Wally Olins, World-renowned brand expert and Author, UK

Marketing yourself as a brand may initially sound and feel too 'commercial' for the artist within, but you're aiming to succeed in this business and those who brand well, earn well and live well.

A brand image has 3 main ingredients all of which have to remain consistent for your audience, that audience is everyone in the industry and the general public: -

- Core essence – the attributes which make you the unique individual your mum always tells you you are. Are you: kind, nervous, adventurous, disciplined, independent? Write a list of ten key words that describe you. Be honest; don't go out of your way to flatter yourself. If you are stubborn write it down, if you are prone to laziness put that in too. You should have a list containing mostly positives and a few negatives. These negatives are things that you should work on; just be aware that they need extra attention. For example, if you are an insomniac, this affects everything you do and it is an important part of who you are. However, this doesn't mean that you shouldn't try and find a healthy sleeping regime; as this will improve your ability to concentrate and therefore directly affect your performing and mood no end.

- Image – the picture that your identity creates generates an emotive response from your audience. This includes the specifics, not just the colour of your eyes but also the tone of that colour and what feeling that conveys. Your physical stance – is it imposing or laid back and congenial. The quality of your voice and speech – is it authoritative, do you sound intelligent and well spoken, is it very street, practical rather than academic, do you sound dangerous? Are you quite wholesome and bit fluffy? If so, we'll expect to see you on kids TV. Do you come across as an East End gangster? If so then we'd expect to see you in an action film with Danny Dyer or Jason Statham (and I hope *not* on kids TV).

- Reputation – Your reputation precedes you (I will cover behaviour in auditions in more detail in chapter 6). This means that you can get marked as rude, arrogant and/or late before you even send in your CV or attend an audition. People in every industry talk to each other, ours is no different. If you are always scruffy and late or you're always impeccably turned out and on time, we get very different feelings about you and we're generally more inclined to favour the latter. You need to identify what your reputation is. *Do not ask your friends!* Instead consider an old teacher, your agent, or a director you've worked with. It must be a candid conversation so flag it up as such. If you have just signed with an agent, they often arrange generals(6) and ask for feedback from the casting directors who will give it honestly, your agent in turn passes those comments on to you.

This establishes how you are currently seen. You don't want to market your *brand image*, *that* speaks for you whether you want it to or not. You want to market your *brand identity*, which is an idealised version of yourself – something that you are actually in control of. If you want to be seen as a leading man, then you might have to work on not only your image (looking more toned) but also your core essence (you may be too lazy to go to the gym so you need to find ways to motivate yourself) and your reputation (always arriving on time looking good and never appearing to have an 'off' day).

- Make an exercise of it – picture yourself as a product. What are you, where can you be bought, a supermarket chain or a boutique? What service do you offer, are you practical, sturdy furniture or a beauty product? Are you a magazine or a book? Are you a sleek flashy sports car or an understated but reliable run-around? Are you a healthy salad or a naughty-but-nice cream cake? How will these attributes about you the product make your audience feel, what feelings are they buying into when they look at you?

The difference between the brand image and brand identity of two of the nations favourite actors seen recently in 'Broadchurch' could be summarised as follows:

Olivia Colman; her brand image was that she is funny, many of her credits gave that impression, but 'Green Wing' and 'Peep Show' in particular brought her to the attention of the greater public as a 'Comedy' actress. Her brand identity that she is a multi-faceted talented individual wasn't quite in line with that. Recent performances in 'Tyrannosaur', 'Accused' and 'The Night Manager' however brought her brand identity and brand image closer together. She is now widely acknowledged as the extremely talented and versatile actor that she is.

David Tennant; his brand image for a long time was that of 'Casanova' and of course 'Doctor Who' – the quirky, Sci-Fi adventuring, Saturday tea time TV heart throb. His brand identity as an intelligent layered actor was known in the industry because of all his fantastic previous body of work, but for the general public this was not widely the case. A sell out stint in theatre as 'Hamlet' with the RSC and serious roles in 'Single Father', 'The Politician's Husband' and 'The Escape Artist' have bridged the gap between brand identity and brand image. Now in much the same way people are reminded that he is more than his past successes, he's a captivating, utterly believable actor in any role he's given.

There are always many variables factoring in the successes of particular productions and how the cast are perceived, as with these examples the roles they have taken have been choices, wise choices which have continued their branding.

YOUR STORY

Now it is time to build your brand, brand building involves any communication that reaches your audience (casting directors, agents, directors) before they directly experience you, the brand. Generally this would mean an advertising campaign but as an actor you are not a normal brand. You are a person and as such your audience are interested in your story. We don't mean your life story; we mean the story of what you are selling, of your brand. Everything should then follow that story and the associated feeling – are you exciting, intriguing, glamorous, sexy and dangerous?

Very successful actors tend not to veer from their story and it works for them. If your story is that you are a young, clean living healthy bubbly type then you want to emphasise information about your working with children, charity races etc. If your story is that of a driven and determined strong action hero, then push your combat skills, your martial arts and your weapons training. This is always in conjunction with your talent so it's not designed to stereotype and typecast but to give a feeling of that type which you will mainly be going for. Don't overdo it, though. Don't punch out photographers or your friends because they took candid photos on their phone of you in a less than 'clean living' moment. Just ask your friends not to post them on the Internet if they are not in keeping with your brand identity. An actor friend asked me to delete an old photo of her on Facebook, because whilst there was nothing inappropriate about it, she was heavier in it than she is currently and she has many industry contacts on her page. I of course deleted it. She wasn't being vain, merely savvy in the knowledge that it may be viewed by someone who didn't notice the date and would assume that it was a current representation of her.

Make the decision about when you're in show business mode and when you're on your own time. Some celebrities are warned by agents/managers not to misbehave at particular events and some are prepped to do just that in keeping with 'bad boy/girl' image. That's their brand and all public communication is marketing. If you want to be an actor whose personal life is private and not for sale in 'OK' and 'Heat Magazine' etc, then it's up to you to stick to your privacy ideals. It can be difficult if you're doing magazine spreads one week and asking for privacy the next. Respect for someone's personal life can be achieved even at the height of fame, Jodie Foster and Harrison Ford are both very private individuals and have always made that clear. If you always maintain your privacy and have it violated, at that point you can involve lawyers.

PRESENTING YOURSELF VISUALLY

Everyone is familiar with brand logos these days. Look at all the clothes you're wearing and your accessories – the chances are that they will be a company name you know with a logo you recognise. In using brand logos what you're aiming to do is instantly interest and reassure your audience.

As an actor you do not need a brand logo, the analogy of you as a brand only travels so far. You do however need to consistently present your brand identity (how you wish to be seen). In many cases your main point of contact will be your CV, if you have an agent use their template. We'll go into more detail on creating and maintaining a CV and associated promotional materials in chapter 3.

BRAND ASSOCIATION

Brand association is so commonplace that you won't realise that it's worked on you, but it will have already. Any item being sold wants an association to quality especially if it is somewhat of an unknown quantity. TV programmes are sponsored nowadays by chocolate manufacturers, theatre programmes are full of sponsored ads for companies who find that a link to the arts helps them and their image as much as it helps the show in question. We, the audience, see the name of the sponsor and have a reaction to it. We have feelings already associated if it's a big airline or fashion house, so for the actor how can we brand associate and with what?

- Where did you train? Does the drama school or university have a well-known logo? – Where you trained should always be on your CV but the placing of it can make a difference in the feeling we get looking at it; especially if you do not already have a long and illustrious list of credits.

Logos work because a picture is worth a thousand words, a small picture which we know to mean quality reassures us as an audience or in a shop looking to buy something. We intrinsically know the British Kite mark equates to goods of sound quality so we relax and buy them.

- If you are currently represented, your agent will have a logo because the industry is all on board with branding. The logo of your agent is of utmost importance on your CV.

Putting your agent's name and logo on your CV should be standard and yet many actors don't do this when they send their own CVs out. It is already a seal of approval and quality; it is assuring us that you are good enough to be represented by that agent. If it's a large renowned agency then by association you are up there with the big boys, as that agency always represents actors who are consistently working. Even if you're looking to move from the agent you are represented by and are writing to other agents, it still says in bold that you have been validated.

- Are you a member of Equity and/or SAG-AFTRA? Again, these are stamps of approval so you want to be associated to that organisation as you are already a part of it.

You want as many positive associations as you can have, the more companies of quality you are linked to the more your name has a ring of excellence to it. And in some small way when the audience next see the names of those companies you are associated to, they will be reminded of you. Have you worked with the R.S.C.? We think of the R.S.C. as the great company of actors it is, but we often assign the names and faces of their most famous actors to it, it makes us feel secure. The aim is to elicit good feelings and the idea that these big well-known successful companies are linked to you:

> *"'They're not stupid, so if they buy me, maybe you should buy me as well. They've made a lot of money, do you want to make a lot of money, so buy me. They've made some really good artistic decisions as well, so their advertising is purely about art and about communicating their product later on, so do you want to make some good artistic decisions, well buy me because other good artists have." So can you, clearly to your audience, associate yourself with other products, other brands that make good decisions?'*
>
> Mark Bowden, Author, UK

IS THE AUDIENCE BUYING YOU?

So you've pictured your audience as buyers purchasing your good self – and remember that audience is everyone, industry and non-industry. What every actor and everyone marketing a product wants is the same, for as many members of that audience to start buying and, more importantly, keep on buying.

With a congruent story and brand, you're working towards creating and maintaining brand loyalty from your audience, your aim being continued success. When brand loyalty works, it works really well; you just need to look at the TV faces the British public love to see again and again or the teen heartthrobs we all secretly like to watch. So if you think you've got your brand consistent and exciting, yet it's not working for you we need to look at why. Is the market already flooded with the same type? Has that type gone out of fashion?

You also need to work out if you're gearing your brand towards the wrong audience. Look at the market you're aiming to break into and check out the competition. What can you offer that is in keeping with the theme of that market be it Soap, Radio or Shakespearean tragedy? Of course you have to have the appropriate skills in abundance and an understanding of what they require. You must offer a certain something which is slightly more alluring and exciting than the other actors who are already successful in that field. If say, you're specifically aiming for a career in TV Sit Com as with Mark Bowden's example:

> *'Can you manoeuvre your abilities and your look into that, can you nudge yourself round to that, can you create a CV which is full of those kind of images? Can you create a CV with as much comedy as possible to show that that's what you do, you're a comic actor, you don't do anything else, you do comedy… If people want a comic actor, they come to you because that's your product, that's what you do, you do it best. Then you're going to be really selling to that market. They're not really concerned I would say, as to are you a good Shakespearean tragic actor. It's of no consequence. They don't want to know that. It might just confuse them.'*
>
> Mark Bowden, Author, UK

Anyone in the position of hiring in our industry; casting directors looking to cast a role, an agent looking for new talent to represent; production companies looking for assistants or theatres looking for stage managers; are all looking for the same thing. We want to meet positive capable individuals who interest us and offer us something different, something more inspiring than others do. We are trying to find someone who makes us feel they are the answer to our unknown question, someone who makes us want to say 'Yes, it's you!'

> *'If you've researched what they are doing, what you have to offer, you can then put the two things together and present yourself as a potential solution to somebody else's problem. i.e. you approach Saatchi and Saatchi, the advertising agency, with three or four commercial voice-overs not with your Shakespeare or your poetry.'*
>
> Bernard Shaw, Voice-over artist and Author, UK

This requires some focussed research from you for whatever the role is you're auditioning for. You need to be adaptable to these requirements.

GIVING YOURSELF THE EDGE

So to give yourself the edge over the countless other actors in your casting bracket what can you do? You need to be self-motivated, because most of the time in a jobbing actor's life the phone isn't ringing off the hook with job offers, it's silent to the point that you might think you need a technician to try your line for you. Chances are, however, that it is just quiet. So, if no one is phoning you and when you speak to your agent you're told 'it's quiet at the moment' don't just sit back on the sofa and whinge to your mates that you can't even get arrested.

> 'You have to think, "What can I do? Can I get together with some people, with some like-minded people; can we put on an enterprise of some kind? What about the people that I've worked with, can I contact them, or can I find out what they're doing?"... You have to rely on yourself, your own reserves, your own resilience, otherwise you are gonna get defeated by the whole process because there is the huge weight of rejection upon you.'
>
> Alison Chard, Casting Director, UK

Alison makes the good point that the contacts you have already made are a great source of tips and leads provided they don't feel 'networked' and they feel that you will give equally in that relationship. We'll come back to Alison's point about putting on enterprises with your friends in chapter 10.

TALKING HEADS

Many actors can feel lost without their script – other people's words for characters they play – dialogue they will give truth to and deliver, but it's not their own truth and not their own words.

> 'I think one of the fundamental things behind an actor as distinct from say a stand-up comedian or somebody else who puts themselves forward in public, an actor has a script, an actor relies on a script. And I know so many good actors who are without a script very pale human beings.'
>
> Simon Dunmore, Director and Author, UK

If you're talking without a script, what can you do to present yourself at your confident best?

Go back to the list you made of your key attributes, think on the positive ones. Are these things you can talk about without sounding egotistical?

- If one of your key skills is comedy but your career so far hasn't reflected that, work into conversation how much you enjoy it. You don't have to tell someone you're hilarious and a comic genius. Instead say you'd like to do more and, at some point make them laugh – if you are naturally funny you will most likely always elicit laughter in person.
- If you're by nature an inquisitive person, use this to your advantage. It will mean you're full of questions for the people you're speaking to. As long as they are not inappropriate, ask them.
- Put a positive spin on an attribute if it's one you feel is negative, i.e. you're not all that physically fit currently and you know you need to improve that, maybe you've been thinking of starting to do an extreme sport, martial art or a trek in Nepal. Remember to steer clear of lies though – they have a habit of coming back to haunt you.

Being positive and appearing confident without being egotistical is a really important part of your marketing in face-to-face situations where you will be networking.

NETWORKING

You always need to be in the know in terms of what's happening in the arts and if realistically you are a good fit for a project. If you've heard on the grapevine that a particular show is casting for a short Afro-Caribbean male and you're a tall Caucasian female do not ring the casting director or your agent about it. It's incredibly irksome to have those 'I thought there might be something in it for me' conversations when they're irrelevant and time-consuming.

I spent 20 minutes on the phone to a very pushy actress whom I'd met previously socially and whose friend had come in to audition for a project. Because the production was set in the north and she is Northern, he had tipped her off, as any good friend would do. Unfortunately she was not in any way right for the female roles. I had to spend part of my incredibly busy day explaining diplomatically why a) as someone who's met her, I would have mentioned her were she appropriate for the project and b) her friend is not the director, casting director, casting assistant or the producer, so does not know how we are casting the other roles. She would have got very short shrift indeed had someone else answered the phone. That over–the-top pushiness and inability to listen, absolutely worked against her for future opportunities.

So back to my example, if you are a short black guy, see what you can find out about the production you've heard is looking for your casting bracket. The Internet is an amazing tool and some of your friends may have been up for it. If you've been in for it and you feel you didn't nail it, do you think any of your friends are right for it? Pay it forward. Call them and let them know about it – and be *specific*. It's a competitive industry but it doesn't have to be cutthroat. We often see actor friends coming in for the same roles.

Networking is a subtle and acquired skill, we've all been networked inappropriately before and we remember it, for me being networked at a funeral was an all time low. Seriously, wrong. Also, out on a hen night. It was more than a little annoying and I remember those actors for all the wrong reasons…

- Choose your moments well, i.e. the funeral, an inappropriate choice and quite desperate.
- If you are out socially and it turns out the person you are talking to is in the business, think about it – they are out socially too. A bit of shop talk is fine but no handing your

CV or business card to some who is dancing or propping up the bar all night next to them.
- Think about what it is you want to say about yourself, this is face-to-face marketing after all. It should be in line with your brand, clear, concise, interesting and exciting.
- Think about the person you're talking to, if their preferred medium is theatre it's not that bright to bend their ear about how you really want to get into commercials or films and vice versa.
- We all network a little when out at industry events and socially if introduced by a friend or colleague. Remember it's a conversation – don't dive straight in there with the thinly veiled 'what can you do for my career' line, we can see through it.
- If you're networking someone in the hopes of them genuinely offering you advice or help, do not turn it into a chat up. It's incredibly unflattering to both parties and transparent, none of which is appealing.
- If when talking you're are asked 'Do you have an agent?' never answer with 'Yes, but I'm looking.' It is disrespectful, if you're unhappy then be proactive, research other agents, don't just try to get the low down of all agents whilst talking to a casting director, producer, actor or indeed another agent.
- It's not a one-way stream. We are a community, there are always ways you can help your friends and peers, recommending someone-else for something you're not available or not quite right for is: a) a good pay it forward kind of thing to do generally and you'll feel all warm and fuzzy if it leads to something and b) it helps the person you're talking to find the right person whom they might not know yet and that makes you look not only like a 'good egg' but also an intelligent professional with a pragmatic understanding of the business.

- Remember it's a conversation not a counselling or careers advice session so converse. Don't recite a monologue – ask the person you're talking to questions as well, because actually it's human nature to want to help people we genuinely like. So take the pressure off it and talk *with* them. The chances are they'll see something they like in you and then will remember you.
- Try to remember their name and face. It's not just unprofessional, it's actually rude to be introduced to someone on numerous occasions who always wants your help and advice but can't be bothered to remember who you are. Americans have a great trick for this which we'll look at it chapter 3.

> *'I wish I'd done it [networking] I didn't, I think I was judgemental about it... If you're afraid of it and you feel it's a dirty word, think of it as helping, not just yourself but helping others... people are trying to help each other. I think in a world that is obsessed with celebrity, obsessed with profile, you have to enter it, you have to, nobody is going to discover you, but nobody.'*
>
> Ann Mitchell, Actor and Director, UK

Good networking pays off. If you're charming, interesting, engaging and sound like you're a committed professional, people will remember you.

HAVING AN INTERNET PRESENCE

Every working actor in Britain should be in the Spotlight directory and IMDB.com (Internet Movie Database), with *up-to-date* credits, the casting process often requires immediate or very quick ideas and answers about actors. If you're not in Spotlight or don't have contact details on IMDB, you don't look committed to the profession because if we can't contact your agent to enquire about you, you're not that bothered about working surely. Having your own website is not enough. The industry is too busy to be trawling the Internet for your specific website, have a link to it by all means, but that link should be on your Spotlight page.

> 'I do look at actors' websites, particularly European actors.'
> John Hubbard, Casting Director, UK

> 'It's a good place to hear someone's voice tape or showreel… And particularly I think, on the Spotlight website, because that's a central base, I think perhaps more than individual actor's websites where you're having to dodge round the web.'
> Alison Chard, Casting Director, UK

Some actors have You Tube channels with vast quantities of their work.

- If you're particularly interested in comedy, put some sketches together on You Tube or Vimeo, you can link these to your Spotlight CV and a website if you have one.

Do you see lots of theatre and love to talk about it?

- Why not blog about it on your website, these are things that your audience can then take the time to look at if a) they are interested and b) they have the time. Just make sure it looks professionally done and is easy to navigate.

You should always have your showreel link on your Spotlight page.

SOCIAL MEDIA

Think about your use of the Internet and social media: which part is for your career and which part is for your social life? Be aware of the difference. Some actors choose to have two pages per site, one for the person and one for their acting persona.

- If you are using the same Twitter, Facebook, instagram etc, accounts for both your professional and personal life, it should have a professional sounding handle, i.e. your name, not a mix of letters and numbers spelling something suggestive. You are a professional and you must appear so.

Also be aware that other professionals in the industry use social media sites such as Facebook and Twitter for the social aspect as we are allowed to have a life outside our careers too. If you friend request a casting director, director or producer we may well ignore your request to retain *our* privacy.

- Don't tweet or Facebook message an individual or company asking for an audition unless they have requested twitter replies as such. Social media is not where or how castings are arranged.
- Are you on Linked-In? Are you trying to connect with industry professionals you already know? Are you making connections here with industry professionals you do not know? Who should you connect with?

Let me be clear – you should only be connecting with people whom you know professionally. It lessens the professional worth of the site if you are trying to connect with all and sundry in the vain hope that it will improve your career. Do not ask to connect unless you have met or worked with the individual. Linked-In provides a way of validating people professionally at a glance,

'Ooh look at all those connections and skills.' This validation is lost if the connections are not real and earned, they then don't mean anything.

- Are you tweeting, instagramming and/or Facebooking snippets about your latest work?

Make sure you have permission to do so first. Many productions require an official press release before actors involved can publicise photos of themselves on set or even mention that they were involved in it. You can always check in with your agent who in turn will check in with the appropriate channels. Once you've had the official go ahead; go ahead.

MARKETING IS A CONTINUOUS PROCESS

Does there come a time when you stop marketing yourself?

No. It's easy to become complacent if you feel you are doing well and have a good body of work behind you, but it's a fickle business. Competition gets harder as the number of performers and reality TV 'stars' increases. Mark Bowden elaborates:

> *'If you look at big brands, Coca Cola, they're market leaders and each year they will pump more and more money into their promotion of themselves because the more you're at the top the more you need to try and stay there, the more you need to try and get your message out to people. I heard one actor say once that it's really easy to get on TV. The difficult part is staying there and staying there requires marketing.'*
>
> Mark Bowden, Author, UK

If you look at stars or huge successful companies they never stop promoting, so you just continue it as part of your working life and business strategy. You need to think about ways to be distinctive and exciting which are in keeping with your brand. Don't lose sight of your goals, you don't want to be driving your career forward to such an extent that you drive past them in a different direction. To a practised hand the marketing of your career becomes second nature and an intrinsic part of conversation and activity. Being an actor is an integral part of who you are but it's not all you are. Whatever and however many your career goals are, like Richard Branson, keep sight of them. You may get all you want and more, just like the bearded man himself, if you keep focused on the end goal you can enjoy the journey as much as the rewards.

SUMMARY

What you can take away from this chapter is that to get the industry's attention and keep it for as long as you wish to perform will take self-promotion. We've looked at the basics of marketing and what that entails, to introduce you to something that will always be a part of your career; taking a realistic view of yourself and your key achievements and attributes and capitalising on them. Deciding on your brand essence, image, identity and story so you can always be consistent. Looking at your goals and tailoring your promotion in order to gain as many opportunities in that field as you can; ways to network appropriately and effectively and how essential it is to have an Internet presence nowadays. Throughout, we have said to be aware and make sure you are always appropriate, never inappropriate or a nuisance as that will work against you. In the next chapter we cover the marketing tools in more depth.

CHAPTER 3

MARKETING TOOLS

We looked at ways to grab and keep the industry's attention in chapter 2. Here we look at the specifics of getting your promotional materials right in their content and presentation. We'll look at:

- Your CV in depth, from content to typography, colour and paper.
- Your photo and what that image needs to say about you.
- Your mail out, the covering letter, why and whom you're sending it to.
- Your showreel, what to include and when to send it.
- Your voicereel, what to include, how to record it and whom to send it to.
- And we'll cover the difference in British and American marketing.

YOUR MARKETING TOOLS

The harsh reality is:

> *'You're a product and you've got to market yourself.'*
> John Hubbard, Casting Director, UK

So what are the basic marketing tools that an actor needs to attract and keep someone's attention? You have to be able to write to casting directors, theatre or production companies and agents alike; be that for theatre or screening invites, if you are currently unrepresented or looking to move from your agent.

> '30 odd years later I've still such vivid memories of the sense of dislocation… as an actor, that writing around all over the country for auditions. And then pleading for auditions and then getting the audition and feeling that you were only kind of just about standing on the gangplank, let alone been up allowed to stand on the deck of the ship.'
>
> Sir Richard Eyre CBE, Director, UK

How can we get you off the gangplank and treading those boards… Materially speaking you need: an industry standard CV; a good realistic headshot; a short, strong, edited showreel; a voicereel if you want audio work and a succinct and well-presented covering letter. In person: a well presented you – the actor, an ability to network appropriately, the charm and apparent ease it takes to pull that off. What are you going to do with these tools and attributes?

The point of marketing is to get someone (our target) to do something we want them to do. This is known as a 'Call to action', you can see it everywhere: 'For more information call this number' and in the Internet world 'Click here' or 'Read more'. The commercials, print adverts and/or websites must be able to explain why their target would want to do the desired action i.e. what's in it for them? In your case:

- Call to action #1 is 'Look at my promotional materials.' Why should they, if they have a pile of 100 or more on their desk?
- Call to action #2 is 'Give me a chance/an audition/the role.' Again, why should the casting director, director, producer or theatre company give you that opportunity?

What will make your CV, headshot, showreel and covering letter get looked at and eventually acted upon? Remember 'standing out' as we will see later does not necessarily equal 'effective' and what you need are *effective* marketing tools.

CURRICULUM VITAE

Your CV is a list of productions you can be credited for working on, be that from a varied career or as a new graduate. Your CV is actually more than just the credits sat upon a piece of paper. Nowadays the presentation of your CV is also key.

Most actors have a generic CV, which they send out to everyone. Your agent will also have one, it will list your credits, most recent first and they will be in categories: film, television and theatre. The actual order of category depends on the agent and if you specialize in a particular medium. Always make sure your credits are up-to-date!

> *'Keep it up-to-date because that's the one thing about Spotlight is that a lot of the CVs are completely out of date. And we do now rely a lot on running off CVs from [the] Spotlight website... therefore the producer or director will not know your recent body of work... actors are not keeping them updated or their agents are not doing it on their behalf.'*
>
> Alison Chard, Casting Director, UK

SPOTLIGHT CV

On your Spotlight CV your characteristics should be up-to-date and appropriate, in particular:

- Age range. If you joined when you were 16 and ticked the 16-21 box, but are now 40, un-tick the boxes which are no longer appropriate. Spotlight doesn't automatically un-tick as you add a new age; think about it, can you really play 16-40? Really?
- Skills i.e. dance, sports, singing range etc. The most infuriating skill actors list is accents. There is a list to tick for 'native' accent/dialect and one for 'proficient.' You CANNOT be native to every regional accent in the UK, across Europe, Asia, Africa and the USA. There are some actors who have ticked as native every accent they believe they can do. They come up time and again on searches when casting directors are looking specifically for native speakers (from wherever). Funnily enough these actors tend not to get called in for audition.
- Categorise your credits so that the person looking at your CV can see immediately what stage, TV, film, short film and radio credits you have, rather than trawling all the way through a long history of credits that has no sensible order.

IMDB is a great resource for the industry, you can have a professional account which requires a paid subscription, or you can use the regular free site. When you want to add any credits if you have not been credited in error or you are adding your agent details on the 'contact' page, there is an edit option on every production listed. IMDB of course verify all these so don't be pretending you're the new James Bond if you're not, you'll just end up in trouble.

Don't think of your CV in a humdrum way. Ask yourself a few questions. What do you want your CV to do for you at this moment? Are you looking for a new agent?

- If you are currently represented, use your agency's CV so it's on their letterhead. They can always email you a PDF of it. It's fine to send your Spotlight CV, as long as it is up-to-date. Some agencies use Spotlight CVs for their clients. Agents who have their own CVs however, always set them out to show their agency branding and look good. You can't hide that you have an agent if you're looking for new representation and why would you want to? Eventually there'll be a conversation between the agents; a list of the roles you were suggested for recently, any headshots etc, will all be sent to the new agent.

- If you are not currently represented then you can use your Spotlight CV. However setting out your own CV – as an agent would have done by taking on board their aesthetics – is quite shrewd. Make sure you put your contact details on your CV if you are not represented, your postal address, mobile number (with spaces so we can read it easily) and your email address.
- If you are sending your Spotlight CV via email, always send the actual link to your page not your pin number. Email yourself your CV and then copy and paste that link into the email you are sending. Make it easy.

If you're doing a mail out to casting directors, theatre or production companies for specific reasons this requires thought and effort on your part:

- If you're inviting people en masse to a play or screening of a film you are in, it makes more of a mark if you've tailored your CV to whomever you're sending it to. Think about the work they do: if it's a film and television casting director or producer, put your screen credits first; if it's a theatre casting director or theatre company put those first. Some won't notice, but the point is that you made it easier for them to glean the information they need from your CV in as short a time as possible. And we are all short on time.

Are you writing a general 'please think of me' letter? If so the same principle applies.

- Tailor your CV for the side of the industry the recipient specialises in. If you don't know because you're going through 'Contacts'(7) from A – Z, then research them! All industry professionals who've been credited on screen work are listed on IMDB. For theatre professionals you'll find information on them if you Google them. You need to show you are interested in *them* specifically.

So, how should you present your CV? How should it look and feel? Where should your name be? Your agent's name? What font should you use? How many colours? So many questions…

There are two distinct types of agency CVs, ones with a small photo and ones without.

If you want a CV that is just words and a separate photo, remember we read left to right and top to bottom. Your CV is all about you. The speed at which we all have to work means we briefly scan everything before *deciding* whether to read it – it's that moment when someone flicks their eyes across the top of your CV that it must grab their attention.

The agent's name and logo reassures us. Your name large and appropriately placed tells us who you are. If you put a small photo of you in the top corner of the page, it gives a physical reality to those credits.

You need to think about your association with your agent as like the sponsor at a theatre event, they are your business partners. If you are not currently represented then there is the Spotlight logo, in itself a seal of approval; a very clever design on their part. It gives you the added stamp of legitimacy even without an agent. Make good use of it.

Even though most recipients would nowadays rather receive it all by email, treat the content and design in the same way as if you are posting hard copies. Send a pdf of your CV if via email not a word document to avoid any mac/pc compatibility issues.

When structuring your CV there are a few useful industry standards to pay attention to.

- Content: The length of your CV can be an issue. Some people only want to see 1 page of your best credits, others are happy with 2. Avoid 3 pages because the chances of all those credits being great (and read) are slim. You may need to cull early credits. The one-liner parts you did 15 years ago are no longer relevant if you're not going for those roles anymore. If you graduated many years ago, get rid of your 'theatre whilst training' credits. John Hubbard's opinion is:

'I've done 150 movies and my CV is on 1 page, I don't see why actors cannot put everything on 1 page. I think what also helps is like a little photograph on the CV as well, so for filing purposes I'm 1 sheet. I'm not 4 photographs, 2 letters, 3 CVs, you know. But everything you've done, what I like is at the top I like film or TV and then I like theatre, that's because I'm a film and television casting director.'

John Hubbard, Casting Director, UK

- Education & Training: Where you trained should always be visible on your CV unless you're at the height of success and there isn't room. For most jobbing actors you can afford to lose one fringe theatre or short film credit in order to have your drama school/university listed.

'What's important to me is where an actor trained, no I'll go back a step, that an actor trained. I think actors should train, there are of course exceptions that prove the rule,

but on the whole acting is a craft and people should train to be actors. So where an actor trained is important to me, who an actor has worked with – the directors on a list, I mean if an actor has worked with a director that I like then I reckon that that actor must be OK to have been accepted to the ranks of that director's cast. If an actor's just played Hamlet or [is] about to play Hamlet of course that will stand out. At the other end of that extreme if an actor hasn't worked for 3 years, that will stand out. I think at the extremes of anything it's very easy to make a judgement.'

Joyce Nettles, Casting Director, UK

- Page Layouts: There are usually 3 or 4 columns of information on an actor's CV. The name of the show on the left, the character you played either in italics on the same column or separately on the next column to the right, (that's why it's either 3 or 4, it's a design choice). Next goes either the director or the theatre company/production company, and channel if it was for TV, these last two columns vary between agencies. I have included templates to help you visualise this more easily. On these templates I've used the example that you played 'Mr Darcy' in 'Pride and Prejudice' directed by Jane Doe, on one I'll put it as a stage show, secondly as TV programme and lastly a film.

| Your Photo | Agency name and logo |

Your Name
Height: 6' Hair: Brown Eyes: Brown

THEATRE

PRIDE & PREJUDICE   *Mr Darcy*   Adelphi Theatre   Jane Doe

TELEVISION

FILM

SKILLS:

TRAINING:

YOUR NAME

Your postal address
Your mobile number
Your email address
Height: 6' Hair: Brown Eyes: Brown

TELEVISION:

PRIDE & PREJUDICE *Mr Darcy* Red Box For BBC1 Jane Doe

FILM:

THEATRE:

THEATRE WHILST TRAINING:

SKILLS:

TRAINING

Agency and name logo	Your Photo

YOUR NAME

Height: 6' Hair: brown Eyes: Brown

FILM:
PRIDE & PREJUDICE (*Mr Darcy*)　　　　Jane Doe　　　　Great Films

TELEVISION:

THEATRE:

SKILLS:

TRAINING

- Type size: Your name and agent (if you have one) need to be in text significantly larger than the credits.
- Typeface: The font you choose should be easy to read and not fussy, we don't have time to try to decipher beautiful but illegible calligraphy on all your credits. Choose a font that's strong, either go for a simple minimal font like Geneva CY, Verdana or Charcoal CY or a serif font like Garamond, Palatino or Times New Roman. Whether your whole CV is in capital letters or not is a design choice but make sure your name is in upper case.
- Differentiation through type: Sometimes the name of the production is in capitals, the character, director and theatre/production company is in sentence case. Remember you can use **Bold** and *Italics* as well, just don't go mad.
- Paper colour: Another factor is the colour of your paper. This background colour can be warm or cold, aggressive, too bright or too dull. In general warm cream or off white colours tend to have a better response than cold blues or aggressive reds. Bright white can be too harsh. Bright Yellow can be too much. Green and pink don't necessarily look serious as background colours on your A4 CV. Think about your paper colour before you start thinking about text colours.
- Paper Quality: This is of course only if you are posting a hard copy not emailing. Is your paper thin and flimsy like copy paper or a bit more solid and reliable? Does it have the texture that older thicker paper used to have, what's the weight of it in your hand? Many home printers can only cope with a limited thickness of paper. Standard office paper ranges between 75-90 gsm(8) but can feel pretty feeble. Home printers can usually cope with up to 120 gsm. Check your printer's specifications. The texture of your paper can have an emotional association worth considering, is it smooth, glossy and slick or matt and understatedly dependable?

- Text colours: Your CV needs to look professional, your credits and your name need to stand out but don't go crazy with all the colours your printer can mix. Brightly coloured wording or way too many colours distract from your credits, hurt our eyes and can look like someone vomited on the page. This does not help you. Keep it simple. Choose wisely, bearing your reader in mind. Those of us whom you'll be sending your CV to, receive more per day than you can imagine. If you want colours like green, pink or red, it can be a stylish decision, if you have black text on top so that we can read it. It will still highlight and frame the text.
- Logos: If you have an agent their name and/or logo is always at the top.
- Photos: It is a really helpful for quick reference and means that, from a casting perspective, you don't have to mess with other pages to see someone's face.

It may feel that I'm being too prescriptive in setting out rules, leaving little room for personality. This is not my intention. It's just that every profession has a standard they follow which has been developed over a number of years. Like it or not everyone within that industry has become accustomed to responding in a particular way to paperwork that feels 'appropriate' to them. Mark Bowden gives his insight into the paper your CV is printed on:

> *'People can feel your CV and people respond to feeling… If you've got it on photocopier paper, the cheap stuff… words go through your head maybe like "flimsy, ordinary, plain, flat" those words frame the rest of that audience's experience of you, every time they read that credit, it's a flat credit, it's a flimsy credit. So can you put it on paper that's maybe firmer, more exciting in some way, it has*

> *texture, maybe it has a feeling of depth to it, maybe it has words that you would associate, that you would like associated to you as an actor... Scientists would say that yellow is the colour that most people will choose if given a choice between red, blue, white and yellow. If I were to say to you pick a colour, you'll all on the whole immediately go for yellow, however yellow and black is nature's warning signal, it says "keep off I'm dangerous, I bite." But if you soften that yellow, you'll notice that every time you bring it in front of your face you get a little warm feeling, actually you'll start to smile slightly. And there is a paper called vellum which has this soft yellow in it, also it's thicker than other paper, it's about 100 grams per square metre and it's bonded, it's laid, it has a texture to it, it's firmer in your hands and it will give you a little smile. Try putting your CV on that and seeing if you come across as more pleasant firmer experience.'*

Mark Bowden, Author, UK

SMILING FOR YOUR PHOTO WITHOUT SAYING 'CHEESE'

The headshot, the first impression you can make for yourself visually before you've met someone. This should be a good quality photo, which you can also include as the small one within your CV.

> *'You need to express a good aspect of your personality, [so] that something shines out of that photograph that shows some kind of spark. "Hi, here I am, I'm me and I'm happy with myself".'*

Simon Dunmore, Director and Author, UK

Ooh we've all seen some corkers over the years. It's surprisingly difficult for many actors to get a good headshot for various reasons, but often it's simply that they cannot just 'be' in front of the camera if not in character. Being comfortable being yourself is key for a good photo and your photographer should help relax and bring 'you' out. Don't use your mate and their smart phone; always use a professional photographer.

What your photo needs to show:

- A flattering but realistic photo of your face, as you are now, not 15 years ago.
- Your eyes looking at the camera and thinking about something.
- Your head facing the camera.
- You as you, not in character.
- You in focus, especially your eyes.
- You centrally placed.
- The not quite smiling yet still inviting, intelligent, attractive expression commonly known as a 'Mona Lisa Smile'.

What your photo should *not* show:

- You in character or costume.
- Your hands obscuring your face to be 'arty'.
- A card with 4 small pictures of you showing your 'range.'
- You wearing glasses, (Specs are a prop) unless you actually wear them.
- You in fussy frilly tops, busy patterns or bright colours, particularly if the shot itself is in colour as these all detract from your face.
- You in a social setting with your arm around someone whom you cropped out.
- A selfie in your bedroom.

> 'The photograph is extremely important and I think it's much more than most actors feel, that they get a very strong accurate photograph of themselves, as they actually are. Now what I mean by that is that, you know sometimes people, you get these pictures divided into 4 pictures: me as a bus conductor; me as hamlet; me as something else. It just doesn't help; I'm not looking at the real you. So I think a full face, very honest photograph, photographed by a professional.'
>
> John Hubbard, Casting Director, UK

You must be relaxed, so you need a photographer with whom you feel comfortable and have a rapport. It's quite difficult to smile slightly at a camera or look enigmatic and alluring whilst someone takes hundreds of photos. You're not in character, you're not acting, it's about capturing you. Outdoor shots often elicit a more relaxed expression than in the studio. They just do. For a good photographer the natural and uncontrollable lighting is not an issue.

Have a look through Spotlight or agent websites at other actors' photos; you'll see the kinds of expressions they have. They tend not to be a broad grin showing all their gnashers, nor be incredibly pouty. What they are is a good likeness with an interesting thought behind the eyes, sometimes a determined set to the jaw or the beginnings of a smile. You'll have to try it out to see what works for you, your face and the feeling you want to convey.

> 'It's a very human interaction between the photographer – actor relationship, it's almost like the actor to actor relationship or the director to actor relationship, or the television cameraman or sound engineer to the actor. You react off each other. And having a good photograph that evokes you in black and white… It can make such a difference.'
>
> Simon Dunmore, Director and Author, UK

If emailing, always use a smaller Jpeg than your original photo, which will be a huge file. If sending hard copy, the standard is 10" x 8". You can get smaller, which admittedly is a bit cheaper, but there is good reason 10 x 8 is the norm. It is nearly life size and you're trying to use your face to make a human connection to someone whilst not physically in the same room. Not in a metaphysics or spiritual way, just practically. Their eyes looking at your eyes, life size, albeit probably in black and white.

Should your main headshot be colour or black and white? This is personal choice, the standard was black and white, but remember that's how film started out. We film and watch in colour nowadays. I would say if your main headshot is back and white, make sure your secondary picture on Spotlight is in colour and vice versa.

Whenever you send a hardcopy of your photo and CV make sure the return envelope you enclose is large enough for your photo if you would like it back. No one is going to go to their own expense to return your headshot, why should they? It shows you've not really thought about what you're doing, which doesn't look very professional or bright.

What feeling should your photo convey?

Well, this all depends on what you are aiming for. You will always have one photo which is your main headshot, this is the one your agent will send out and will be used in theatre programmes. The beauty of the Spotlight website is you can have secondary photos, this is where more characterful photos can be used and you can have production stills here. You can have an intriguing main photo or a friendlier one and your secondary photos can be darker, more dangerous… a bit more sexy. It all depends on what you want as the main feeling. Make sure you keep in line with your brand and your story, which we covered in chapter 2. Mark Bowden's thoughts on the feeling of your photo are:

> 'Your photograph to be a good tool has got to give across the feeling that you're trying to sell, it doesn't want to be bland... But it's got to produce some kind of excitement, it doesn't have to be a good feeling either, remember negative feelings or feelings that we might consider to be negative can sell as well, actors like Leslie Grantham make a business out of being "bad."'
>
> Mark Bowden, Author, UK

Most casting directors are Internet friendly these days. They are used to being emailed small Jpegs and looking online. However the look and feel of a hard copy 10 x 8 is always better than one they've printed out on whatever office printer they have. Some 'old school' casting directors still prefer to receive hard copies in the post because ultimately they will want to show a good quality likeness to the directors and producers they are working with. Emailing or posting is a judgement call you have to make, if they have a website it may tell you their preference.

> 'It becomes important if I want to promote that actor, suggest that actor for something and I need to show that headshot to somebody else.'
>
> Joyce Nettles, Casting Director, UK

> 'It is more tangible and when you are sitting down with the director and the producer, you're showing them something actual, rather than them scrolling down a computer screen. And they like to take it away and have a look at it and see if they've worked with somebody before. So yes, hard copy is still the way to go I think but just for swiftness and efficiency email has helped considerably. But people do have to use it wisely really and not just bash off things in great volume. I think I'm not the only one whose computer has jammed and crashed whilst receiving

some probably rather marvellous showreel, but [laughs] it hasn't come through.'

Alison Chard, Casting Director UK

One last thing on headshots; either stick a printed label with your name and agent on the back of the photo, or write it on. This provides quick reference for who you are and how you can be contacted if your headshot becomes separated from the rest of your details, which it will.

THE MAIL OUT

Mail outs are one of those strange phenomena in our industry. None of us really like them, but they are a necessity. The success rate of a mail out can't really be measured, because it's all so subjective. Good occasions for a mail out are:

- If you'd like to invite people to a stage show or a screening of a film you are in.
- You're looking to change or get an agent.
- You're graduating from drama school and you're inviting casting directors and agents to see you in the showcase.
- Work has been quiet so you're trying to remind the industry that you're here, ready and able to work.

Don't send out a generic mail out. They are lazy and that is not the impression you want to give of yourself as an actor, because you are not. Targeted mail outs have a higher chance of working in your favour.

So how do you target your audience? Research who you are writing to and think about why. Seriously. I'll say it again and again, look on the Internet, find out about the person/company. If you don't, at least half of your mail out will be a pointless expense. It also annoys the recipients no end. Everyone in the industry is a very busy individual if they have taken the time to read your letter, the very least you can do is know to whom it is you are writing to.

This may seem obvious, but often eludes those sending mail outs, if it is postal the presentation includes the envelopes you send out and your SASE (self-addressed stamped envelope).

> *'If somebody sends me something in a scruffy brown envelope, it doesn't make an impression. If it's in a white envelope, preferably a padded envelope with a nicely printed label saying who it's from, what it is they have to offer – that's interesting, because I know the person has a grasp of how the business works.'*
>
> Bernard Shaw, Voice-over artist and Author, UK

COVERING LETTERS – PERSONALISING THEM EFFECTIVELY

How do you personalise the actual covering letter to your targeted audience? At the risk of teaching old ladies to suck eggs… this comes down to research and presentation.

If your mail out is to casting directors, what is your reason for it?

- If it is a general 'Hi, remember me, I'm available for work', then make sure you send it to appropriate casting directors for the work you're interested in. As with your CV, tailor your letters appropriately. It makes a difference to the person opening their mail.
- Have you met the casting director before? If so remind them in your covering letter, perhaps they came to see you in a show or met for a particular production.

- If it is specifically an invite to a show/screening or to tell them about a TV show you're currently appearing in, make that apparent. Include a flier for the show, put the dates of the show clearly in the letter in case the flier gets lost. All the relevant information together, concisely. When and where it is on is – bizarrely – often missed out. Including the flier alone isn't enough; it *will* get separated from your letter.
- Be realistic with location; what are the odds that a busy London casting director has the time or inclination to see you in fringe theatre in the Shetlands really, or Stoke-On-Trent? I'll tell you now, it's slim to none.
- If they accept the invitation, do NOT seat them on the front row – it is way to close.
- Have you seen their work? Do you actually like their casting choices? Have you ever thought someone was a really brave, inspired idea and that excited you? Tell them, not for flattery's sake, but because you're showing you put the time in to research them, you understand the industry and like their taste.
- Don't just generically say how great they are; those letters go in the bin.
- Casting directors usually use their full name; so generally you can tell their gender, do not open with "Dear Sir or Madam". It's strange after having addressed an envelope or typed in an email address.

The implications of not researching the person you are writing to are huge. It makes them question the likelihood that you'll research for roles if you get meetings or the part? No one likes a lazy actor because those who are committed work incredibly hard and sacrifice a lot of their time to make their performances the best they can be. So you don't want to mistakenly appear apathetic. Mark Bowden and Joyce Nettles make their points on research:

'Making sure that you're telling people that what they've asked for, you've got. If somebody's looking for a Shakespearean actor you better reply to them "I am a Shakespearean actor." If they are looking for a film actor you better say "I'm a film actor", tell them what they want to hear.'

Mark Bowden, Author, UK

'I would say between 40 and 50% of the letters that I get that the actor doesn't know who I am or what I do. Mistake number one. Now I'm not saying that because I'm particularly grand, I'm not saying every actor should know what I do, but if he wants me to help him, if he needs me more than I need him, he should make a little bit of an effort. I mean I wouldn't make a job application (and that's after all what a letter from an actor is) without finding out a little bit about the person to whom I was writing. And as I said these days with all sorts of ways of finding out more about people that we don't always want them to know, there's really no excuse for a "Dear Sir or Madam" letter I don't think.'

Joyce Nettles, Casting Director, UK

If your mail out is to find new agent representation:

- Go to the checklist at the beginning of chapter 2 about picking the right agent and follow those points.
- Market yourself as a solution to their problem. Is there a gap in their client list which your 'type' would fill? That's what you need to concentrate on and express to them.
- Have you met them before? Mention if so.
- If you particularly like some of their existing clients and would like a career that mirrors theirs, tell them.
- Are you currently in a stage show or have a screening you

would like to invite them to, or in a TV show that they can see you in?
- If you're looking to change agents ask yourself why? Be honest. If you feel there was a lack of communication and/or you were getting meetings for work that didn't interest you then mention it, but always in a positive way. Do not bitch about your current (or old if you've left already) agent, it's bad form and those agents may be friends.
- Don't keep emailing/writing to the same agents repeatedly if they've said No before or not replied. If they said their books were closed that was a polite No, so move on.

Regardless of whom you are writing to, always:

- Spell-check your letter. And make sure that you have their correct contact details, they are listed in *Contacts* but you can always check the Internet.
- Check on their website how they prefer submissions, via email or post. *Never* just turn up with your CV and headshot hoping for 5 minutes… You can guarantee it will be the worst day you could have chosen.
- If you have written to the individual/company before think about how often you should send them updates, mail outs, invites, etc. Personally I would say not more often than four – six months. Updating someone every five minutes about your latest commercial or guest role in a TV serial is not necessary and can make the recipients feel annoyed or harassed. Update people when appropriate, invite them if they have not already seen you in something similar.

'If you get a 10% response, most of which will be negative, you've done something… If your paper promotional package looks good and is well laid out and is well constructed and is well written you can up your response

> *rates to at least 50% if not more. It's amazing how many paper submissions are pushed to one side because they are badly constructed in some way, or many ways. You should see the rubbish that comes through and the number of agents and casting directors who've complained about various aspects of it to me is extraordinary... Spelling, I find it deeply annoying if not offensive sometimes, with name spelling especially of people.'*
>
> Simon Dunmore, Director and Author, UK

Postal Mail outs are expensive; this is why a targeted one makes much more business sense. It's time to consider the financial implications.

- List everyone you are writing to before you start. If you can only afford a set number of photos and hard backed large envelopes, don't start alphabetically and miss someone who may be more appropriate for you.
- Add up the cost per individual mailing, i.e. the 10 x 8 headshot, the nice thick textured paper for the letter and CV, the stamps for your SASE and the outgoing envelope. If you include a hard copy DVD showreel, the cost of that DVD and its case. It all adds up.

Once you see how much it costs to send one, you can decide realistically how much you can afford, then you can choose whom to write to.

If it's a 'Please remember me' to people you've met, if you're in something on TV for example; Simon Dunmore has a nice way that's cheaper than a full on mail out but still looks professional:

> *'Sending out reminder postcards, well designed simple reminders saying "I'm doing this"... A simple postcard*

> *that somebody can read, it attracts their attention, they can look at it. "Ah yeah, I remember her" and you put it in the bin, the casting director or agent or whatever, but it sticks in there. It takes time, it costs money, but it's a much much cheaper way of doing things, just to keep people reminded, but you've got to have a certain track record before you can do that.'*
>
> Simon Dunmore, Director and Author, UK

Keep your letter short. Everyone you are writing to is being written to by countless other hopefuls as well. Show some of your personality whilst still being succinct. We don't need to know the name of your long dead pet and how it inspired you to be an actor. Think about what you're writing.

Casting directors or their assistants read every letter and email sent to them. Some will of course end up filed in the round filing cabinet under the desk, that gets recycled on Wednesdays... that's inevitable.

> *'I personally check all of them and I will give them I don't know 5 or 6 seconds, I think the first thing is the photograph... then my judgement is backed up by the CV or the letter. For example I mean I can look at a face and go "Interesting, there's something interesting there."'*
>
> John Hubbard, Casting Director, UK

Some actors send novelties in their mail outs to make more of an impact, should you?

No. Really, No. It doesn't look professional. Give your friends or loved ones random gifts. Don't include them with your 'please consider me' letter.

The use of gifts between companies is very different to an actor sending a half box of Celebrations to all and sundry. Alison Chard explains why not to do it:

'I do get strange things, you know written in crayon on sort of torn out bits from notebooks and I'm afraid that kind of gives off waves of strangeness really, so those do tend to get put in the bin I'm afraid. Nice conqueror notepaper [laughs]... I don't necessarily like the kind of out of the ordinary, I mean I get all sorts of things from tea bags to sweeties, to Shakespearean poetry and I kind of think "Well yes that's very creative and nice, but really it's not the point actually."'

Alison Chard, Casting Director, UK

If you are emailing rather than posting:

- Copy and paste the text from your covering letter as the body of writing in your email, make sure you check the formatting so that there are no problems with accidental changes to font size, etc. This can happen when pasting into emails and is not always apparent to the sender.
- Always title your emails appropriately so the recipient knows that it is not spam and opens it. The amount of show invites that an email service provider will automatically put in the junk folder because of the title or lack thereof is staggering.
- Make sure your email address looks professional. i.e.: yourname@yourprovider *not* dragon@, fluffybunny@ or any such nonsense, if that is your personal address, then use it just for personal things, but for your career it needs to feel business-like.
- Think about your timing before you hit send. If it is well past business hours, save it as a draft and send in the morning! Being woken up in the wee hours by an email for new headshots or an invite to something in a town far, far away does not endear the actor to the tired recipient at all. If it is apparent from their social media that they are away on holiday – wait till they have returned to send your email/

letter; saying 'I hope you're enjoying your holiday, here are my new headshots' is not a great idea – yes I did receive that email…

Should you ring or email to check that they received your letter or first email? *No.* Even just for courtesy? *No.* It just wastes everyone's time, no 'ifs', no 'buts.' Send your letter/email and if the casting director, agent, producer, or production company is interested – they will be in touch. Have some faith in your presentation of yourself and then leave it with us.

The double check can give the impression that you are a nuisance. Another point on unsolicited phone calls is – don't make them:

- Don't phone up just to introduce yourself as an actor. You don't need to if you are on Spotlight, IMDB, have an agent and/or are doing a mail out at some point.
- Don't call and insist on trying to talk to the casting director in person and not their assistant. It annoys the pair of them and works against you getting an audition.
- Don't ring every few weeks asking to speak to them. This just comes across as really pushy, which is not how you want to appear.
- Don't call a casting director or agent on their mobile just to introduce yourself, that is not an emergency.
- Don't call casting directors or agents at unreasonable hours or on public holidays. Understand that other people in the industry also have right to a life outside work too.

How about writing to directors? The success of those letters relies entirely on the director in question, if they like being written to and/or read those letters and if so, how they are presented. Many resident theatre directors will automatically just pass them on to the casting department.

> 'They can write to me personally, but I always hand it on because there's no point in me trying to create lists and things. We've got a wonderful casting department and so it goes to them and they sort it from there.'
>
> Braham Murray OBE, Artistic Director, UK

REELING THEM IN WITH YOUR SHOWREEL

Showreels can be incredibly helpful nowadays when so many casting decisions require just that bit more information for the director or producer. Sometimes producers can understandably be scared to take a risk with either an unknown actor or an actor in a different kind of role than they are used to seeing him/her in.

So if you don't have a showreel already:

- Get one.
- If you have a body of screen work already, get one.

If you're doing a mail out there's no reason not to include a showreel. You don't have to send hard copy. You can give a link to one that's online. Always link to it on your Spotlight page regardless of whether you have your own website or not.

UNSOLICITED SHOWREELS

Do casting directors watch unsolicited showreels? That depends on the casting director but for the most part, yes, even though they are bombarded and would sometimes rather not. If it's not the casting director themselves, then their faithful assistant/associate will watch and flag up those worth a look. Everyone wants to find new talent.

'Dan's [Dan Hubbard] quite good, I mean he goes home with 30 showreels and he watches them... However, if I get a showreel where it says "Dear John, it's 4 minutes long, it's got some nice stuff on it" I might put it on because it's 4 minutes long.'

John Hubbard, Casting Director, UK

What should you include on your showreel:

- The title should have your name in large, bold, clear text and that of your agent if you have one, if not say C/O Spotlight and have your mobile and email details. It's pointless and tiresome to watch a showreel which has detached from it's letter, or attached itself to the CV and letter of someone else only to find that it belongs to God-only-knows-who contactable by God-only-knows-how.
- Short edited clips of your best screen work, showing you in different types of roles, this is where you show how versatile you are. Don't just use 3 clips which show a similar character and/or situation or you could look like a one trick pony.
- The beginning montage of everything is incredibly popular these days. It doesn't help casting directors, so make sure it's not too long. Lots of 3 second images over 2 minutes tell us nothing and give us a headache. Watching the actual clip of your great work *is* informative however and therefore beneficial to those viewing it and in turn to you.
- Give each clip a title, so we know the name of the TV show or film.
- Choose clips of your best acting and dramatic, emotional or comedic content, not just ones where you're with the most famous co-stars from each show.

If you don't have a wealth of screen work to use because you're new, work primarily in theatre or your screen work is not recent then it may be worthwhile taping some scenes for your showreel.

- You can use a showreel company who specialise in filming scenes and cutting reels together, there are plenty.
- If you're not using a showreel company because of expense, then get a director friend to help. Someone has to hold the camera, someone has to hold the boom (directional mic) – and have someone direct you and anyone else in the scenes.
- Film in an appropriate environment, not your messy kitchen or bedroom. Depending where the scenes are set, hire a studio or use a theatre set if applicable.
- Choose scenes with good dramatic content, of which you know the full story. If it's from a film, watch the entire film or read the full script. If it's a stage play, read every word. You always need context or you lose truth.
- Light it properly
- Make sure you can be heard. Does the camcorder have an external mic or can you hire/borrow a directional mic for it?
- Avoid choosing monologues because a huge part of acting is in fact listening and reacting, so the viewer needs to see that. They also need to see you thinking on camera not just talking, apparently to yourself.
- Do not look directly into the lens.

Ideally try to keep your showreel to somewhere between 2 and a half to 4 minutes, its function is quick visual reference to you and your talent. The casting director/director/producer can always ask for the full episode of whatever show your clip is from should they need to.

> *'They build up until I just can't move for showreels… I'm having to give up my Saturday evening and I watch 20 or 30 over a couple of hours. When you see somebody – and I'm about to be a little bit cynical, I mean I've seen some really*

really dreadful showreels and – there's no point in doing "I left me ring with her, what means this lady?" in your kitchen. You get no flavour of what that person can be like on stage, it's probably very bad quality, it's badly shot, it's not helpful.'

Joyce Nettles, Casting Director, UK

VOICE WORK REQUIRES A VOICEREEL

If you have a voicereel there's no reason you can't include a link to it with a mail out. If you want to get voice work, be that voice-overs or radio drama you need a voicereel, as this work tends not to go via the audition route for casting but from reels. Like your showreel it can be hard copy or an email link to Spotlight, your agent's and/or your website. Marina Caldarone states your voicereel needs to be:

'Instantly recognisable as you so that when someone is casting for a commercial or a documentary they think "Ah, we want 'that', that's what she does."'

Marina Caldarone, Radio Director and Producer, UK

Voicereels differ in terms of what content you should include. Where a showreel is trying to show how versatile you are, voicereels want to be specific and offer a particular identity be that gruff cockney, urban teenager or sophisticated, sexy older woman.

'One of the guaranteed ways of not finding employment is to offer yourself as versatile; it's a fact of life that very few people cast 'versatile'... They know exactly what they want and the cliché I use is: they use a 21year old female Geordie, educated husky voice, with a sense of fun and so the guy who's sent out a CD with 40 minutes worth

of material demonstrating 67 different voices and who has found himself filed under V for versatile doesn't get a look in, because they'll look under [G] for Geordie.'

Bernard Shaw, Voice-over artist and Author, UK

'In terms of who can be a radio actor, there is this sort of idea that in order to work on the radio you have to be able to do a wide range of accents from all parts of the globe and all parts of the country and I really don't think that's true.'

David Thorpe, Voice Actor, UK

WHAT SHOULD YOU INCLUDE IN YOUR VOICEREEL

This depends on the kind of voice work you are going for. There's no reason you can't have more than one voicereel for different purposes.

Think about the media. Radio drama, audio books, commercial voice-overs and documentary narration are different genres, it requires thought as to how you approach them for the best chance at success.

If your voice reel is for radio drama or audio books you need to include:

- Short, strong excerpts that show character.
- Clips which focus on the feel of the character and scene, not the accent – which ideally should be your own.
- Clips which have different pace and energy (back footed energy is laid back, front footed is positive and driven).

'Back foot and front foot and centred so it's energetically moving forward or it's relaxed or it's centred. It's in it's own space.'

Marina Caldarone, Radio Director and Producer, UK

Voice acting work is different to screen or stage acting. Of course that's obvious – there is no visual side to it. That lack of imagery however, is a *huge* part of it. Everything visual has to be created by suggestion and sound effects for the listener. In terms of emotion you'll have to give more in your voice than if you were visible so the scripts are different.

If your voicereel is for commercial voice-overs, you need to include:

- Commercial voice-overs you have done which have aired.
- They should show the aspect of your personality you are trying to sell yourself on, your brand. Is your voice commanding or congenial, relaxing or motivational? Chose wisely and don't try to be too many things.

If your voicereel is for documentary narration, you need to include:

- Any narrative work you have done.

Documentary narration is different to drama as you are evoking what the audience is actually watching at the time.

If you have not done professional voice work before, you can have a voicereel for any of the above purposes recorded at one of many studios which offer this. If you can't afford the outlay, which can be very expensive and are recording tracks yourself, have an industry professional friend listen to them. It is virtually impossible to be objective when listening/watching ourselves. You don't want to send out something of poor quality that makes you look or sound unprofessional.

Whichever area of voice work your voicereel is for, keep it short with only a handful of tracks on it. Bernard Shaw explains how people feel when they play your CD (or more commonly, listen to your voicereel online):

> '*When you put a CD into the tray, the first thing the machine tells you is how much material there is on there. And if you put one into a CD [player] which says 45 minutes, one kind of groans and thinks I'll do something else instead. If you put one on that says 20 seconds, 30 seconds, 40 seconds, a minute, you're fairly confident that you're dealing with someone who knows what they're doing, knows how the industry works and that is an example of the kind of focus that people need.*'
> Bernard Shaw, Voice-over artist and Author, UK

When sending your voicereel always include your CV and photo. Why do this when the audience won't see your face? Well, for the recipient it's always good to see the face of the person they're listening to. There may also be a reason for wanting a specific ethnicity for a particular voice job. Gone are the awful days of actors 'Blacking up' thankfully, even on radio.

> '*You may not be able to tell from a voice nowadays what their particular ethnic origin is. But you may want to cast somebody for admirable reasons, you may want to cast a black man to be a black man rather than a white man to be a black man and so although the voices may be indistinguishable it's useful having a photograph.*'
> Bernard Shaw, Voice-over artist and Author, UK

RECORDING YOUR VOICEREEL

When you actually record the tracks for your voicereel there are two technical aspects you should always be aware of:

- Firstly the mic. This is twofold: 1, speak into the mic (obvious but often forgotten, the consequence is poor audio, so keep still and direct your speech toward the mic); 2, think of the mic as the person whom you are conversing with, imagine them if it is a particular person/character.

'The microphone is the person you're speaking to. Whether that's a novel, so say it's Harry Potter, you've got to create a little boy listening to every word. You've got to see him, smell him and actually see him so you play to the mic by looking at it on the full stops.'
Marina Caldarone, Radio Director and Producer, UK

'Your relationship, be it love, be it hate, whatever it may be is with that piece of metal and wire in front of you and that's what you have to remember and bear in mind at all times.'
David Thorpe, Voice Actor, UK

- Secondly don't rustle your pages. Find your own way of holding them in order to make little or no noise, see what works best for you. Some actors like to turn the pages as they go, some recordings have 2 actors standing close together using the same mic so sharing a single script is easier and one of the actors will hold it, sometimes the script will be put on music stands. Whichever way, at some point the page will have to be turned and you must limit the sound.

'The prime technical considerations: remembering to speak into the microphone and keeping your pages silent.'
David Thorpe, Voice Actor, UK

A COUPLE OF COMMON VOCAL ISSUES IN VOICEREELS

The falling inflection is often a problem in voicereels from less experienced actors. This is how statements are made in ordinary conversation, the final note of the end of the sentence is lower. The problem with this in terms of voice over work, in particular commercials, is that the client would want you to lift the product name. And in general not letting the end of a statement fall flat sounds more optimistic. Bernard Shaw has a trick for combating this: his example is 'Bombay Sapphire Gin', you will have no doubt seen similar by nervous or inexperienced singers on TV talent shows:

> *'Speech and gesture come from the same part of the brain. Basically if you put your hand in the air your voice will go up, if you put your hand down your voice will go down. So when fighting for the rising inflection it's worth conducting oneself with the hand, often with a pencil held in it to get the rise, so you would say 'Bombay' put your hand in the air 'Sapphire' and surprisingly the voice will have gone up.'*
>
> Bernard Shaw, Voice-over artist and Author, UK

The second issue to avoid is eliding words. This is when you merge the end of one word and the beginning of the next so they become one word in effect. In everyday speech it's fine, we understand they are two words. Again, if it's a commercial voice-over you want to make sure you pause slightly in between, back to Bernard:

> *'"Our English breakfast tea" two 'T's one at the end of "Breakfast" and one at the beginning of "Tea." In natural speech we probably will say "Our English Breakfastea"… Introduce a pause between the words "Breakfast" and "Tea."'*
>
> Bernard Shaw, Voice-over artist and Author, UK

Not everyone makes full use of a full stop. They give you a

chance to breathe. But more importantly they mark the end of one thought and the beginning of a new one.

Giving appropriate inflection, meaning and gravitas to something that you can't see can be difficult. Imagine seeing what you are saying. It will give the words the truth they need to convey their meaning.

In documentary you would watch a monitor and deliver your narration alongside, in drama, audio books and commercials – use your imagination.

> *'Actually see what's coming out of your mouth. If you're saying the blue ball bounced twice against the wall, you've got to see it as you say it.'*
>
> Marina Caldarone, Radio Director and Producer, UK

If you are doing a mail out specifically for voice work there is a book called 'Voiceover Contacts.' Go through the companies listed and do some research… there's that word again.

THE USA/UK DIFFERENCE IN MARKETING

There is a huge difference in how American actors promote themselves in contrast with Brits – it's a completely different culture. I'm not suggesting everyone get uber white teeth and botoxed beyond the point of any facial expression; there are however definitely some things that we can learn.

Stereotypically speaking Americans as a nation are more confident, not as quiet or apologetic as us Brits.

> *'I think the measure of any country's level of self-promotion can be found in their television advertising. Because that's the most expensive form of advertising you can buy so a lot of thought goes into it and you can measure how to*

promote yourself from looking at television advertising and in this country it's largely very subtle.'

Simon Dunmore, Director and Author, UK

If you look at their front-footed 'Yes I can' tradition as opposed to our 'Oh I'm really not sure' one, you'll see that American actors (and many Americans in general) like to think positively. US actors market themselves all the time, it's a subconscious part of that front-footed behaviour. We should take some positives from our pals across the pond:

- On meeting someone for the first time, they will maintain eye contact, give you a warm smile, a firm handshake and repeat your name back to you in conversation as though they're checking they understood it correctly or the pronunciation. The more you say someone's name whilst looking at them and/or are in physical contact, the more likely you'll remember it. It's a memory aide, but it makes you feel important and flattered, all very pleasant. What do Brits do? Often it's a handshake so limp John Inman patented it, half-hearted smile or desperate 'give me a job' grin and they'll forget your name as soon as it's said. The key difference is the American is making an impression, a good one. At that moment the person they're meeting: director, casting director or producer is more important than themselves. They want to remember the important person, hence repeating their name to aide memory and they will be remembered.
- They *always* prepare for their auditions. Competition is so fierce there with millions fighting for the dream that they really pull out all the stops. Here we can get actors turning up to audition who haven't read the pages, or even gone home and washed since they returned from Glastonbury – that was an interesting and aromatic experience…

We do borrow culturally from the US and water it down for our own very British palate; 'Have a nice day' has become 'Have a lovely weekend'. We could borrow a little more and apply ourselves to personal marketing so much more effectively.

> 'They have to push themselves forward much, much, much more, they do do the rounds and... It seems finally to come down to how much you're prepared to put yourself out there. Whereas... there's still this fundamental British thing is we don't like people to be too pushy.'
> Simon Dunmore, Director and Author, UK

Another difference in the way Americans approach their CVs from a marketing/branding perspective, is to state if a role was a lead, some UK agents do this on their clients CVs. Mark Bowden explains why:

> 'The standard in America is to put the type of role that you did on the CV – whether it was a lead part, a character part, a series regular... We don't help ourselves by not helping people to understand what our credits mean in terms of what we do. So put that you were in Great Expectations, played the lead "Pip" put "Lead" and then the name of the theatre that it was on at, the Queens Theatre, West End – West End, it's a brand name, it has a lot of feelings that go with it... feelings that are associated with "Lead", "Pip" might have no associations whatsoever. They might just go "What?" And each time somebody reads your credit on a CV, you want them at some point to go "Yes" as they read down going "Yes, Yes, Yes' not "Oh, What, Oh."'
> Mark Bowden, Author, UK

As I said in chapter 2, marketing has to be a continual process, so you have to keep on top of your brand, using all your marketing tools. Your CV needs to be up-to-date, your showreel needs to have recent screen credits, you have to network where appropriate and be remembered.

> 'When William Shatner won his Golden Globe, he went up to the podium and the first words of his awards speech as he held up that award was the words 'William Shatner'. He says his name. He reinforces his brand. There's somebody who manages somehow to keep on the television or keep in film, when really he should have gone by now, but he keeps on going. So even he knows that it's about him constantly reaffirming who he is and what he does and that he is there and doing it.'
>
> Mark Bowden, Author, UK

SUMMARY

What you can take away from this chapter is that your marketing has to be continual and you can't be complacent with it. The presentation of your promotional tools i.e. your CV, headshot, showreel, voicereel if appropriate and your covering letter is of utmost importance. These tools all require time, research, effort and finance and are not to be underestimated or done half-heartedly. We've covered in depth each of the tools. We've looked at the way in which competition and marketing is considered differently in America and a few stateside tips we can put to good use.

CHAPTER 4

THE CASTING PROCESS

This chapter focuses on how you get chosen to come in for an audition, the things that are to do with you and those which are not. We'll look at:

- Who the creatives want to cast and why.
- The process through each stage.
- Things you can do to help you stand out from the rest.
- The difference between auditions in the UK and US.
- Producers and exec producers.
- It may not be about you if you didn't get the part.
- Dealing with constant rejection.

WE WANT THE BEST ACTOR, WITH SOME PROVISOS

If you ask a casting director, a director and the producer on a production who they want to cast and why, their reasons will often differ. Of course, *of course*, everyone wants it to be a great actor – that said – there are other influences for each creative on those choices due to the nature of their job.

THE CASTING DIRECTOR: He/she wants the best actor for the job, someone who will enhance the character when they bring it to life. But they also have other considerations:

- Is it a new stage, screen or commercial production? Part of the joy of casting a new production is that it's ideas heaven for a casting director, a fresh canvas for a whole production.
- Are there already actors attached to this new project? Bear in mind this could be how the project acquired its original funding. If it does have actors associated, then the casting director needs to cast around them. Casting around other actors means the casting team have to consider physical 'type' more than usual as some of the actors auditioning may be too physically similar to someone already cast and that can confuse an audience… or a producer.
- Is it an ongoing TV show or film franchise? If so the casting team have to worry about whether an actor has appeared in it previously. You'd be surprised by how many fans will write in to the production company to say someone played Joe Blogs in 2007 so how can he play Jack Smith in 2015?! Long running TV series have a time limit before an actor who played a smaller role can appear as a different character, some 18 months, others 2 years. If you have already played a recurring character you cannot appear in another role within the same production. Certain episodic 2 part dramas will not have you appear twice at all, regardless of the size of role. For theatrical productions an actor can reprise a role they played before or take on another role in the same show.
- Are you auditioning for the ensemble in a stage show? If so there are physical characteristics for an ensemble that have to be considered. Height and physique are important to the look and feel of the ensemble as well as acting, vocal range and dance/movement skills.
- Is it a double cast stage piece? This is when two shows are put on using the same cast. The shows sometimes alternate performance days. The casting team will have to look at which skills the actors need to have specifically: do they need Actor-Musicians for one of the shows, is physical type

essential for any of the roles, is there a specified gender or ethnicity bias, how are they going to work the double casting?

'When I did "Hamlet" in Regents Park for example it was double cast with "Midsummer Night's Dream" and there were certain people who spilled over into "The Card" which was the musical which was on that year. And there was a day when I discovered that all my soldiers had to be able to sing... they were great guys but they tend to be a bit camp and you needed butch boys to play the soldiers... When you don't get a job it might be because you're the wrong height, I mean it was a long time for example before I knew if Ophelia was going to play Helena or Hermia in the Dream, well Helena's very tall and Hermia's very short in the text, so you're either going to end up with a very tall actress or a very short actress. So what happens to Hamlet, what if you cast a 2' Hamlet and you end up with Helena, they look ludicrous together.'

Tim Pigott-Smith, Actor and Director, UK

- Have the shortlisted actors worked together before and had any problems? Sometimes people have relationships that end in messy divorces; understandably it's not great to put them together again. If the team knows about this they will try to avoid it. Agents will often ask if there is anyone else cast yet and if so at that point can let the casting director know of any unforeseen personal issues.
- Are you available? We need to know if the actors we would like are fully available or technically/partially available and how many of the ones we want have been cast in other shows during the dates of the production. Not only do actors get offers for other jobs whilst the casting process is going on, but also if some are available and others aren't we may need

to re-evaluate some of our other choices to make sure they work together. More ideas are always necessary.
- Are any of the shortlisted actors known to be tricky? It is best not to put two 'trickies' together.
- Are there any restrictions on the character descriptions? If a character is described as a particular ethnicity for example, unless it's a focal point of the character and the story, can we open it up for all?
- How open-minded are the director and/or producers to left-field choices? Casting directors love to find new talent and to cast against type. This is not always appropriate for the director's or producer's needs for a particular production.

THE DIRECTOR: He/she wants the best actor they can work with, but has other concerns:

- Are you someone they've worked with before? Some directors will always want the cast to include at least one actor they've worked with before because they feel secure in those actors' abilities and personalities. This shows loyalty and can foster great working relationships. It can however lead to actors who are not quite right being seen for parts and resistance to other casting options. Directors simply can't know as many actors as casting directors do. That's the nature of the job. But a director will know several actors infinitely better than a casting director through having worked with them.
- Do you have a believable interpretation of the role? A director wants an actor to come in and really nail the role. Most directors are absolutely open to having an actor come in with a completely different perception of the role. If it is convincing, feels real and rounded, it gives them other characterisation ideas and interpretations to work with. The director wants to see extraordinary talent and intelligence walk through the door.

> *'I'm looking to be surprised actually, that's probably the thing that's the most important thing. I'm looking for somebody who is going to bring something to that part that I didn't necessarily know that I wanted before they came in. I'm looking for chemistry that's going to exist between that actor and that actor. I'm looking for unpredictability and some sense of danger I suppose is really what I'm looking for.'*
>
> Peter Cregeen, Director and Producer, UK

- Do you want the job for the right reasons? Directors want the actors who really want the job, who love the role and the script, who can really throw themselves into it, they want to create stage/screen magic.

> *'My instinct is always looking to see whether the actor really wants the part... even for smaller parts, if you're going for the part – again for the wrong reasons, it may come out and you may spot it. So I'm always looking for the actor that wants the part, that wants the part for the right reasons, they've got something to give, they've got something extra they wanna share.'*
>
> Robert Bierman, Director, UK and USA

- Will you fit in with their team? They want a cast who will be a united and fun team working together under their vision. So they are always looking out for tell tale signs of actors who may be tricky or perhaps just don't listen all that well. They want actors with whom they feel a professional, creative and emotional kinship.

> *'It's pretty important from my point of view that they can actually excite me about the part that they're in for... I also want to feel absolutely confidant, not*

only that they're going to able to play this part... but also that they're going to be able to deliver that performance on the sort of schedule that we've actually got... I don't want to hear somebody saying "Well I think I might be able to do this." I need to feel that they are going to be able to cope with it and I need to be able to feel that it's going to be a creative relationship, working with them and that it's going to be extra fun working with them.'

Peter Cregeen, Director and Producer, UK

- Are you a quick study? They want actors who'll understand their vision swiftly and not need too much direction on set as there's less and less time for rehearsal nowadays.
- Do you listen to notes? They want actors who will take notes well in the audition room because, in theory, that foretells how they will take notes in rehearsal and on set/stage.
- How will the fully assembled cast look and feel?

'*We all have certain actors that we've worked with over the years like Tom Courtney and David Threlfall, Bob Linton, people like that who are heart actors and we like that... But, to also understand that to have such an important job is a service in the highest sense so the wrong kind of ego doesn't help you do that job. You have to know if you're playing Hamlet that this is almost like a sacred mission. I don't mean that in a heavy way, you're there to entertain of course you are and be brilliant and extraordinary, but you're actually enacting a work of art to an audience who, if you do it well – will be immensely strengthened by it and exhilarated by it in the best possible way. So it's that, it's to convey the heart of the play.*'

Braham Murray OBE, Artistic Director, UK

A PRODUCER: He/she wants not just the best actor but also one who will bring them the best return and is of course reliable, their priorities are:

- Does your fee fit within their budget? In particular they look at how many well-known actors they can attach to the production within their financial constraints.
- Can they utilise new talent and still be economically sound? They also like to introduce lesser-known actors for budgetary reasons as much as anything else. Though they need to feel secure that their faith in the unknown actor is not misplaced. They're always aware of the numbers they need for the show to go on: theatre ticket sales/TV ratings/cinema box office figures, etc.
- Do you have a reputation for being difficult? They will often ask if any of the actors they've shortlisted have any prior bad reputation as it wastes time and money.
- Do they consider you physically attractive enough for that role? This is not a judgement about their particular aesthetic preferences; they try to look with the eye of the perceived audience, exec producers and the networks. The financial landscape has changed over the decades; culturally we're all getting a little shallower. Don't just take my word for it, take a look at some re-runs of TV shows from the 70's and tell me that there weren't some odd looking actors doing very well just on their talent. Nowadays – not so much.
- Will you fit in to the fully assembled cast?

So, as a team, the creatives have to think about their various considerations as well as making sure the shortlist of actors are all capable, charismatic, talented performers.

THE PROCESS, BEGINNING, MIDDLE AND END

The actual process of casting a production, whichever medium, usually follows approximately the same route. A casting director is approached by a producer generally, or the director if they've worked together before.

The casting director is sent the script for initial ideas. Sometimes producers approach more than one casting director and meetings will be held with to see if they are all on the same page in terms of how they see the roles and, that they want to work together. Frequently a meeting is set up and financial offer made without any others in the running. Many casting directors have agents too – so they don't have to negotiate their own deals.

The casting director and their team will read the script and come up with various ideas for the lead roles, the smaller roles will be looked at later. The director will also have ideas as will the producers and execs, some producers are very creative, not just concerned about the financial and business side of production.

The casting office will check the availability of all the actors they are interested in and usually send a breakdown of the roles to the agents they choose to, ordinarily via Spotlight (here in the UK). This is why it is imperative to be a paid up member of Spotlight if you want to work. Agents will suggest clients they think are appropriate and a few ideas that are against type (agents are also creative). The casting office will narrow down from the available and technically available lists, frequently through discussion with the director and producers, which actors they want to bring in to meet for each role.

Sometimes the casting team will make it known via Spotlight and other casting breakdown websites and/or the press that they are looking for submissions so that actors can submit themselves. Even if they haven't, you'll hear because news gets round in our industry. In either case be realistic, if you have no lead credits they are unlikely to see you for a lead, look at the supporting and smaller roles –depending on your level of experience.

The casting office will set up audition sessions from the reduced lists often adding in other actors whom the casting director feels appropriate. Scripts and sides (scenes) are sent via the agents to the actors coming in, for them to prepare. The casting director or their associate/assistant will often do the first round of auditions without a director/producer. They then recall the actors they felt really got the character and brought something interesting to it back for the director and/or producer to meet. Occasionally a production will start casting without a director attached in which case the casting team will audition the actors with the producer. How much time the casting team have with the director will affect how many actors they can bring in. Directors audition at different paces so time slots are allotted accordingly. Some US shows have a UK casting director who will put people on tape here without a director/producer present and some UK shows also follow this pattern when the team are not available.

Open auditions are not commonplace for most professional work in the UK; they are time-consuming and financially unsound for the slim chance of a positive result. Open singing and dance calls are however held for stage musicals. If auditions via children's agencies and stage schools have not found the right child for a part (in whichever medium) then opens will be held.

If an actor is not available to audition for a screen project, casting directors will also now for the most part accept self-tapes(9). The agent will email the self-tape links to the casting director who watch and decide whether to pass it on to the creative team.

After recalls, there will be a shortlist of actors per role; this can vary from one to a handful. If it is for screen work they will usually be uploaded to a secure website where only the creative team, exec producers and network (if applicable) can view them to discuss the final choices. If it is for stage work, there will be a casting meeting with the creative team and exec producers in which all the CVs and headshots of the shortlist choices per role will be looked at for how they could work together and the discussions begin, this can be lengthy and requires caffeine. Recently it has also become the case with musical theatre finals for long running international shows, that they will be taped and those links sent to the international creative team if they cannot be in attendance.

During the selection process, when the shortlist has been refined to two or three choices per role, 'pencils/holds' are put on the first, second and third choices via their agents. Pencils are put on actors whom the production is interested in but not in a position to make an offer to at that moment, this means the agent is obligated to tell the casting office of any other offers which come in. As soon as decisions are made offers will be put in to the agents of the first choices. At this point it varies from production to production. Generally for screen or stage the casting director will usually work out from the casting budget what they can allocate for each role and then negotiate with the agent. In some cases the producers want to be the only ones discussing the budget, if so they will do the deals.

Once the financial offer is accepted, the casting office releases the other actors on pencil and let the agents know that an offer has been accepted elsewhere. Some casting teams try to contact the agents of everyone who was recalled, to let them know if they didn't get the part, though many are too busy. The casting office will send CANS (casting advice notes [10]) to the agents for the actors being hired (for screen work), these documents cover in brief what is being contracted. These are signed and returned. Production in turn send contracts to the agents to be signed by the actors and returned.

Peter Cregeen puts in perspective how you've been narrowed down and everyone wants you there:

> *'You wouldn't be there at all if the producer and the director didn't believe that you were going to be smashing in that part. You know the casting directors are freelance like the actor so the casting director is really only as good as the people that they actually put up. And when you were put up for it you were probably one of 5 people who were put up for that part, you know, 25 names perhaps originally. People who are brought in, there's not time to see more usually than 5 or 6 people for any one part. And if you were brought in in the first place the casting director believes that you were going to be wonderful in it, otherwise they don't bring you in. The director when he casts you is going to believe the same thing and the producer is gonna believe that you were gonna be great in it. So you go in there knowing that everybody believes in you in the first place.'*
>
> Peter Cregeen, Director and Producer, UK

STANDING OUT FROM THE REST

So what makes an actor stand out from the others who've met for the same role? There are a few intangible internal qualities, the 'X-factor' if you like, that a person can bring with them to an audition:

- PRESENCE. Some people have that thing, when they walk into a room or on stage, they mesmerise you. It's a bit like being attracted to them. It is *not* however actually about their physical attributes contrary to popular belief, it's just a certain something, sorry – je ne sais quoi.
- CONFIDENCE. You can work on your confidence, as self-assurance and confidence are attractive qualities. Not arrogance. Never arrogance. These qualities make an audience feel safe that you won't let them down in your portrayal of that character.

- INTELLIGENCE. An audience responds to an actor who really thinks about the role and story. Someone who has insight, an opinion and uses their instincts.

    'When I meet an actor for the first time, I don't know what it is, but, it is instinct. It is a sense of something interesting, I don't just mean visually, (but that's an important, important part of it, especially today in Hollywood and it's creeping into the industry now). Also I think it is an intelligence, I think it's a sort of drive that's communicating itself to me, there's a sort of ambition.'

    John Hubbard, Casting Director, UK

- IMAGINATION. An actor who really runs with the script, is excited by it and brings the thoughts and images in their mind with them.

    'We're looking for something that's going to be different, something that's going to bring something interesting to that part... I try and build in, when I'm working with the actor, some sort of life to the character some sort of back story that is actually more than just the dialogue that's there on the printed page.'

    Peter Cregeen, Director and Producer, UK

- INNER STRENGTH. Does this actor have the right psychological make-up to cope with the demands of this production? e.g. If it is touring theatre, is the creative team sure the actor will be happy away from home for that long and be a positive member of the cast.

    'I did turn down some people on occasion because I thought they weren't the right psychology.'

    Tim Pigott-Smith, Actor and Director, UK

However, there are also important practical things that make an actor stand out from the others in a long day's casting session. These things can often be overlooked if you are only thinking about those internal qualities; but they are just as vital to your success in an audition room:

- PREPARATION. The actor who is prepared, has read the full script and thought about it all, not just their character and scenes in isolation.
- PUNCTUALITY. The actor who is well presented and punctual doesn't ring instant alarm bells.
- RESEARCH. The actor who has researched who they are meeting and drops relevant things into conversation where appropriate will be remembered as someone who is well informed and personable. This doesn't mean crowbarring snippets of information into a conversation, just at appropriate moments.

AUDITIONS, LOVE THEM OR HATE THEM?

Auditions are a completely different experience for actors than for the creatives. This is true even if you are an actor who loves to audition – a rarity.

> *'I think everybody hates doing them, they're so peculiar, they're so unnatural. And you know sometimes you find yourself on stage with a terrible sort of glare of lights and a body of people out there. You don't know who they are or where they are, you don't know whether they're at the back or in the middle or the front, you can't see. You're petrified, I mean it's just, it's deeply humiliating, horrible.'*
>
> Tim Pigott-Smith, Actor and Director, UK

As a rule, casting directors, directors and some producers love being in the audition room. Seeing you bring the script to life. We enjoy the diverse ways different actors see the same role and what those actors bring to it, Alison Chard explains:

> 'I enjoy the actors' creativity actually, the chief thing I enjoy is reading with the actors actually... It's kind of play time I suppose and obviously you're striking a balance, you're not giving the performance, but you're striking a balance between being helpful to the actor and actually being objective. So that you're trying to sit outside yourself as you're reading with them and of course you've got the director and/or producer and nowadays you've got the wretched camera as well in there.'
>
> Alison Chard, Casting Director, UK

We empathise and get apprehensive for the actors because we can see and feel their nerves. For a director the appreciation of nerves is even more acute as they may have been an actor previously, consequently some directors find the process hard.

> 'One; I suffer with the actor because I know what they're going through, the absolute [fear]... Two; because it is so important if you're casting a play, I mean it's nine tenths of the job. If you get the casting right you're likely to be OK and if you don't it doesn't matter how clever you are you're not going to be. And auditioning is a very false process, it would be much better to go and see each actor act, so I find them quite tense.'
>
> Braham Murray OBE, Artistic Director, UK

CASTING DIRECTORS ARE ON YOUR SIDE

Quite why so many actors think casting directors are not on their side is a mystery to those of us who work in the casting side of the industry. We are always supporting actors. We have a duty to the director and producer, but we are constantly looking out for and trying to make things work for the actor.

> *'Usually, I get very nervous, I mean I get almost as nervous as the actors do. Because what actors forget, or maybe what actors don't know is that when an actor walks into the room for an audition, I am sitting there thinking "Please let him get the job, please let him get the job". We want the actor to get the job.'*
>
> Joyce Nettles, Casting Director, UK

We want every actor who walks into the audition room to get the part. You've been brought in because you are talented and right for the role, regardless of our personal feelings about you as John Hubbard illustrates:

> *'Even if it's only the casting director and you know certain parts of the business there's not much respect for casting directors. People feel we hold people back or we don't like people... in this company there is absolutely none of that and even when we've had big big rows with actors... If that person's right for a job, I'm gonna get them in, if that person gets the part it's gonna make me look good. So it's very, very unashamedly unbiased, looking at every actor that's been submitted or that we're thinking about.'*
>
> John Hubbard, Casting Director, UK

Actors sometimes think if they get a meeting at short notice that they are brought in just to pad out a session, someone else can't attend and there is a gap to fill. Why would we do this? If no one else whom we want can make that slot, we simply alter the schedule. If an actor gets the role, the casting director's name is attached to that choice evermore. If they turn out to be an inappropriate choice then it's the casting director's reputation at stake. So no one is there just for numbers.

> *'If you're called in to an audition, because there are so few people coming in for that part, you at least can feel the confidence of knowing that you're extremely likely to get the part. You may not get it for reasons beyond your control; you may not be how the producer visualises the part. There's nothing you can do about that when it comes down to it. But at least if you've been called in you have some assurance that perhaps will settle your nerves that you know there is a willingness to cast you in that room, so all you can really do is confirm the expectation really.'*
>
> Alison Chard, Casting Director, UK

There is a personality trait that seems to go along with being in casting. Whatever other character attributes individual casting professionals possess, we have a kind of selflessness *in this context* and a confidence that is borne of our role of supporting others to achieve. We all intrinsically know that 'it's not about us.' For example, at college my sight-reading was awful. My voice teacher asked the whole class to let her know of any dyslexia issues that any one of us might have… As I didn't put my hand up to voice any concerns she naturally asked me, by name, in front of everyone. So I had to do it, again, poorly and slowly. Thanks for that, not scarred at all… But that's the interesting thing: in the audition room I sight-read perfectly well. This is because I am there to facilitate the actors. I don't get the nerves associated with performing so I can be selfless in the moment giving the actor what they need, not thinking about myself. Like many in casting I enjoy reading in auditions whilst viewing the actor and aiding them.

Sometimes actors think they want to get into casting or agenting. Many of us, from assistant to award-winning casting director or agent, will talk to these actors about their potential career in this field. We can see the ones who genuinely want to retire from acting and honestly want to move into these challenging, incredibly rewarding but often thankless jobs. There are also those who have a reasonable interest, but the potential career change is more down to disillusionment with how often they are cast. This can be a conflict of interest where the actor/casting director/agent may think *they* were a better choice for a particular role than other actors. If an actor still wants to act, casting other people or being an agent and doing the deals for other actors probably wouldn't make them happy in the long run. Many casting directors and agents were actors originally who actively chose to leave the profession and move to this side of the industry.

> *'One thing I learnt from advertising is that you must always think about other people all the time… it is not about me… how you apply that to the business is that you must think about everybody else, I must think about everybody in the room, I must think about the actor, I must make sure they are happy.'*
> John Hubbard, Casting Director, UK

As well as this facilitating role there are numerous other things the casting team do in order to aid actors:

- Move appointments because of actors' childcare issues or other meetings.
- Accepting self-tape auditions if actors can't re-arrange a trip or a day's supply teaching.

- Argue for the best actor, not the celebrity or prettiest actor.
- Put our industry standing on the line when they bring any actor in for an audition.
- Go to the theatre every week, including fringe theatre and see as much TV and film as we can so that our knowledge base of actors is always growing and current.
- Go to as many showcases and drama school shows as we can to make sure we're aware of any interesting new graduates.
- Some arrange 'general meetings' to see actors we've not had in before.
- Help actors we know tape for productions which we are not casting, sometimes for American or other overseas projects.
- Work much longer hours than you would think. TV and film casting often involves dealing with America, that is a different time zone, New York is 5 hours behind the UK and LA is 8 hours behind.

'I'm putting my reputation on the line as well as an actor's for the producers and director.'

Alison Chard, Casting Director, UK

'We are willing somebody to get the job. Because we wanna do our job as quickly, and I don't mean rashly… I mean it quickly in the sense of [as] efficiently as possible. And so I want an actor to get a job when he comes in the room.'

Joyce Nettles, Casting Director, UK

However, even with all this support and goodwill on the part of the casting director there are times when the creatives of a show will realise pretty much straight away in the audition that the actor is wrong for the part. Occasionally it can be that the actor can't get their own preconception of how to play the role out of their mind and if asked to change their portrayal does not respond to direction. This is a difficult and awkward situation for all involved of course, but it does happen. All anyone can do is be diplomatic about it. Alternatively it's because a director or producer will be very rigid and want everyone in the cast to conform to a particular vision. You would still read for the part but maybe your meeting wouldn't be as long as you would have hoped for. In both situations the creatives will smile the *warm smile* and say those words savvy actors have come to recognise 'Well it was lovely to meet you. Thank you for coming in' Google translate = 'So sorry, you're not going to get it, but we don't want to embarrass you.' Not as merciless as it used to be as Sir Richard Eyre CBE remembers:

> *'It can be terrible when first of all when you realise as soon as an actor comes in the room that there is no way in which you are going to consider them for the part... When I was an actor, in those days auditioning was much more brutal than these days, you would walk on a stage where the director or casting director were sitting in the auditorium with the house lights off and you would just see a glimmer in the stalls of a little desk light and you'd be blinded by the stage lights peering out there talking to this disembodied force in the stalls. And you'd be stopped if you started off and they didn't think you were getting it, they'd say "Thank you!" and you'd just be yanked off stage.'*
>
> Sir Richard Eyre CBE, Director, UK

Once a handful of actors have been shortlisted, each bringing something different to the part, a final choice must be made. The process of whittling down the list depends on the production and the team. It can be a battle of wills, a general consensus or a determined dictatorship. This is the point where the casting director's diplomacy and ingenuity come to the fore. It's not that we're Machiavellian, but sometimes you have to let people think an idea was their own in order for them to see the bigger picture.

Like my dad always says… 'Slowly slowly, catchy monkey.'

> *'It's always instinctive and sometimes you do have that debate, that people like different people and you have a discussion about it. In most cases I will win and it's not just because I'm older than most people in the room. But it's because I'm used to speaking up about a particular actor that I'm sometimes more articulate about why they're right for the part. I'm not saying… [it]'s the same in every case but the only thing, the only way to make a decision about that is: what is your heart telling you?'*
>
> John Hubbard, Casting Director, UK

HOW BRAVE ARE CASTING DIRECTORS IDEAS?

There are always going certain roles where the creative team in unison think it has to be 'So-and-so!' Most likely because the actor in question has played a similar role to great acclaim in the past, or because it's the sort of role they've always dreamed of working with said actor in. This does not mean however that the casting director won't still have a list of ideas for that role which are entirely different.

Gender, ethnicity and age will always be played around with. If there is no real specified reason a role has to be the particular physical description in the script, nowadays casting directors will largely ignore that description.

What would constitute a left-field choice?

- Frequently female characters are written as slim, blonde and in their twenties, often writers are male; this may be their personal preference. If she is not Scandinavian or her blonde tresses are not integral, don't be surprised if when the show

is aired the actress cast in that role is in fact South East Asian, Afro-Caribbean or a curvy redhead.
- Sometimes there is a rather violent character, written as one would assume as male. Every now and then not only the casting directors but also agents will suggest actresses, because it would be a more interesting choice – it would bring another rather chilling dimension to that role.
- If we have to build a family or a street of families, the casting team will usually do this colour blind and with an open mind to age. There is no reason teenager couldn't have for example a young father and slightly older mother and so the age of the grand parents can be played with, we could have one set of young grandparents in their 50's and one set in their 70's. In real life people often remarry later in life and have another set of kids so this can be realised on stage/screen too. Again, the ethnicity will be left open; we will see which combinations of actors make a realistic family and work around the ethnicity of those choices. i.e. two great mixed heritage teenagers, means we then look for the parents and grand parents accordingly.

ARE CASTING DIRECTORS AND DIRECTORS ON THE LOOKOUT FOR NEW TALENT?

Part of the joy and satisfaction for casting directors and directors alike is finding and nurturing new talent. From drama school showcases/end of year shows, fringe theatre, to a trusted agent's new find – an ingénue or rough and ready bad boy/girl. Casting directors and their assistants sit through many a production in the hunt for new talent.

> *'Talent is talent and we're all looking for it in a kind of vampiric fashion, you know 'New blood' is what's exciting about casting really. It's finding something different,*

> *something new, something unexpected and trying to help it along really, that's why I do it at any rate.'*
>
> Alison Chard, Casting Director, UK

There are individuals who have a charisma, which is palpable, and they will be given the chance for a general meeting and possibly to audition regardless of where they were spotted.

> *'It gives me the biggest thrill; it's like discovering somebody. I think of all the first times we saw Colin Farrell and Kate Winslet and Jonathan Rhys Meyers... Ros found him in a pool hall in West Cork and dragged him straight to the director and we had the first thing of him on tape, it wasn't even an audition just a chat... So we love discovering people and new faces and new talents, so it is not a disadvantage... to have done no film or TV.'*
>
> John Hubbard, Casting Director, UK

So whilst often the decision about who gets cast in a role may come down to the other actor having more experience in front of the camera or on stage, that's not always the default decision. Brave choices are made, new and exciting careers launched.

PRODUCERS SEEM TO HAVE THE FINAL SAY

Producers tend to have the final say on the casting decisions; it is part of their responsibility to the production. Some are more creative than others and really want to be involved with the whole process and this can lead to great partnerships with the director and casting director. Executive producers are usually involved on long running TV series, so there can be more hoops to leap through and more recalls for the shortlisted actors to come back and meet them, or links to the uploaded auditions will be sent to them. For theatre they will often come in on the last round of finals so the team behind the desk has multiplied each time an actor comes back, with musical theatre it can feel like the team just keeps on growing in numbers.

> *'[It] goes beyond the walls of the audition room and through at least one producer and probably three or four by the time a decision is reached and then it comes back again at you and then you can go and argue. And sometimes you win, but sometimes you don't, so the producer is the final arbiter... It used to be the director; it's almost always the producer because of pressures beyond any production company's walls. You know they have the broadcasters and the networks to please basically, so it's out of your control to a certain extent. Although you're bringing people in that you think are going to get the part, you kind of have no control beyond your immediate producer in some cases, which is not a good thing I think. But we live in the real world and that's the way we have to operate really.'*
>
> Alison Chard, Casting Director, UK

If the director is particularly sought after, rather brilliant or somewhat difficult, then producers are less likely to argue. In theory what the creative team is trying to achieve is fashioning a complete cast that everyone is happy with and excited by. There are always discussions; there is no lone, bald overweight producer in braces enjoying a cigar and all the power, as depicted in old Hollywood films.

> *'I'd meet them, cast them on tape, they were fabulous, I'd say "I love you" and then the producers would say "Well there's some other people you need to see"... then they had to go through this process again and again and*

> *again and again and this is often how casting's become now. It's become a problem of executive after executive after executive level wanting to be involved and so the actor has to be prepared to do it again and again and again, just don't take it personally. It's not that they don't think they're good enough.'*
>
> Robert Bierman, Director, UK and USA

WHAT ARE THE ODDS?

Naturally when the casting process for a production comes to an end most actors didn't get the part and one did. There are a variety of reasons why you may not be cast in the part you auditioned for.

Often it's just not about you, though it always feels like it is. There are a multitude of considerations when choosing from a selection of talented actors.

> *'Don't take it personally. You're there to do a job; you're a skilled person. You know when someone's doing heart surgery they don't get upset that if there's some old biddy they don't like when they go round to the ward before hand, who's rude to them. They don't say "Well I'm not gonna do a good heart job on this one because she was a miserable old cow"... You do a great job of saving that life and as an actor you've just got to do a great job within the confines, the bubble of your character.'*
>
> Robert Bierman, Director, UK and USA

When the feedback you get is 'They went in another direction' or 'They really liked you but you're not how the director/producer/Exec/Network saw the role' usually that is exactly the case. If the reasons were personal, the feedback would be specific to you

'You were late/unprepared/rude' or 'One of the team had a bad experience with you' etc.

Try to take as objective a view of your auditions as you can. If you did your best and didn't get it, chances are, it wasn't about you.

> *'You've got to somehow learn to shrug that off, just take it as part of the whole process that it's not personal. That it's perhaps circumstances beyond your control or, if you're going to be really really rigorously honest with yourself after an audition – 'Was there something that I didn't do?'*
>
> Alison Chard, Casting Director, UK

YOU NEED A THICK SKIN FOR THE CONSTANT REJECTION

No one likes rejection, at a bar, on the school sports field picking teams and certainly not in the work place. Actors know this only too well yet non-industry people are often oblivious to the rejection actors face daily. An audition is essentially a job interview, on a good day you could have 2 or 3, then you may have weeks of nothing and then a week with a few again. What are the odds that you'll get many of those jobs? Often it's between Bob Hope and no hope – and Bob Hope's dead.

> *'The actor... of course get a lot of flack from all sorts of people, they get rejected so many times, it's a terrible profession for rejection, I think it's a very honourable profession.'*
>
> Richard Briers CBE, Actor, UK

It's hard, at the end of the day when you don't get the part, whatever the reason, Tim Pigott-Smith empathises, it feels like it's *you* being rejected:

> *'I don't like that endless sense of rejection which goes with the business. It's horrible because it's you, not your painting, or your book, or your piece of carpentry. It's you that they're rejecting, so it hurts at whatever level you're at.'*
>
> Tim Pigott-Smith, Actor and Director, UK

You just have to be a bit Zen about it. For some reason it wasn't the right part for you, perhaps there's a better one round the corner. Don't take it to heart, it's not a judgement on you personally. Continue to work your hardest for your next job.

THE DIFFERENCE BETWEEN THE UK AND USA

I've talked about the difference in competition and marketing in the States. Americans approach their auditioning, differently to us Brits too.

TV and film auditions here have over the years started to expect a more American approach from actors, in a nutshell:

- Learn your lines for your meeting.
- Dress with a hint at character.
- Preparation and research.
- Be punctual, personable and well presented
- Be brave and go for it.

> *'These guys work really, really hard, they work harder than anybody that's why they're at the top. I mean they don't just work hard, but they will use any technique they can to create the part, they will do anything technically to make sure on film they look right.'*
>
> Robert Bierman, Director, UK and USA

> *'I've directed in North America quite a lot and there it's extraordinary, they learn the part, they'll do anything you want them to do. There was a time when English actors kind of felt it was a bit of a dig to audition... In America they are emotionally freer, they are quicker than English actors, the same in the rehearsal process. I'm not saying that's good or bad, but they'll come out with it fast, they don't stalk it, they're much less inhibited. As I say in New York if you're auditioning there's nothing they won't do, and the grandest actors, I mean if they know you're an English director directing in New York they think "Well fair enough, he can't know me, I'll come and I'll do an audition."'*
>
> Braham Murray OBE, Artistic Director, UK

They also have a completely different system over in the States. Actors have managers as well as agents, and the more well known they are they are likely to have lawyers too. A whole entourage.

Here everything pretty much goes through your agent. If you would like to find work in the States too, Pilot season is a great opportunity to do so. Many shows make a first 'Pilot' episode and then the networks choose which of the many options to commission. Pilot season is January to early April. Many US shows have UK casting directors as well so Brits are auditioning in the UK for those shows all year round. Pilot season is an incredibly busy time. Let your agent know if you are particularly interested in this, though they'll likely be suggesting you anyway. Remember, if you're thinking of just jetting off to LaLa Land (Los Angeles) on the off chance of being discovered, that as a British citizen you need a Green card or A1 visa to work in the US. So in real terms it may save a lot of heartache and expense to just let your agent know you're interested in UK castings for Pilot Season.

SUMMARY

What you can take from this chapter is a deeper knowledge of how casting works, the process, the priorities the creative team have, that producers tend to have the final say on casting decisions. An understanding that casting directors *are* on your side and only bring in actors whom they believe in. Casting directors are always looking for new talent and want to nurture young actors at the beginnings of their careers. We looked at the fact that it is a tough business, full of rejection and that you have to find the inner resources to deal with it and not take any of it personally.

CHAPTER 5

PREPARING FOR THE AUDITION

This chapter covers the professional preparation you need to do during the days prior to your audition. We'll look at:

- Reading the full script.
- Learning your lines.
- Sight-reading.
- Making decisions on your character and researching your role.
- Researching whom you are meeting – and yourself.
- Dressing for the part.
- Working on your confidence.

PREPARATION IS THE KEY

When the casting director's office calls your agent to book you in for an audition they will:

- Recheck your availability for the production.
  Handy tip: always tell your agent when you are going away for trips, weddings, if you have any odd days work not booked through them – teaching, corporate work, etc.
- Arrange a date, time and location for your audition and tell them whom you will be meeting.
- Give the agent any further information about the project and/or creatives involved.

- Email the agent the audition information, what you will be required to do, any accent etc, the full script (not always but wherever possible) and sides if they are pre-chosen or you may be asked to pick scenes yourself. Depending on the casting team sometimes a brief character description. Your agent then sends the information and material to you.

Although some audition sessions are set up for the next day, most casting directors try to avoid that whenever possible. This is so that you the actors have longer to *prepare* in order to give you the best chance possible.

I've said before and it is reiterated by the many industry professionals quoted, show business is very competitive. What sets jobbing actors apart from each other, if equally talented and charismatic, is the preparation they are willing to put in. This is highlighted before the auditions. The basic elements for your homework are simple. Putting them into practice takes time and a little effort on your part.

READ THE FULL SCRIPT

In order to bring truth to a piece you have to know it in context. The reason we send full scripts (when possible) is so actors have a perspective on the whole story. If you only read your speaking scenes it's difficult to extrapolate your character arc, all your character motivations and relationships to others and your character's history if it's given. This all helps you find your character's truth and depth. You also need to see the other roles within the entire story to understand their motivations and all the subplots.

If you are sent the full script and you don't read it, only checking for your character's lines, what it says to the creative team in big flashing neon is that you are lazy. That is likely not the case. There may be many circumstances in which you genuinely didn't have time to read it all, but that is not what will be remembered. As Robert Bierman points out:

> 'It's about reading the part, if it's a full script, a lot of actors do not read the full script, they only read their part. They don't know what the rest of the script is; these are terrible, terrible problems for real screen acting. You must read the full script, understand what your part is in the script and if you gonna read some scenes really know them well, know them very well.'
>
> Robert Bierman, Director, UK and USA

And by read the full script I don't mean skim read, I mean *read*. Even if you get it the night before your meeting and you're currently working in a theatre production. Read the stage directions, because there are often descriptions and actions that give a lot of detailed meaning. There's also the interesting stuff which makes the audience use their brain, you know the bits which the execs will have often cut by the time a TV show is actually aired. Read that, it's an insight into what the writer intended and director finds compelling, even if ultimately the execs don't.

> 'If you've thoroughly prepared yourself and you've looked at the stage directions, I mean good actors read everything, bad actors just read the dialogue, there's just so much information and sometimes it catches me out.'
>
> John Hubbard, Casting Director, UK

LEARN YOUR LINES

There is a difference between theatre and screen auditions when preparing your scenes.
- For theatre auditions actors are not usually expected to be

off book for the first round, you can have pages in hand. However you need to be familiar enough with the lines to be performing not just reading off the page. It also gives you the flexibility for movement.

- For screen auditions it is better to have learnt them, even for a first audition, though you can usually hold the pages for reference should you need them. Screen auditions are taped, the camera needs to see your eyes. It is much more difficult to convey all that you need to to the audience if you are constantly looking down or worse still holding up the pages you are reading from. The viewer needs to believe what you're saying and this generally is emoted through the eyes.

Be familiar with the lines so you can have thought about the motivations for your character in that scene within the context of the story as a whole.

> 'To prepare for a TV or film audition… if you have the chance and you get the script before learn it. Make no mistake, if you get it even the night before, the difference it makes to have learnt it is tremendous. You won't get your eyes dropping to a script you won't get the rustling of the script. You'll show them that you're serious, the whole package of things that come with learning it, so I would say if you can, learn it.'
>
> Mel Churcher, Acting and Dialect Coach, UK and USA

There's a fine line between learning the lines well enough for an audition to nail it and still being open enough to change what you are doing if asked to.

The danger in learning too well can be you become set in those scenes with the choices you've made and then can't take notes and you must always take notes if they are given.

'I don't mind an actor holding a sheet of paper and looking at the lines, absolutely not, but I do mind him holding it in front of his face. We can't see you; I thought the point of you being here was that we could see you... Learn it if you can, but don't learn it to the extent that you can't change what you've learnt... you have probably learnt one way of doing it, because in learning the lines you learn an interpretation of the lines. And if the director suddenly says to you "Can you do it this way?" you might think 'Well no I can't because I've learnt it that way'. So I suppose I'm going for a happy medium.'

Joyce Nettles, Casting Director, UK

Certainly for a screen casting session, links to the uploaded auditions will be sent to producers, execs and eventually, at recalls, to the network too. If they were not in the room personally and didn't meet you during your audition and chat, they need to glean everything they can from those moments on camera. So, you need your eyes to be engaging with the person with whom you are reading... as opposed to looking down at your page.

Alison Chard explains the more you can do to better your chances, the better your chances will be:

'Whereas in America they all believe that they should work for something and they're quite happy to come in and show that they've put in the work and I think part of that is learning the part... If you're making a connection with the people in the room and with the camera then you really are going to show up on the tape itself. Therefore when the producer sees it and of course they haven't had the advantage of meeting you and so they don't know what you're like as a person and they don't know the context of your performance all they can see is what's on

> *that tape. So if you can learn it or become at least largely familiar with it then you are gonna really give yourself a leg up actually and again it shows that you've done your homework... Things are so expensive now that they want you to be completely prepared and ready to go really, so that is an indication, "Oh, you've learnt it, oh great, let's see what we can do with it" you know, you do it the way you want to do it and we'll have a chat about it.'*
>
> Alison Chard, Casting Director, UK

If you find learning lines hard, try recording the other characters' dialogue on your phone and playing it back, so when you practise aloud you learn your cues as well.

Some productions have confidentiality clauses, which mean they can't send out sides prior to the meetings so you get sides on arrival. If this is the case and you are dyslexic, make sure your agent knows. If they know, they will ask if an exception can be made in your case, if it is not possible, the casting office will let you arrive much earlier in order to have longer with the material so you are not at an unfair disadvantage. You gain nothing by not sharing this information with your agent.

Whether your scenes were specified or you were asked to choose, you should still be familiar with them for stage or screen. If you've read the whole script, you will understand the character's journey and have been thinking about it. I'll say it again – American actors are more prepared, *always*, and that's a leaf we should take out of their book.

> 'In the States it tends to be on the whole I'd say more enjoyable because the actors are so much better prepared... In the States it's as if they say "We all know that this is a terrible ordeal for all parties, but let's get that aside and get on with it."... They will know the sides and they will have worked on them so what you're

watching is an actor who has thought about the part and tried to apply themselves to it, whereas in this country it's much more slap dash on the whole.'

Sir Richard Eyre CBE, Director, UK

Occasionally, on the day, the director or producer may have decided that, in fact, they want to look at scenes different from those that were sent out. In such circumstances there will be a flurry of activity when you arrive for the audition. A casting assistant will apologise, explain, then hand you a photocopy of the side(s) the director wants to look at. You may only get 10 minutes or so to look at these before it's time for you to go in. Again, if you are dyslexic tell them, the casting assistant will make sure you can go and get a cuppa and read them in your own time and space. In these situations a number of things are important: your composure, (we'll look at that in chapter 6)… and sight-reading.

SIGHT-READING

This is a skill that is always worth keeping up and it gets easier over time. At certain auditions you will be handed pages on arrival. So, accept that you just have to do it. It is essential that you get on with preparing yourself in the few minutes you have rather than complaining about the situation. The reason we're looking at this here is because it's a skill you can practise at home before an audition so that you're not flustered on the day. There are some straightforward steps you can follow:

- Read the scene through first, so you've understood the context of that scene and your character's intentions within it.
- Place the thumb of your left hand holding the page to the

beginning of the line. When you finish your dialogue move your thumb down the page to the next section of your dialogue. This means that when you're reading with another person you can look up at them even though you don't know the scene that well yet. You can watch and listen to them and flick your eyes down on your cue. Miraculously your thumb is pointing to your next line. So instead of just reading and then waiting for your next line cue, you actually engage with the other person.

- It is possible to quickly skim-read the rest of the sentence while you are reading the beginning of it out loud to the other person. This however takes practise. So practise.

'One of the pieces of advice I would give is learn how to sight-read. It's really important. You're gonna walk into an interview, especially for movies you know, when someone thrusts a couple of pages under your nose... have a look and make an instant decision about how you're gonna play it. And then committing yourself to that and being able to do it while a camera's on, without keeping your nose on the script – you know there's a real knack to it. It's the first thing I learnt when I was a kid. My eyes would skim to the end of the sentence while I was still reading the beginning, and that's really important and that will really help you.'

Phil Davis, Actor and Director, UK

MAKE DECISIONS ABOUT THE CHARACTER AND HOW YOU'LL PLAY THE SCENES

Having read the script and familiarized yourself with the scenes, you have to make decisions about how you will play the character and therefore those scenes within your audition. The implication of an actor's decisions or the lack of in an audition is always compounded by time constraints:

> 'Make absolutely sure that you know it really well. I always want people to come in with a very clear idea of how they want to play that part too, there isn't time for somebody to come in and say "I've no idea how to play this part, mould me"... You've got to have made up your mind exactly what it is that you want to do with it and know it very well. Not necessarily because I'm going to want you to play it exactly like that but unless you go in absolutely secure, there isn't actually time to work on it and turn it upside down if you want to.'
>
> Peter Cregeen, Director and Producer, UK

Of course there will be indications in the stage directions to help you. However mostly you will have to make those decisions based on where the scene is trying to get to within the context of the story as a whole. For example:

- If the stage directions say your character is angry and raises their voice, consider why you are angry, what's the backstory to this? Why are you losing your temper now? Is it revealed entirely in this scene or has it been built up to this point? Do you raise your voice in this scene but go on to a violent or emotional peak in the following scene in which case you need to consider the levels.

> 'Very simple textual analysis, I might say: does the character talk a lot, or does the character ask questions, or does the character respond to questions? I might ask myself about the fixed givens: which are facts which are not open to interpretation.'
>
> Sam Rumbelow, Method Acting Coach, UK and USA

- Are you telling someone in the scene that you never loved them and that's why you're leaving? There may be myriad reasons for this. Perhaps in the previous scene someone blackmailed you to do so and you're trying to protect your loved one(s). How on the nose are you going to play that scene, which of the motivations are you going to choose to show the director, casting director and producer? These are *your* choices.

> *'If you go in sitting on a fence thinking "Not really sure about this, I'll just kind of like say the lines and leave it open", you'll give them nothing, and so I suggest that that won't take you to that next stage. So, I would say you have to be like a detective in that waiting room, or on the night before when you're learning your lines, and really have a look and think about who you are, what the relationship is with the person you're talking to or the people you are talking about and most importantly what do you want? And then really play it. Really think and make your choices really important to you. That doesn't mean you have to show masses of emotion, but it means that you have to make what you're thinking vital, so that we see something happening.'*
>
> Mel Churcher, Acting and Dialect Coach, UK and USA

Be brave about your decisions and see them through. Even if your take on it is not how the creatives envisage it, you'll give them something interesting. As long as you can back up those choices, knowing the script gives you that insight.

> *'If you hire me to play the part then I'll play the part. I take responsibility for it and directors like that. You go, "Alright, I'll have that, I'll do it" and they don't have to worry about it… as a director I love it when actors come in and they really want to play and they say "Give it to me" and you hand it over gratefully. You think "I don't*

have to worry about that anymore because I've got this guy and he's gonna be good."

Phil Davis, Actor and Director, UK

Seeing the way a selection of actors work with the same material is a joy for casting directors and directors alike. You will make idiosyncratic choices, distinct from the other actors because you are individuals with different life experience. So, whichever methodology/technique you trained in, you still employ *your* choices to give the character an inner depth – which differs from actor to actor.

RESEARCHING YOUR ROLE

Your decisions on how you play the role should be coming from your instinctual reaction to the script. What makes these choices have a deeper resonance is research on the role. We'll come back to this in chapter 9, but key points you should consider are:

- Do you understand their job, is it something you can find things out about if it is completely alien to you? I don't mean staying up all night reading medical journals if it's a doctor. But if it's say a farmer in wartime Britain, they would have had a lot of stresses, a hard life in hard times.
- Are they damaged? What history are we given? If it's someone who left an abusive relationship are they in a refuge? You can always find survivor accounts of most things on the Internet.

That bit of research can add such depth to characterisation, that it can be invaluable.

RESEARCH WHOM YOU ARE MEETING AND THE PRODUCTION

Research the people that you will be meeting. You may be asking yourself why you need to do this, after all you have a lot to do, learning your lines, working on your performance, characterisation – and your nerves… For the same simple reason as with your mail outs. It can come across as complacent and rude if you haven't, as though these people are far less important than yourself. And no one likes to think that all their previous experiences and work are irrelevant. Why should the creative team research you and have an opinion on your work if you don't take the time to look at theirs? Remember your audition is a job interview. Turn this on its head, how committed and serious about the production and your craft do you appear if you *have* done your homework – *very*.

There is another crucial factor in this research; it will inform you as to whether you actually *want* to work on this production, or with the creatives making it. Find out:

- Who the team are: the director, writer, producers and casting director?
- Have you seen any of their previous work before?
- Did you like it? Did you watch it and think you'd love to work with them? Here's where a practical application of reading scripts and plays can come in, it could make all the difference in a meeting having already read someone's previous work for pleasure.
- Are their choices brave, interesting, right up your street? Would you give your right arm to work with them?
- Is it a long running TV or stage show that you are meeting for? If so have you seen it?

It is so exciting to work with a team you genuinely respect and whose vision is one you want to work towards. So if you have been excited by any of their previous work, you want to know this when you go in to meet for the project so that you can talk about it and how it affected you. They will love to hear that, if it is genuine.

> *'Find out something about the programme before you go. If you're going to go in to play a part in an episode of... "Holby City" or whatever. You mustn't lose sight of the fact that particularly the producer and the casting director and probably the director are very enthusiastic about the programme. And if you go in and say "Well I don't know anything about this, I've never watched it" that's not actually the greatest start in the world.'*
>
> Peter Cregeen, Director and Producer, UK

Knowing who someone is when you talk to them in an interview isn't purely about professional courtesy and respect, it demonstrates you understand the business you and they are in. Before you meet someone for the chance to work on their project, know that a little research can go a long way.

> *'I think actors should do homework. I cast a production of 'Death of a Salesman' in the West End – I happen to think, and I'm not alone, that 'Death of a Salesman' is not only one of the greatest plays of the 20th century, but one of the greatest plays ever written. When actors came in to audition for that, without having read the play, I was shocked and I was angry and I was upset on behalf of Arthur Miller who was about to die. So do your homework, this is my advice. And learn a little bit about the people you're meeting... and find out a little bit about what they've done, so that you know whoever you're meeting.'*
>
> Joyce Nettles, Casting Director, UK

SO HOW DO YOU RESEARCH THE PRODUCTION AND CREATIVE TEAM?

Nowadays this is not remotely difficult. It's not like the early 90's when you still had to go to your local library to find information and photocopy or God forbid – write things down… The chances are you've got access to the Internet at home and on your smart phone. It's easy as 1, 2, 3, a, b, c… well I, M, D, B.

- www.imdb.com
- www.google.com

It's that simple.

IMDB them first. You should be listed there with your screen credits and have your headshot and agent contact details there. So put the name of the casting director, director, writer and producers into the search box. Bear in mind that if their main body of work has been in the theatre you will need to Google them as IMDB only refers to screen work. If you have time, watch something they previously worked on if you are not already familiar with their work, finding Internet links to TV shows is easy enough. If a stage show they wrote, directed or produced is currently running go and see it. You should be in the habit of seeing theatrical shows and not just productions your friends are in.

If it is a long running TV show, watch a recent episode before you go in, even if you have seen it in the past. So that you are up-to-date with the current storylines and cast, style and feel of the show as it may have changed over the years.

READ YOUR OWN CV

It seems an odd thing to suggest, but think about it. Everyone gets nervous before an audition, when you're in the room and your adrenaline is pumping away. Even if you've managed to start out the pre reading conversation in a seemingly relaxed way and you're being quite charming to the creatives you can still be thrown off your stride. Someone asks you what you've been up to recently and your mind goes blank. How are you then going to regain your composure to read your scenes well whilst fighting your inner monologue – the voice inside your head that's shouting 'How could I have forgotten what I've done this year. . ?' To begin with, don't beat yourself up as it happens to us all, actors or not. But don't take that to mean there is not something you can do about it.

> *'I'm constantly surprised by the number of people who you ask about a particular show that they were in on their CV, and there's no director's name on it. And you say to them, "What did you play in that?" and they can only just remember what they played in it and then you say "Well who directed it?" and they can't remember the name of the director at all. That seems to me, not to be particularly sensible.'*
>
> Peter Cregeen, Director and Producer, UK

So take a look at your own CV the night before you go in, or on the morning of your meeting. You did the work so you don't need to study it just refresh your memory so you're calm and no information will evade you. This way you can expand on something as John Hubbard explains:

> *'It happens you know. "What have you been doing recently?" "Um, God, what have I been doing recently?"... don't go "Well I've just played Horatio at the Exeter theatre". Think "Well, I've just worked with this exciting new director, John Bloggs"; "Oh, what was that? Tell me about it, why did you think he was good?" You know you*

might get that. Just give them one thing to hold on to, because if you reel it off they're not taking anything in.'

John Hubbard, Casting Director, UK

DRESSING FOR THE PART

Dressing for the part is not for the benefit of the casting director, it is for the producers. Many directors aren't overly concerned about what you wear and are perfectly able to see beyond it.

'When you're going to an audition, if it looks like you've over dressed for the part, there is an initial problem you think "Why is this person dressed like this, are they going to a wedding or did they do this for me?"... Again, if you come off a building site, that can be off putting as well you know... I'd always say the classless dress is the easiest way because then you're not worried about what people look like, you're concentrating on them, their characterisation, their face, their features, all those things.'

Robert Bierman, Director, UK and USA

It is a question that comes up a lot, there are always exceptions but there are rules of thumb:

- Commercials – dress for the part.
- TV – British TV come as you are with a hint at character. You will be advised if you need to do more than that.
- American TV or co-produced by Americans – dress for the part (within reason), use your common sense.
- Film – dress for the part (within reason). You'll be notified beforehand.
- Theatre – come as you are, if specific clothing for say movement is required you'll be told in advance.

- Musical theatre – first round come as you are, recalls dress for the part. Dance calls always require dancewear.

Generally speaking there is a smart-casual sort of uniform for actors; jeans and a casual top or shirt for both genders is fine.

> *'If I don't have the imagination to see through what somebody's wearing to their, sorry to sound so frightfully pompous, but to their soul or whatever, then I shouldn't be doing my job. However, having said that, there are certain directors that I've worked with and still work with... whom I believe would be happier if somebody came in dressed relatively appropriately. And if I knew that I would say to the actor "This is set in the 40's", so I suggest that perhaps if you're a woman that you come in a skirt or a dress rather than in jeans, because that will give you more of a feel and make you look slightly better. It's not that important to me.'*
>
> Joyce Nettles, Casting Director, UK

You will be advised if you need to dress up for the part but it is always worth hinting at it. If you're coming in to play a nun or a priest, don't come in a habit, dress conservatively. If you're coming in to play a sex worker, dress a little more provocatively *within reason,* e.g. tight jeans and a vest top. For many American shows casting here or UK shows co-produced by the US, the producers will want to see your physique. So that will mean dress attractively and for women vest tops or dresses which show your arms and give an indication of your torso. Don't wear a vest top lower than your bra – yes I've seen it; no she didn't get the part.

> 'You should come in suggesting that you're aware of the part, he's an accountant – so he probably wears a

suit, you know, he's a fashion designer – sort of smartly casual with a little flash of flamboyance. It just helps the director to see. You're not doing the whole job of the wardrobe lady. But I don't say if it's an athlete's part come in shorts, you might come in I don't know in a white shirt and something like that just to give the people looking at you, judging you, saying "I know what I'm testing for", you know.'

John Hubbard, Casting Director, UK

For the ladies, well actually for some of the guys too, don't wear too much make up. It can be really distracting. I've seen actresses asked to go to the bathroom to tone down their make up before their meeting which of course makes them feel a little foolish and doesn't help their audition nerves.

SELF-ASSURANCE / CONFIDENCE ARE ATTRACTIVE, ARROGANCE IS NOT

Presentation when you are in the audition room and on your way to it is really important – you never know who's walking up the stairs behind you. It's something to think about before you are there.

You must be able to present yourself as a confident actor and self-assured person, never arrogant. No one likes arrogance, even for the most talented individual in the world. We'll go into more detail on presentation in chapter 6, but this is something you need to work on before the day of the audition.

> *'I think you can smell real talent… that's not always true – because sometimes people don't present themselves very well.'*
>
> Tim Pigott-Smith, Actor and Director, UK

If you're naturally a shy person, you have to work at finding a way to bring yourself out of your shell and engage with the people you're meeting with, because talent alone will not get you the job.

> 'Really work on your person skills and your kind of social skills because, that is I've noticed, over the years, that it's increasingly more part of the package really, part of the audition process really. So if you're kind of shy and retiring then, I think, you've got to get out there and practise not being quite so shy and retiring. Particularly, as I can't really think of many kind of monster directors that I've worked with in recent years, most of them are extremely nice, love actors, love what they do.'
>
> Alison Chard, Casting Director, UK

Jeff Turner is a Life Management and Performance coach; he has various strategies for managing a person's emotional state in order to get through situations like auditions. He talks of using a role model to find a resourceful state of being and asks you to think about:

- Do you have a role model who can be your source of inspiration for your required confidence?
- Physically how you sit or stand to appear confident?
- How you move?
- What expressions you make, what you give away in your face?
- Vocally what qualities of your voice will you use?
- How are you breathing, is it helping your current state or making it worse?

This summarises his process of state management before going into the audition. The theory is think about all these things, imagine how your role model might do it, imagine how you might do it and then work on those key elements. In doing this you will appear and feel more centred and confident. Where's the harm in trying?

> 'One of the things you might like to do before you walk into that audition is just to think "Who am I? Who do I choose to be in this?" You might step into the shoes of a chosen role model of yours – someone that you know would act confidently in a relaxed and resourceful way in this rather tense environment. So let's just go through those five things again in order for you during this audition to give the best performance that you can. Who do you need to think of? Who do you need to be for the purposes of this episode in your life? How should you sit or stand in order to appear more resourceful? How will you choose to move – perhaps checking in with your role model? What facial expressions will you allow the director to see? (Only resourceful ones). How will you speak, not only whilst you're reading for the part but as you? What qualities in your voice will make this person invest in you? What will make them believe in you and also how will you support this process through your breathing? So just thinking about the future, how you gonna use this, how will this be valuable to you?'
>
> Jeff Turner, Life Management and Performance Coach, UK

This is a process you can be working on all the time but certainly a few days before going in could help. Trying it out while sat in the waiting room for your audition isn't the place where you would be able to calmly think about all of this for the first time. Think about it before and then perhaps try out some of those techniques on the day – they may help.

You will have had movement and voice training when you were at drama school or university, here's your chance to put it back into practise, if you don't already. We all witness people (and know some personally) who exude confidence without being arrogant. Ask yourself how they stand, sit, walk, smile, start a sentence. Don't copy that person just think about how they use their physicality to own their space, how do they use their voice to communicate and get their message across. This, as an actor, is part of your training; so don't leave it by the door with your bag. Breathe calmly and take the confident talented actor inside the room.

That's one coping strategy but there are different schools of thought. As you're not in the audition room yet you've time to try these things at home.

What you're doing on a personal level in an audition is making a connection to another human being so you need to be in a relaxed state, or as near to relaxed as you can be, in the artificial situation that auditions are. By that I mean you're acting for a very short period of time in order to get the chance to play the part in the actual production. You're on your best behaviour and all charm and grace to woo everyone without being smarmy or dishonest. You're sat in a chair opposite the team reading the lines with the casting director or a reader, in a small room, not how the scene would be on stage or on set. It's a manufactured circumstance, but we *all* have to suspend disbelief for fifteen minutes or so.

Simon Dunmore has a theory about absorbing the ambience of a room. Each audition will be different but you can practice this technique wherever you happen to be in the days before an audition.

> *'Just take a moment to absorb the ambience of the room that you're walking into, it's a new space – even if you've been in that room before, don't presume it's going to be exactly the same. OK, you may be meeting the same people but the interview table or the interview*

area might be in a different place. Too often people walk blindly in without connecting with the space. I suppose another way of thinking about a lot of what I'm talking about is just have that moment to connect, and it takes half a second to do it. But too many people walk in blind and make silly clutzy mistakes, which are forgiven, but they throw themselves [off their stride]. There's a lovely phrase in the novel "Howard's End", they cut it from the film unfortunately, which is "Only connect". And I think that sums up so much and I suggest to people – just take a moment, in any situation, then say "Only connect" in your head and that is sufficient time to adjust to this new circumstance.'

Simon Dunmore, Director and Author, UK

Try it prior to your next audition, absorb the atmosphere of a room you're in, tube carriage, lift, supermarket and do not let it interfere with you. So that when you come to the casting venue no awkward atmosphere can unsettle you and you can fill the room with your own good vibes.

DO YOU WANT TO WORK ON THIS PRODUCTION?

This is something that some actors don't appear to think about till after they have auditioned.

- Only meet for a production whatever medium if you actually want to work on it.
- Never attend an audition because you want to meet any one particular member of the team but not the show in question.

Have you considered the practical implications of the show?

- Long term filming in another city or abroad can put huge pressure on family life, especially if you have a young family. You need to discuss these practicalities with your partner and children (if you have any).
- A theatre tour for a year could mean weekly venues which though it can be great in terms of differing audiences and seeing the country, can bring its own stresses.
- Can you afford to be in a profit share fringe theatre production if you can't quite make your rent/mortgage?
- Do you want to be in a micro-budget feature film where all hands are on deck? They can be a wonderful experience and some fantastic films come from this, but do you mind the prospect of potentially sleeping in sleeping bags, 5 people in someone's lounge or hosting 5 others in your lounge, etc for a couple of weeks or so?
- Short films (be they student or industry professionals) vary tremendously in how smoothly and professionally the production runs and how beautifully executed the end result is. Some win countless awards and you can build some great contacts and working relationships this way; but some fall by the wayside. Some are paid properly and some are expenses only.

Be sure you want to meet on something before you say yes. *Never* attend a meeting, then turn the job down based on the specifics. It wastes both yours and their time when they could have been meeting someone who actually wanted to work on it.

READING YOUR AUDITION DETAILS EMAIL

One last point, I've saved this till last so it works as a reminder. Always read the email your agent sends you with the script and sides thoroughly. Often when they give you the details on the phone you'll be out and about without a pen to hand, it will be noisy and possibly your mobile reception isn't all that great. You will not remember all of it. Casting offices give all the relevant information for what you need to prepare and work on to your agent, usually on the phone and reiterated in the email with the material.

- You should *never* go for an audition at a home address. Even short and low budget films use appropriate venues.
- What day, what time and where is your audition? Very importantly: make a note of this either in a diary if you're old school and still use paper and pen or on your phone.
- Does the character have an accent?
- Have they specified a dress code?
- Which scenes are you meant to prepare?
- Will you be doing any improvisation around the scenes and characters?
- Will you be auditioned in pairs if they are looking at characters that are partners, colleagues, friends or family members?
- If it's musical theatre or a play with music do you need to bring your own choice of song (always with sheet music) as well as the material they are giving you?

These are all things you need to consider and work on prior to your meeting and it's surprising how many actors turn up on the day saying they weren't told any of this… whilst holding a print out of the email they were sent. Read it thoroughly so you can do your best work with all your bases covered.

SUMMARY

What you can take away from this chapter is the knowledge that your preparation before going into an audition is vital and that it is down to you. You should be reading any full scripts for context and preparing all the material sent to you, giving yourself enough time to do that effectively. That done you can then make decisions about how you are going to play each scene and the character as a whole. You should always be working on ways to improve your audition technique; your confidence, how to manage your emotional state, sight reading, knowing your own CV. Also of utmost importance: researching the creatives you will be meeting and the production you are being brought in to audition for. Always know something about each individual in the room and the project. Read the email you were sent containing all the information on what to prepare.

CHAPTER 6

THE DAY OF THE AUDITION

This chapter covers what happens and how you should present yourself on the day of your audition. It looks at what you should have considered and how do you need to behave when you get to the audition itself. We'll focus on:

- Punctuality, Presentation and politeness.
- Etiquette for the waiting room and the casting studio.
- Being yourself and as relaxed as you can.
- Psyching yourself up to a confident state.
- Listening to notes.
- What stands out for a director?
- Common mistakes.

PUNCTUALITY, PRESENTATION AND POLITENESS

At this point it is important to remember that you've been whittled down from a long list of ideas and suggestions of actors for this role. Also, you're being given the opportunity for what could be a great job, possibly the one which will be your break through role…

> 'Getting that appointment is such a massive achievement for an actor, it therefore needs to be respected, so you need to know exactly what you're gonna be doing.'
>
> John Hubbard, Casting Director, UK

Here are rules of thumb for punctuality, presentation and courtesy that cross each medium of casting, be it theatre, TV, film, commercials, corporates, fringe shows or student films:

- Be punctual – always.
- Be presentable – always.
- Be polite, have some manners – always.

It sounds so obvious but you'd be amazed how many actors are routinely late, unkempt or not yet ready. And, sometimes rude. Despite the fact that an audition is in effect a job interview, some actors confuse its informal appearance with informal requirements. This is the *professional* setting for this industry and it beggars belief, that anyone could treat any aspect of this interview less than professionally. This is a more common occurrence in young actors but it applies to all.

PUNCTUALITY

Not every casting office is overly concerned about actors' time management, it depends on the casting director and the creatives involved, it also depends on how much time they have. Some individuals are more relaxed and their offices will just bring the actors in in the order they arrive and the session is more fluid. But you can't work on the assumption that everyone is that easy going or accommodating.

Punctuality is not something that happens to you. Trains and tubes will always be subject to delays; buses invariably get stuck in traffic when you have somewhere to be. Even pre-booked cabs can arrive late.

- Get an earlier train, tube or bus – then go for a coffee round the corner from where your audition is, so that you're on time. Don't be late. Conversely don't turn up an hour early because you were trying not to be late (I'll come back to this).

What are the consequences of late arrivals?

- If you are 10 minutes late and everyone has waited for you that encroaches into the next actor's timeslot. What if the director/producer has to leave on time today? Who should lose 10 minutes – the actors after you, or you the latecomer?
- The following scenario could be fairly typical in any audition; slightly disorganised actor A would have been running 5-10 minutes late, actor B would have been on time and uber organized actor C would have had time to freshen up before going in. But what if these first three actors all had problems with public transport because of one signal failure on the underground? Now they're all late. The casting office calls the agents of A, B and C then that of actor D asking if he/she happens to be in the area already and wants an earlier audition. This is *not* a question of scheduling – casting assistants are perfectly capable of moving a few names around an audition list. It is a question of human psychology. The casting team are trying to help all the potential candidates and the creatives. Everyone gets stressed out and not going to be at their best, actors and creatives alike. If actors A and B had been on earlier transport, by the time it was C's timeslot the signal failure would likely be sorted out and no one would be feeling frazzled.
- What does strolling in late tell the creative team about the professional respect you have for them? It says you can't be bothered and if you can't be bothered to present yourself in the best light at the audition what will they get if they offer you the job – the same level of professional courtesy? Could you be relied upon to arrive on time for rehearsals? For the shoot or theatrical run?

- Worse still is strolling in late with a friend. Why have you brought them with you? If you need a chaperone because of your age, it's usually a parent, sibling or teacher. If you're an adult *no one* should be holding your hand to go into a professional situation like a job interview. Do you think barristers, brain surgeons or bus drivers take their mates with them, I very much doubt it.

> *'The days when bad behaviour like turning up late or not knowing your lines or what-have-you were regarded as a sign of genius, which was kind of in the 80's I think is gone, long gone... "Oh, you've learnt it, oh great. Let's see what we can do with it" You know, you do it the way you want to do it and we'll have a chat about it. Whereas they can't necessarily do that if your appointment's at 4.00 and you turn up at 4.10. You haven't got time to look at it and you're crashing into everybody else's audition time and we have to call you in kind of right now and you've given yourself a kind of real handicap.'*
>
> Alison Chard, Casting Director, UK

Why do some casting offices send actors away when they arrive early?

- Sessions are often organized so that actors for the same part do not follow each other and meet the competition (of course this depends on the production and creatives, but casting directors will always try to avoid you seeing each other if possible). Seeing an actor you may know already going for the same part tends not to help nerves for various reasons for example; it feels like they always get the part and you don't or they are very different to you (and you start to think that you're the leftfield choice that no one is going to choose).
- There may not be a particularly large waiting area available

and when there is it is often next to the rooms which the auditions are being held in. Actors understandably tend to start talking to each other in waiting rooms; this can sometimes be heard by the team or on camera within the audition studio if it's a taped casting. The sound travels because actors naturally project their voices even when whispering to each other. It's part of the training. So what is being said 'quietly' as an aside *actually* the whole casting office can usually hear.

- Ring your agent and ask them to call the casting team, or call yourself, if you're hoping to get an earlier appointment. Don't arrive super-early unannounced. Casting teams are always helpful, changing actors' meeting times because of childcare issues or other appointments, if we can help we do. Don't just turn up and expect to muscle-in in front of someone else's pre-arranged time, you wouldn't do that at your DR's surgery.

PRESENTATION

Presentation is also key in an audition. There are many reasons why you need to look appropriate to the situation and not like you just rolled in from clubbing the night before or a camping holiday. This meeting is for a professional engagement. Even for non-paid work there should be an understood professionalism.

> 'It's no good coming into a casting, with a voice that says "I left Soho House at 4.00 this morning" waving two sheets of paper and going "Um, was I supposed to look at this?" You're dead, you're dead, you know.'
>
> John Hubbard, Casting Director, UK

- If you need to change into clothing more suitable for the character, get there with enough time to switch outfits in the ladies/gents at the venue or the nearby coffee shop (where you've been relaxing with your latte because you were really early). Don't arrive with 2 minutes to spare all flustered because someone else is occupying the only available space. Could you have travelled in your outfit? Is it that difficult? You can always ring in advance to check what facilities there are.

'What I don't like is when people come in looking as if they've just got up and really, really, really scruffy, because I think you've got to make a little bit of effort. I'm not suggesting you have to go to the hairdressers and Harvey Nicks and completely get a new set of clothes, but coming in bleary eyed with a lot of holes in your clothes is not my tip for how to get on in life when you're going up for a job.'

Joyce Nettles, Casting Director, UK

POLITENESS

Why do you *need* to be polite and courteous? Well, for one: manners cost you nothing and two: everyone you come into contact with is a person, with feelings just as real as your own.

- Don't be rude, dismissive and/or sarcastic to the assistant who is offering you water and making sure you got your script and sides.
- Don't be rude, dismissive and/or sarcastic to the assistant operating the camera, or the pianist if it's musical theatre.
- Don't be rude, dismissive and/or sarcastic to the creative team.
- Turn off your mobile phone because it is rude and dismissive to all of the above.

I put them in that order because that's generally the order in which you'll meet the team, but they are all people. Just because an assistant is not the person making the final choice on whether you are going further for *this job*, does not mean they won't in the future. They are also often asked how people behaved in the waiting area, it is after all an indication of temperament. Like the bad funeral networking; we all remember those who are inappropriate or unnecessarily rude. Like elephants, we have long memories. John Hubbard expands on the knock on effect of bad behaviour:

> *'Behaviour everywhere has deteriorated... People are very disrespectful... Everybody's under pressure and we just have to recognise that and recognise they're other people under pressure. It's a horrible, horrible process but I can't think of any way round it. That chemical meeting, face-to-face meeting is very, very important. A lot of it, of course, is behaviour, like looking at you and saying "Do I wanna work with her for two months? Do I wanna see her morning, noon and night for two months?" You know, because what I'm getting from her is I think she could be trouble.'*
>
> John Hubbard, Casting Director, UK

It is often those who've not been out of drama school that long who have developed these very bad habits and I suspect it's because they've not been told otherwise – at home or when training, bring back the stocks I say. But seriously, if you are new to the profession you shouldn't have any sort of bad attitude. You often find that those with the most experience and standing are the most polite, punctual, personable and generous natured.

> *'Some of them they come in, you know, like immediately "Are you gonna give me a job or not?" With terrible*

> speech, bad tone, perhaps not quite clean enough and hair probably hasn't been washed and you think, 'Well that's so unpleasant.'"
>
> Richard Briers CBE, Actor, UK

SAT IN THE WAITING ROOM

Sitting in a waiting room is uncomfortable for anyone; whether it's at the dentist's, train station or audition venue. While I can't advise what might help in the other situations, the following would make your time in the audition waiting area better spent all round.

Do:

- Whatever you need (within reason) to centre yourself, focus and relax. We looked at State Management in chapter 5 – now would be a good time to implement some of those techniques.
- Go over your scenes quietly.
- If you're catching up with another actor you've not seen in a while chat *quietly*. Do remember, they also need to prepare, so keep it brief, swap numbers for a catch up later, rather than now.
- If you have pertinent questions regarding the production ask the casting assistant, they will be happy to answer as long as the phone isn't ringing off the hook.
- Take a moment before you enter the room to remind yourself/check the names of who you are meeting and if you have met them before.
- If you are at an open audition; expect it to be a long, *LONG* time before you are seen, use your time productively.

Don't:

- Talk loudly to the other actors waiting about which role they are coming in for.
- Talk loudly to the other actors about whether they are working and the state of the industry.
- Talk loudly whilst chatting up another actor.
- Talk loudly on your mobile phone.
- Run through your scenes loudly while walking around the space.
- Complain that the session is running late.
- Complain that you never get a job through this casting director.
- Discuss the creative team or the production in any way that is negative.

Remember generally we can hear actors' whispers like theatrical asides – we understand we weren't supposed to hear them and yet we did…

PUT YOUR BAG DOWN AND BE UNCLUTTERED

Actors often arrive at auditions with an array of bags – and it's not just the ladies actually. Whether it's: overnight bags because you've travelled from outside of the city for your meeting; your gym bag, your laptop bag, your handbag/man-bag; or all of the above; as Simon Dunmore explains, it is clutter.

> *'When you're walking through the door, first of all if you've got any baggage with you, try and leave it in the waiting room. If that's impossible, you know somebody's got to look after it, put it down by the door before you start trying to shake hands.'*
>
> Simon Dunmore, Director and Author, UK

The chances of theft at an audition are slim, though of course that depends on the venue. If they are at the casting director's office: Leave your bags in the waiting area, there will be no through traffic and if you have valuables i.e. laptop, ask the casting assistant if they can keep them by their desk. If it is at a public venue with other people walking around not involved with the auditions, or you don't want to be parted from them take them with you, but put them down to the side out of the way, the moment you step into the audition room.

> *'Come in un-encumbered, the actor walks in and there's nothing, he's not carrying anything, he's turned his mobile phone off. I can't tell you, out of every 20 actors, there'll be 5 mobile phones will go off in the middle of the read.'*
> John Hubbard, Casting Director, UK

This is a very important point, wherever you put your bags turn off your mobile phone. Turn it off in your back pocket. Turn it off on the chair. Turn it off in your coat pocket. Turn it off.

BEING PERSONABLE AND YOURSELF

You want to walk into the audition room free of baggage of all kinds, emotionally and materially, so that when the casting director smiles and introduces you, you are ready for all the hand shaking and face-to-face charisma time before the read.

> *'When the person walks into the room, sometimes you think "This person looks like the kind of person I'm looking for," then it is either confirmed or unconfirmed the moment they start talking and start presenting what they have to offer... I think also basically within all this conversation we have to accept the fact that we*

are talking about people who are talented for the job so you know (so we're not just talking about someone you've met in a bar, so that's accepted) we're talking about equal talent.'

Peter Egan, Actor and Director, UK

Be personable, whether you want to view it as manners or more practically as 'they will remember me and be good to me now or in the future'. A warm smile and a firm handshake do more for your career than you realise.

'If you're open, friendly, flexible, all of those things, it's only gonna help your cause really. And be natural, be yourself. I mean directors these days are much more interested as well in you as a person, not just in what you're gonna bring to the role. They have to work with you so they need to know a bit about you. And a lot of actors have extremely fascinating backgrounds. A lot of actors have peripatetic childhoods, you know army backgrounds or just that they've experienced many different things before they've got to the audition room and they like to know that they can utilise that if it's there.'

Alison Chard, Casting Director, UK

When you enter the casting venue, greet everyone with a friendly attitude, that is a great start.

'It's vital for actors when they meet directors or producers for the first time to find a way of presenting themselves in as open, committed and clear a way as possible… a lot of [the] time an actor's mood gets in between them and the job, because they're meeting someone they don't know "How am I going to impress them?" The best thing

> *is always find a way of being yourself, present who you are and allow your energy to come from you as freely as you possibly can.'*
>
> Peter Egan, Actor and Director, UK

Meetings are often more chat than read, so you have to be able to talk once you're in the audition/interview situation and that takes preparation just as the read required learning lines.

> *'That connection, making a connection with the person you're talking to – very quickly when you're meeting them – is absolutely crucial.'*
>
> Simon Dunmore, Director and Author, UK

Work on being charming, not in a overly flirtatious 'Prince/Princess Charming' way, but in an honest, 'interested in other people' way. Have you met any of the team before? If so isn't it lovely to see them again, especially as it may lead to working together this time? Tell them if you mean it, it's not fawning if it's sincere.

This is where that research on the creative team comes in, so you can talk without floundering about some of *their* work. This can make that essential human connection between you and them, showing how compatible your creative views are and how it added to your interest for this particular production.

> *'They've thought about the character and that they like the piece too. I mean it's interesting how directors are human too and they do like it if you've done a bit of research on the Internet yourself. And you know what they've done or you know the context which they're operating at the moment. And if they've chosen to do a project then you can be sure that they've invested a commitment to it and they want to see that you're prepared to do likewise really.'*
>
> Alison Chard, Casting Director, UK

You cannot walk into the audition room and let your nerves get the better of you. You need to appear as a relaxed, confident version of yourself. Remember:

- You can do this part.
- You want this part.
- You want to work on this production with this team.
- You want the team to work with you on this production because of what you can bring to it: your intelligence, preparation, your ability to work with everyone and have fun and, of course, your talent and imagination.

PSYCHING YOURSELF UP TO APPEAR CONFIDENT AND RELAXED

You have to understand and feel the difference between the two states of being: a *confident* state and an *arrogant* state.

If you were looking at another actor and they said 'I believe I can do this and give you something interesting and unexpected' you would hear it as confidence. If they said 'I'm the only actor that can do this part justice' you would hear it as arrogance.

> *'Don't make the mistake of confusing confidence for arrogance. Arrogance isn't actually a resource state. Arrogance in fact is an over compensation, arrogance is never borne out of confidence, it's usually because on some level we're feeling insecure and we tend to over egg the pudding. We tend to overdo it.'*
> Jeff Turner, Life Management and Performance Coach, UK

The difference between appearing confident and relaxed and presenting as arrogant is key. Often arrogance masks fear and we on the casting side understand that, but it's not pleasant to deal with.

Most actors are nervous before auditions, so you will likely need to psyche yourself up before your meeting; the day before, that morning, on the tube, walking up to the venue, sat in the waiting room and finally in one last deep breath before you enter the audition room.

> 'Actors' fear (with which I sympathise) expresses itself in very different ways with different actors. And an actor should be aware of how his or her particular fear expresses itself. Sometimes it's literally in the shaking of the paper as they're reading the scene. Sometimes it's not being able to speak, I mean just kind of freezing up and not having any answers to any questions.'
>
> Joyce Nettles, Casting Director, UK

Tim Pigott-Smith had a rather lovely succinct way of making himself feel more confident because like all actors he hated the audition process:

> 'I think everybody hates doing them, they're so peculiar, they're so unnatural... I used to convince myself I'd get it I suppose, "Oh they're bound to want me" [laughs] you know "It'll be alright."'
>
> Tim Pigott-Smith, Actor and Director, UK

Though he laughs about those nerves, the advice is actually great. It's not arrogance, trying to convince yourself that they will want you. This way when you go in you can appear more relaxed and you can concentrate on just giving the best performance without trying to over sell it in your chat.

Directors can smell fear, casting directors can smell fear, producers can smell fear. Most actors get nervous before an audition, it feels like an algebra equation you've no way out of – creatives to the power of 3. The thing is the team are aware that actors are nervous; that the audition is a false way of seeing how someone will be on set or on stage (this is an unspoken given). The purpose of the first stage auditions is to see that you've understood the material, if you will get on with the creative team and if in person you have the right feel for that role and have brought something to it.

> 'A director can smell it as soon as you come in the room. I can smell the fear and I can smell the desperation, the need, all the things that are sort of the dreads of actors are kind of written all over your face and body and they're trailed behind you… Get yourself in the position of saying "I don't need this part, I'd like it, but I don't desperately need it" that's a really important thing. That's a sort of mental level to get into.'
>
> Robert Bierman, Director, UK and USA

If you've been brought in, there is an assumption that you can act, so rest assured of that at least. Try to work on the appearance of confidence and eliminating the presence of fear.

> 'I think that's what you do when you're acting anyway, you know, "I will get through this part somehow" [laughs] keep the demons at bay.'
>
> Tim Pigott-Smith, Actor and Director, UK

Sometimes actors forget their lines in an audition, if it happens to you don't let it affect your confidence and focus. You are there for the creative team to see your interpretation of the role, not a perfect recital.

BE HONEST

Everyone embellishes their stories a little to add an extra element of intrigue, danger, comedy, or whatever they feel will enhance them. You have to be careful however not to lose sight of the truth in these anecdotes and prevent them becoming tall tales, as Alison Chard suggests:

> *'I would say that directors can spot bluff at kind of 100 paces really these days. And they don't particularly want to work with that kind of person.'*
>
> Alison Chard, Casting Director, UK

The risks you run if you over embellish to the point of fabricating:

- If you invent an anecdote about a person you've worked with (just to name drop them into a conversation).
  One of the creative team may have worked with them previously and so they can check what happened, this will not reflect well on you.
- If you're claiming to have a skill that you in fact don't have: like horse riding (having been on a donkey ride at Skegness when you were 10 does not count); or driving (you only took 3 lessons and got fed up of your Dad shouting at you); being fluent in a foreign language (when actually you can only ask for a beer).
  These can backfire and cause the production problems, not just your reputation for telling pork pies. There is insurance to consider as well as not actually wanting any of their cast or crew to be potentially injured. They may not have the time or budget to teach you these skills once on set/in rehearsal. They may however teach you them if they want you and you were honest about not having them at the start.

- If you say you had a larger part in a production than you actually did or worse still weren't actually in it.
  One of the team may have worked on it and this will all unravel around you.

> *'"I did such and such" and the director will know jolly well that you didn't… or "I ride a bike" or whatever. You know, don't say that unless you do, because it's dangerous. So be yourself and be truthful, just bring yourself along to the party.'*
>
> Alison Chard, Casting Director, UK

CONCENTRATION

So that your time in the audition is used to its full potential you need to concentrate your attention appropriately. Keep your nerves under control and remain calm and alert:

- Pay attention to what is being said to you or asked of you.
- Be aware of your surroundings.
- Focus on why you are here, not your nerves.
  You are here to have a chat and read the scenes to show your interpretation.
- Keep your breathing calm and your shoulders down and relaxed.

> *'If I walk into an audition and I say "OK I need to concentrate on the scene and the character," at that moment I'm just aware that this is a very famous casting director and a very famous director that I'm about to meet, so I'm incredibly nervous. So I have to get myself away from all that fear, right. So I might be able to relax, breathe… and then I might say "OK, let's look at the script."'*
>
> Sam Rumbelow, Method Acting Coach, UK

EYE CONTACT – LINES LEARNT LEAD TO A BETTER READ

Though the requirements for learning lines differ for theatre and screen auditions, generally you're best to be very familiar with the scenes and keep your eyes up, not on the script.

It is not a memory test for exact word-for-word dialogue, but the creatives need to be engaged with you and the person reading with you needs your eye line as much as you need theirs for your performance. It is a communication, we need to be engaged to receive your message. We'll go further into where to focus your eye line for taped auditions and for theatre auditions specifically in the two subsequent chapters 7 and 8. The rule of thumb is – don't perform to the floor, ceiling or to camera. In brief:

- TAPED AUDITIONS – don't look directly into the camera unless asked to. In a normal audition it makes the viewer uncomfortable and takes away suspension of disbelief.
- THEATRE AUDITIONS usually have a larger audition space and you have more chance for movement. Be aware not to go overboard with moving around and focus your delivery towards the creative team. If you're delivering lines and there is no reader because it's a monologue or if you're delivering a song; deliver it to the creative team as a whole. Not two feet above their heads or to the floor, neither of those spaces engages with you. If there is a particularly large panel of the creative team, then think of them as your audience, you can deliver towards their desk, or at head level if you want to avoid picking out eye contact with any one particular individual.

'One of the most important things (from anybody who's gonna look at that tape is concerned) is going to be that they can actually see the actor's eyes... Don't get buried down into the script.'

Peter Cregeen, Director and Producer, UK

John Hubbard makes the point that you're unlikely to have been sent such a wealth of material that you couldn't learn it:

> *'I think you should be off the page... we tend to send out quite short two-hander scenes, never more than say three to five pages and it's part of the actor's job to learn lines. That's what you do and I think that to come into a casting and it's a three page two-hander and you're not off the page – you're stopping yourself getting the job.'*
>
> John Hubbard, Casting Director, UK

The sight reading technique covered in chapter 5 also works if you are not quite off book.

LISTEN AND BE FLEXIBLE TO NOTES

The number one thing actors should always do in an audition yet often don't – generally due to nerves, occasionally down to a lack of flexibility – is *listen*.

You need to listen to the creative team once you're in the audition room because:

- The casting director is always on your side and trying to help you.
- The director will give you notes for various reasons; to give you more of an idea of their vision for the production so you can alter your reading in the room; to see what else you can pull out of the hat performance wise which will give you the edge over the other actors coming in; to see that you are flexible and can take direction quickly as there is less and less time to rehearse nowadays.
- The producer wants to see if you'll listen to the director or anyone else for that matter and take the notes quickly and

effectively. One of their concerns will be 'Is it ego?' will an actor take notes from the creatives or their assistants if necessary, or will their ego get in the way and hold up production?

'A lot of actors don't listen in auditions (they're too nervous) to what the director is telling them, you know like "That's really good, this time, this time just play it, play it a little more lightly." You know and they just do the same read again because they're nervous and in a panic and they didn't actually hear. They heard it but didn't go in and work the cogs and make the adjustment.'

John Hubbard, Casting Director, UK

Part of the ability to listen and take notes comes from concentrating on where you are, why you are there and also relaxing enough to be able to hear above the sound of your own heart beat and veins coursing with nervous blood. As Sam Rumbelow said 'Relax, breathe.'

TALK ABOUT YOUR IDEAS

You've read the full script and are familiar with some previous work of the creative team. Now's your chance to weave into conversation things you genuinely liked about their previous productions, when relevant to this one.

Why would you want to share your thoughts on the script and the role?

- Your ability to turn your interpretation of the script and character into a performance is why you are here, your opinion counts. Tell them your positive thoughts and feelings about the script as a whole and about your character's development.

- Directors love to talk about the journey, the character arc, the story as a whole, and their vision for it. They are generally open to someone else's input; this is where the magic can happen, two imaginations sharing ideas. Don't be afraid of your ideas.
- If you are familiar with the director's style and choices you can converse and bring your ideas to them in a way that makes sense. Even if your ideas are very different, you'll know where they are coming from so the way you approach it will be more open.
- If you love the story, the role, where the journey takes the audience; tell them why.
- You can explain what your reasons are for seeing the character in the way you do. Everyone is different. We have all come to where we are today through individual paths, varying experiences, diverse world views, contrasting tastes and outlooks, particular choices. How is your interpretation the right one for the director?
- Share what intrigues you about the project, what did your imagination run away with? How can you see the partnership of actor and director bringing not just your character but also the production as a whole to life?
- Just a note on the discussion, make sure you don't argue with any of the team, your opinions can differ, but don't talk over them or you'll talk yourself out of a job.
- If you tend to get nervous and forget what you liked about the script and the role, make notes, take them with you and re-read them before you go into your meeting.

'When you go into an interview, an audition, decide what they want and decide what you want, how you would play it and tell 'em that, you know don't be too eager to please.

Claim it, claim the part, claim the role. It's a relief you know. I just know as a director I love it when actors come in and they really want to play and they say "Give it to me" and you hand it over gratefully.'

Phil Davis, Actor and Director, UK

WHAT STANDS OUT FOR A DIRECTOR?

What directors are looking for is a creative meeting of minds; so if you want to give yourself that edge to stand out, put all the preparation to good use.

Everything we've mentioned above:

- The research of script and creative team.
- Vocalising your ideas and impressions of the role and story.
- Engaging with everyone in the room confidently and intelligently.
- Reading with your eyes up and sides down.

How badly do you want the part and to what level should you show that. You may operate a 'Treat 'em mean to keep 'em keen' MO in your love life, but that won't work in the audition room. Nor will the super keen/desperate 'Date two: I'm ready to move in together' mentality. Robert Bierman describes the fine line you must draw:

> 'It's like a love affair, if you think like you're gonna meet someone for a drink, almost on a blind date, how are you gonna be attractive? If you come on strong, are you cool? All those kind of things that you do when you're meeting someone that you want to perhaps have a date or have an affair with, is very similar to an audition… So if you want

it too much that can be smelt. So this the desperation of wanting the part is a real problem.'

Robert Bierman, Director, UK and USA

IF YOU TAKE NOTHING ELSE FROM THIS CHAPTER; BEAR IN MIND THESE COMMON MISTAKES

Everyone has had a bad meeting, interview or audition before regardless of their career. Here are some common mistakes that actors often make in a casting situation and ways to avoid them:

- Auditioning when you don't want the part. That colours the creative team's opinion of you and it *will* last.
  If you don't want to play the part, do not meet for it.
- Saying you are wrong for the part.
  If the description of the character is very different to you and yet you've been called in it is because the creative team have opened up the way they see that character.

  'What annoys… me is an actor coming in saying "Well, I'm, I'm just too old for this part" or "Too young for this part." You know, you're here because I think you're right. I know it says 50 and you're 38, but you know the director said he wants to bring the age down or I feel we could bring the age down.'

  John Hubbard, Casting Director, UK

- Your reputation preceding you if it's a bad one: you're rude, always late, difficult…
  Behave better, period.
- Not preparing well enough for your meeting, not knowing the script or learning your lines properly.
  Read the script. Learn your lines.

'I can sort of understand it and forgive it but there can be a sort of maddening diffidence about "Yeah, well, you know I'll come in." I don't know, "Have you read the play?" "No" "Do you know anything about the part?" "No, no, I don't" and you think "Well put a bit of effort into it."'

Sir Richard Eyre CBE, Director, UK

- Not reading your audition email properly or researching the team.
  Spend twenty minutes on the Internet researching not shopping.

'You need to know exactly what you're gonna be doing. You need to know everything, you need to know where is the casting, who's in it, what have they done? I think anybody who [goes] to a meeting with a director and not really know what they've done; I think it's rude. I mean, I think it should be good behaviour to know that the director's done nothing, or it's Ron Howard and boy! – you know, I'd better check what he's done.'

John Hubbard, Casting Director, UK

- Not listening when being given notes by the director.
  Take a moment and focus on what is being said to you and what is being asked of you. If you need to, repeat it in your head before you start to read the scene again.

'The most common is not listening, some directors are not very forthcoming with notes, but a lot increasingly these days are what I call "Actors' directors" and they do try and help give the actor what they are wanting, how they visualise the part. And a lot of actors, I don't know if it's nerves or what but they do come in with a fixed idea and they sometimes (and I'm generalising madly), but they

sometimes can't move beyond it or along side it or what-have-you even if the director is really trying to convey what they want.'

Alison Chard, Casting Director, UK

- Being rude to, or taking your frustration out on any member of the creative team or their assistants.
  Remember the manners you showed your Grandparents. Also remember that you may have been from a list made by the assistant, not the casting director or director as is often the case.

'Sometimes you have to warn directors about something you've heard, I mean there's so many stories about actors you know: they get drunk; they take drugs; he didn't turn up... he was rude to the wardrobe people; he was completely loony because he wanted his hotel room moved three degrees to the east. I mean I've heard them all.'

John Hubbard, Casting Director, UK

- Coming across as so arrogant that no one warms to you, maybe assuming you're too good for a part because you'd rather be meeting for a larger role.
  There are reasons you will have made the list for one character and not another, you may be a more interesting choice for a role, which is not the lead. Trust the creative team's judgement and vision.
- Rolling up looking like you haven't been home the night before suggests you don't take it seriously.
  Make sure your presentation is appropriate. Take a moment to think about how your tone of voice and body language is perceived by those around you.
- Moving around too much in camera auditions, often the person reading with you is also doing the camera operating, so you end up out of shot and the audio is often compromised

when you turn your head too much as the mics on the cameras are not that powerful if not recording audio head on.
Keep relatively still and speak in the direction of the camera.

- In taped auditions having your pages in shot and/or rustling them.
Keep your pages on your lap and keep a finger on the next page to make turning them quieter and more seamless.

> 'The prime technical considerations: remembering to speak into the microphone and keeping your pages silent.'
>
> David Thorpe, Voice actor, UK

- Being put off by the number of people on the creative team watching you audition.
Don't be flummoxed by how many people are in the room with you, there can be an array of producers. If it's Musical Theatre there will be the resident director, musical supervisor, choreographer, casting director and the international team of creatives.
- Over acting because you're really nervous or too enthusiastic.
Calm down, take a moment and remember Michael Caine 'Less is more'.

> 'Over acting and often in auditions, because today lots of auditions are held with a video camera pointed at you, people give a performance to fill you know, a theatre. And a performance needs to fill literally the intimacy between you and the director or you and the casting director, whoever's working with you so there's a natural quality between the two of you rather than a performance quality and this is something that when the tapes played back and you've left the room, as an actor you see this terrible over acting.'
>
> Robert Bierman, Director, UK and USA

- When asked to prepare a monologue, choosing something completely wrong for you just because it's a lead role with a great monologue.
  Be realistic about both the part you're going up for and yourself and choose appropriately.
- Arguing with the creative team.
  Remember, sharing ideas and discussing is not arguing, never argue in your audition. If your view of the role differs from that of the team explain why. Be aware so that you do not appear inflexible or aggressive.

Try to enjoy your audition, hard though that sounds. Remember everyone there wants you to get the role and wants to meet you. They want to see your interpretation of the role, try to enjoy giving them that, the chat should be pleasant as most folk in the industry are actually very nice and funny.

SUMMARY

What you can take from this chapter is an understanding that how you present yourself before you read your scenes has a great impact on your chances of a successful meeting. Manners, a firm handshake and a warm smile are important and will be remembered. How the points you considered prior to the day of your audition, i.e. all the preparation and learning and research etc, all has to be revisited on the day. Knowing whom you are meeting and their work is vital. Being brave enough to explain your take on the role and why you want to work on this production, what you feel you can bring to it. These all go part of the way to a comfortable audition technique.

CHAPTER 7

READY FOR MY CLOSE UP

In this chapter we'll look more specifically at the points to consider when auditioning for screen work. Many of these techniques are beneficial when your audition is filmed for any kind of acting work. We'll be looking at:

Technical considerations:

- Where to look, stand and direct your focused attention to: eye contact, hitting the mark, keeping relatively still.
- Voice projection for camera work.

Techniques that work well in front of the camera:

- Knowing your script scene by scene, out of sequence acting, knowing your character's journey.
- The difference in acting for Television drama, Soap and Film.
- Everything shown on camera needs a reason.
- Don't overact or under focus.
- Cameras can smell fear and in-authenticity, you must be able to appear relaxed.
- Tips for close ups.

FORMING A RELATIONSHIP WITH THE CAMERA

As an actor, working in front of the camera, you have to develop a relationship with it. You need to trust it to pick up your performance. The camera is in effect your audience's eyes. The viewers see you, observe you, resonate emotionally and intellectually with you through the camera's eye. Don't lose sight of that (no puns intended).

In order to know how the camera sees you, you need to watch yourself recorded on camera. It seems an obvious statement, yet few actors who have worked primarily on stage and now want to focus on screen work have taken the time to watch themselves. It is a completely different medium from theatrical work. It is probably fair to say all aspects are different except for the fact that you are communicating the truth of the story. In order for the screen actors, whom you know and love, to appear so at ease when in front of the camera they need to consider many things and they may have completely different approaches to doing it.

> *'The relationship between the camera and the actor, it's a fascinating one. Some people have a particular relationship in that you turn on a camera and it's as if they're transparent you can see everything that they think and those people have to make sure that thought is strong but not add anything. Other people, their faces are more closed and they have to maybe work even harder at what they're thinking for it to come across on the screen.'*
> Mel Churcher, Acting and Dialect Coach, UK and USA

We'll look at the technical aspects first because whilst you must bring the performance techniques to the role in order to represent the truth on screen; if you are physically looking in the wrong direction, or are in fact not in view, then it's all a moot point.

WHERE TO LOOK?

Unless specifically asked to, never look directly into the lens. A direct look is an acknowledgement of the audience and this technique is used for presenting rather than acting on screen.

The Fourth wall is a theatrical term now used for both stage and screen productions. It means a wall of the room has been removed and the audience (as voyeurs) are looking in from there – like a theatre audience/sit-com studio audience like 'Mrs Brown's Boys' or 'Friends' for example. Mel Churcher explains the phenomena in terms of screen work:

> *'We, the audience, are observing you not interacting with you. What that means is you can never look straight into the lens, that is you can never "spike the lens." But you can look terribly close to the lens so that we can see into your soul and what I would say is, well [what] Scorcese calls the 'Psychic strength of the lens' is true: that if we can see into your eyes but with you not quite looking into the camera, we can see what you think.'*
>
> Mel Churcher, Acting and Dialect Coach, UK and USA

When acting, the direct look is for comedy asides or if the piece as a whole is taking down that fourth wall and letting the audience be a party to what is happening rather than solely observing as in 'Peep Show'. In 'House of Cards' the original British political drama with Ian Richardson and the current American re-imagining with Kevin Spacey, both shows use this device with the lead actor intentionally letting us into his life and his Machiavellian plotting. Occasionally it's a device to let the audience into the heart of the piece, but again this is rare. The TV adaptation of 'Persuasion' directed by Adrian Shergold, Sally Hawkins lets the audience into her heartbreak at particular moments; the rest of the cast do not see the camera nor the shared moment, she is only confiding in us.

When auditioning for screen work the casting director if they are reading with you, or reader if there is one, will generally be sat just to one side of the camera so you play to their eye line. This is deliberate, so that you end up looking as close to the lens as you can without it looking directly into it. Your performance and emotions manifest much more naturally on screen this way and we get more of your face not your profile.

Next time you watch TV or a film, take a look at the eyes of the actors. Then try it yourself:

- Have a friend tape you reading a scene where you look just to the side of the camera at the reader. Then do a take where you look directly into the lens. When you watch it back you'll see the difference and will feel as uncomfortable as your audience would when the scene is delivered directly into the lens.
- If you are in close proximity to the other actor, choose one of their eyes to focus on, if you flick between the two you look nervous on camera. It can be jarring for the audience or seem like you have a tic. Try it where you attempt to look at one eye, both eyes and where you flit between. Watch the clips back to see how where your field of vision is focused affects how we see your eyes and the emotion you're trying to convey.

EYE CONTACT AND LEARNING YOUR LINES

We've said already, countless times in fact, *learn your lines* in particular for auditions for screen work because we need eye contact in the room and your face high enough to see more than just your forehead or bald patch on playback of the tapes. As Peter Cregeen points out:

> 'One of the most important things from anybody who's gonna look at that tape is concerned is going to be that they can actually see the actor's eyes.'
>
> Peter Cregeen, Director and Producer, UK

The links to these auditions are sent to the members of the creative team who cannot be there and countless execs. They need to get as much from that taped read as if they were in the room with you. Those present also receive the links of course, as how you appeared in the room and how you playback on tape can feel very different.

The technique for sight-reading also works with prepared sides. Reading scenes is always nerve wracking; even lines which you have rehearsed can be difficult when sat in the actual audition. Having the sides in your hand is usually fine as long as they're out of shot. It's often better for an actor's nerves to have the scene on their lap and unused, rather than across the room in their bag if they suddenly draw a blank on their next line.

So, common techniques for delivering lines on the day if you are using your sides as a memory aid but not actually reading from them are:

- Hold the pages in the direction of the person you are reading with.
- Listen to the reader when they are reading and flick your eyes down to your lines and then back up to them so that you can see your cues and quickly remind yourself of your dialogue while listening.
- Hold the pages as high as you can but below the camera, this keeps your head up and importantly your eyes up. It's OK to ask the camera operator how high you can go before they are visible.

A tip from Robert Bierman:

> 'You don't have to tip your head up and down and again,

the camera can see your face. And sometimes you can actually make the look down at the dialogue as if you're actually thinking about what the person has just said to you, and you can actually use the reading as if it's like there's something else going on in your mind. So you can use this trick to make you look even more convincing, when actually what you're doing is just reading the scene, "Where do I come in, what's my next cue?" All that panic looks like you're in deep thought about the great characterisation that you've invented. So keep your head up, that's a great tip for casting.'

Robert Bierman, Director, UK and USA

WHERE TO STAND AND SIT

For auditions the casting office will have set up the audition room well before the creatives and actors arrive. The room will consist of:

- Enough chairs for the actor, director, producer, casting director and a reader if there is one.
- A table for the creatives' scripts, audition lists, CVs of actors attending, cups of tea and water, etc.
- Lights if required.
- Possibly a backdrop.
- The camera on a tripod.

So there is no need to be nervous of the contents of the room. Everything will be arranged to everyone's best view point; for the creatives and camera to get a good view of the actor and, for the actor to have a direct eye line to the casting director/reader for when the actual read is taped. The auditions may be held at the production company offices, those rooms are sometimes not ideal, so the team will do their best to make the actor as comfortable as possible. All because, as mentioned previously, casting directors are always on your side and aiming to facilitate everyone in as effective a way as possible.

Generally you'll be sat down to chat and read, some scenes require standing for delivery and you may need to do an ident:

An ident is something which is done for film and commercials, less so for television. A long shot will be taken of you as you say your name, height and agent's name to camera, you would then turn to the right and left for profile shots.

N.B. This use of the word 'ident' is not to be confused with other uses of the word which can mean the 10 second adverts that top and tail commercial breaks. These are used in sponsorship for a particular show for example Cadbury's long-standing relationship with 'Coronation Street.' Or the television channel's own idents for self-promotion, which they all make. You may well do an audition to act in those types of 'idents'.

HITTING THE MARK

Whilst for the majority of auditions you are sat in a chair, if you are following stage directions in the script which are quite physical then you may have to be on your feet. The reader will most likely be stood with you, or your fellow actor if it is a paired recall. You will sometimes rehearse once through without taping. If you then completely ignore that rehearsal when you are taped and half of your performance is off screen then you won't be giving it your best. The assistant behind the camera will be doing their best to keep you in shot the whole time but you have to work together, especially as sometimes they will be reading and taping you. Everyone in this process is working with you, in order to help, but if you don't put in some technical practice beforehand then you will be working against yourself.

Everything has to be a little closer on camera than it would be on stage or in real life – unless many of your acquaintances understand very little about personal space. Everyone stands and sits closer in order to appear in the shot together, otherwise some of the intimacy is lost.

'Hitting the Mark' is the technical term in filming when actors walk or run into shot, or turn round and stop in exactly the spot where they should be for the camera to see them, in focus. This is a skill which has to be technically mastered. Once acquired it looks effortless, however those actors know precisely where they will end up when they walk into a room, dance, fight or embrace. For close-ups: where they should turn, how far to turn or lean, where their eye-line should be and where their gaze should land. On set these actors do have markers to tell them where they need to end up but you never notice them looking at them because they have learnt to hit their mark.

> *'Film, like all great pieces of art is all about bits of sticky tape. This is it, without sticky tape we wouldn't be able to make movies... They're always out of shot, so your trick is to hit the mark without looking at it... back pace yourself, so if you're coming in a door and you're gonna walk up to someone, back pace from the mark to the door and see how many paces it is and make sure that you do those paces, so if it's 6 paces don't do 7, don't do 8. Don't feel like doing 8, don't think "My character felt like he wanted to walk a bit further, because that's how I felt when I did it" the camera's not interested in how you feel, it's only interested in if you're there.'*
>
> Robert Bierman, Director, UK and USA

If you need to be on your feet for a scene that requires some action or movement, prior practice and rehearsal will help you no end. This tends to become more relevant at recall stages than first reads. Scenes with for example a kiss, a shove, a slap, can make the actors involved and/or reader uncomfortable; you don't want to go too far but you're worried about not going for it… You need to be sure how much is being asked of you, the director or casting director will usually tell you.

- If it is particularly physical and the director/casting director has not explained how much action they want to see (perhaps they think they've already explained), don't just try to wing it – ask, both you and the other actor/reader need to know.
- If you're not sure where the edge of the camera's field of view is – ask the camera operator how much space you have to play with whilst still in shot, so you know the boundaries.

If you're not already au fait with camera work you need to practice. Have a director friend tape you and other actor in scenes with movement, with any of the examples above. I'd leave out doing a chase scene at home as you'll break something. Try the easy going 'We'll just film whatever happens' approach, then try choreographing the action, whatever that may be; including just walking into shot. Ask yourself:

- How many paces do you take?
- Should your left or right side be nearest the camera?
- Which actor should be closest to the camera?
- Where should you be looking?

Watch the takes back and work out where you were in relation to the camera so you get a sense of where you were in the shot. Do more to make sure.

Know in advance what you want the end result to look like and then try it a few times and you'll see that these are all technical factors which you need to think about. Another technical consideration is – on which foot are you actually standing? A lot of filming is in close up and as explained, it is easy to be out of shot. Experienced actors consider each of these points all the time.

> '*So you've hit your mark and you've got two feet and you can put your weight on your left foot or your right foot and, particularly in a big close up, it can make all the difference to being in shot or out of shot, in your light or out of your light… You have to remember all these things. But sometimes all the great emotions; you've just lost your father and the person you're talking to is gonna kill your sister and your life's in a mess – you know that's all very important, but have you got your weight on the right foot? That's far more important because you're gonna put in all that emotion but you're not in shot. So film acting is a horrible mixture of deep emotion, deep concentration, being very sexy, being charming and having your weight on the correct foot. This is why people get paid lots of money because they can do three or four things at once.*'
>
> Robert Bierman, Director, UK and USA

In an audition the camera is never in motion just for artistry (unlike on set) if it is moving it is to follow you to make sure we can see you. Be aware of it.

KEEP STILL

Having covered movement, we are now going to concentrate on your reading if you're sat in a chair, I'll repeat the heading – keep still.

Generally taped reads are shot from the shoulders up in a relatively tight shot, if you suddenly lean in, or to the side your head will no longer be on camera. If the camera is on a tripod the footage is more stable but trying to open up the shot and track your head whilst reading with you can be quite difficult, something will lose quality. Also, watch out for too much 'Hand acting', 'Sigh acting', hair flicking and other needless gestures.

It is infuriating viewing a taped read where an actor moves about un-necessarily. It looks unnatural and detracts from the performance, frequently half the dialogue is compromised. Stillness in front of the camera is great for audition purposes and a useful skill to acquire. Technically there is good reason for this – camera mics are not that strong so if you turn away from the camera your speech is muffled.

If you've ever seen 'Singing In The Rain' remember when they make their first 'Talking picture' and the audio goes all wrong... We the audience, hear the actress's costume rustle but her dialogue goes from very loud to extremely quiet as she needlessly swings her head dramatically from side to side.

It is the thoughts and emotions playing across your face we want to see. You'd be surprised how many actors want to do their scene at an angle for dramatic purposes... the drama is lost if we can only see your ear and the back of your head. You are not on set with other cameras shooting different angles and you're not wearing a mic. Leave those choices for the director on set.

Actors often ask if they can read a scene standing, we sometimes oblige. But ask yourself *why* you want to read it on your feet in the audition? Again it's often to make a dramatic turn at a crucial point. Why? Trust your characterization and delivery, if you don't need to read it standing and are not asked to, then you're better off sat down. Especially if you need your lines, as you can have them on your lap. Remember the casting director/assistant will most likely be filming and reading, hand held camera work whilst reading is pretty hard.

- Try rehearsing your lines sat down at home, so you feel more comfortable with delivering them that way in the audition because sometimes it's all down to the actor having rehearsed their lines stood wandering around their kitchen.

VOICE PROJECTION

Casting offices use camcorders to tape readings, we tend not to use directional mics or booms just for audition purposes. You need to project your voice appropriately. You will be in a room with a small number of people and that camera.

Technically there are a few points you can bear in mind to help:

- Direct your dialogue towards the reader and camera.
  Project your voice, remember that you are not on stage and there is no need to fill an auditorium, but we need to hear you and that requires projection even when intimate.
- The creatives in the room will hear you but the camera does not process like a human ear which blocks out other sounds and concentrates on you. The camera and mics simply records what is there.
- Try to avoid the 'TV whisper' – which frequently takes over the moment there's a camera in the room. Think about where your voice needs to reach and project accordingly.

  'In film you are only talking to the person that you need to be talking to in the scene, with the amount of voice that you would need to use in the scene. That doesn't mean that you have to be on a breathy whisper and in fact I would urge you to be on a similar supported voice but at a low volume, the volume you need for the task in hand. If it all goes whispery then you're gonna have trouble finding any emotional resonance in that sound. So vocally

the difference may not be as much as you think but you only need the voice to travel to where you are sending the thought to.'

      Mel Churcher, Acting and Dialect Coach, UK and USA

SELF-TAPES

If you are unable to attend a particular first round audition, casting directors will for the main part accept a self-tape. A self-tape is you being filmed reading for the role, filmed somewhere other than the audition session, then emailing a link of the scenes to your agent/the casting office.

Some things to consider:

- Don't look into the lens.
- Ideally have someone else film it for you so your camera/camera phone is not balanced precariously on a desk; never film yourself with your phone in your hand at arms length.
- *Always* have someone reading the other character(s) dialogue though they should not be in shot. *Never* just read your own lines and pretend to listen to someone else, it looks terrible on camera and suggests a lack of understanding of the industry standards required.
- Film in landscape rather than portrait, it gives you a widescreen shot which looks much more professional and savvy.
- Don't shoot in a messy room or a noisy environment, as this is very distracting for the viewer.
- Make sure that you've lit it well enough that we can see you.
- Make sure that we can hear you and the other unseen reader throughout the scene.
- Always shoot more than one take of each scene.

- Always choose the best takes to send. Don't just send all of them.
- Title it, this is relatively easy if you are using iMovie on a Mac or Windows Movie Maker on a PC. It should give your name, agent if you have one or your contact details if you're un-represented, the production title and character you're reading for.
- Whichever site you choose to upload it to, e.g. You Tube or Vimeo, remember to set the video as private and downloadable, choose a password so it can be viewed only by those with the password. This is for reasons of confidentiality, which all productions need.
- Email the link *with the password* to your agent to forward to the casting team, or send direct to the casting office if you are unrepresented.

So, those are the technical considerations you need to be aware of for auditioning for screen work. Whilst I have been very specific about paying great attention to all these factors, it should not come at the expense of your performance and emotional responses in the room. Paying such close attention is important when you are not used to cameras; the more experienced you become, the more this all becomes second nature.

Now we'll look at the techniques for your performance, confidence and conduct.

OUT OF SEQUENCE ACTING, KNOWING YOUR SCRIPT SCENE BY SCENE

Film and TV work is shot out of sequence, the order of shooting is dependent on: availability of location and actors, number of performers required in the scenes, number of background artists and for external scenes it is often reliant on the weather.

As you will be going in and out of the linear course of the story and your character's journey within it, you need to find a way to keep track of your character's circumstance (emotional, physical and practical) throughout.

Mel Churcher has a great technique for this:

- Make index cards for each scene. Detailing what's just happened, what is about to and what will occur next, also any important key character wants for the scenes.
- String the cards together in order so you can find them easily.

Whilst this is conducive to working on TV or film, you can use the basic principles for auditions if say you were sent two episodes to read and a number of scenes to prepare. It is particularly beneficial if various plot points happen in between. Scenes are not always read in linear order, because a different order may be better for audition purposes in terms of what they show of your character.

For the audition you have to understand the script and get a good handle on your character relatively quickly. Having read the full script if you've had it, knowing it well and *preparation* (there's that word again) is key. So when you've been given or you've chosen scenes to prepare, don't just learn the lines. Break those scenes down in terms of your character's plot points, wants and needs and get to the heart of what the scene is conveying.

Think about your scenes:

- What is happening to your character?
- Who is in this scene with your character?
- What does your character want?
- What does your character need?

- Where has your character come from – physically and emotionally?
- Where is your character going – physically and emotionally?

'It's about knowing where you are in the script, that story, that script is so inside you that if you are asked as an actor "right, we're gonna do scene 37," which is pretty early on, you know it's ten minutes into the story, you know where you are, you know your arc... And that often is about looking at the scene and saying "Why are we doing this scene? What is it doing? What story is it telling? What's the point of the scene?" And if you can analyse what the scene is and what you as a character are doing in that scene, then you will know where you are in the script. So going through the script, knowing which each scene is, what it does to your character, where it builds your character.'

Robert Bierman, Director, UK and USA

You will, on occasion, be asked on the day of your audition to do different scenes than those you were sent to prepare. Sometimes it can't be helped. This is where knowing the story, your character arc and having ability to sight read will help no end. You have to be flexible about this and not let it affect your belief in yourself, or let your nerves get the better of you. Remember if you're dyslexic always let the casting team know and they will give you time to take the scenes away and come back.

THE DIFFERENCE IN ACTING FOR TELEVISION DRAMA, SOAP AND FILM.

As camera equipment for film and TV is getting more and more similar nowadays, one of the main differences between film and TV (except budget) is time; Time in rehearsal, time on set, time in pre and post production. In the UK creatives often work on both film and high profile television dramas.

When it comes to rehearsal and filming this is something you have to consider when auditioning and tailor your audition technique accordingly. For TV productions the director and producers need to feel you have understood the story and character, their vision, that you have come to the role with a great interpretation and can take notes quickly.

Sometimes it's all a bit quick on set even for directors; this applies in the audition room too.

> *'It's getting even quicker, I've done stuff and it's gone "OK, that's one take, that's great, let's move on." I'm like "What? Can I have another?" "No, no, we've already moved the camera." That's absolutely true... Most shows if you're on camera at 8.00, you'll have that first scene in the can by 9.30 that's probably a page and a half – two pages! If you haven't the producer's probably looking at his watch saying "What's going on here?"'*
>
> Peter Cregeen, Director and Producer, UK

In terms of performance, TV acting is more immediate than film. Film is rehearsed for longer and has more time on set for different angles, shots and takes. You can afford to give less away on film and have the time to convey those thoughts and feelings.

> *'You will go in longer chunks [in TV], that there'll be slightly less waiting around or quite a lot less waiting around if you're on a small budget thing because the lens doesn't have to be changed so much or hardly at all... But you will have very little time to prepare and very little time for anybody to allow you to have second or third or fourth or fifth chances so you'll go for kind of instant things. And I think what that can do to an actor is they can start*

getting a lot of tension in and then they can start showing the audience so you'll have these classic looks on Soap opera where people stare into the camera and you see all sorts of things cross their faces, because they're telling you that they're jealous or whatever. Whereas in film they just think and I think in film that's all you need to do is think, but think hard'

Mel Churcher, Acting and Dialect Coach, UK and USA

Television dramas and soaps have different styles again. Soaps by their nature are heightened in that there are multiple story lines running through each episode which are dangerous or heart wrenching.

'Within half an hour you may have 25 or 30 dramatic things so when you watch 'EastEnders' within half an hour so many things have happened to these people in their lives, as a viewer you're kind of exhausted emotionally which is what they want to do. So the actors are having to deliver high emotions all the time which is incredibly un-natural, you know all films are condensed time, but in soaps they are really condensed. And also usually the stakes are quite small, you know they're not saving the world, they're dealing with a problem with the babysitter, but it's sensational, it's exciting so the acting level has to come up to that.'

Robert Bierman, Director, UK and USA

The pace of emotions the actors have to go through is quicker than a drama, which has more time to build on the plot points and characterisation.

Although film covers many genres, they are an escape from the audience's reality. Dependent on the production; emotion and thought can be played at a slower pace than TV would require. Frenetic shoot 'em up action films are a different ball game of course, because that's all fast and exciting with perilously high stakes. However with slice of life and character driven films, thrillers, even Sci-Fi and intrigue based action films like the 'Bond' or heist films; there are opportunities for moments within scenes without huge drama. Instances where the actors are reflecting on what has happened, or are considering their next move for example. In these situations, on set and in the audition room, that stillness I mentioned, allowing yourself the time to let the emotion and thought pass through you, your eyes, your face, your body, is more appropriate.

Great actors are mesmeric. They are able to do ordinary actions such as drinking coffee and yet you are unable to take your eyes off them. This is not about being attracted to them per se, but how captivating they are, they reveal aspects of their character even in incidental things. 'Montalbano' the Italian cop show, was a huge hit in the UK, Luca Zingaretti the actor in the title role spends a good portion of each episode eating and drinking wine at lunch, but as an audience we are still fascinated.

> *'The really good film actors have the ability to appear to slow their feelings and thoughts down so what you're looking at is a thought going across an actor's face, you know let's say in close up that in some ways you follow it like a cloud going across the sun.'*
>
> Sir Richard Eyre, CBE Director, UK

Another distinct difference between screen formats is of course the size of the screen; it is evident that a cinema screen is immense and a home TV a comparatively small square in your lounge but the very real implication is often missed. It should have a bearing on how you tailor your performance in your audition. You are magnified on cinema screens and this provides another reason for keeping your performance a little smaller than for TV.

> 'Film is seen in the dark and it's blown up, if you see somewhere like Leicester Square, about 50 times real size, so you have an enormous close up where you'll see everything happen in your face. I know things are changing, television can be on projectors and film can be seen on a television, but in basic terms film is likely to be seen in a larger format than television and television is seen in the day light or in your electric lights, whereas film is seen in the dark. So I think we're a lot more forgiving about television… we are much more detached I think in a cinema, we get involved in the story but we are observing much more, we're the voyeur perhaps in the cinema, you're much more aware of anything that strikes you as untruthful. So it's a bit like a microscope for film.'
>
> Mel Churcher, Acting and Dialect Coach, UK and USA

EVERYTHING ON CAMERA NEEDS A REASON.

Cameras pick up whatever happens in front of them so everything you do on screen must have a reason. It can be jarring to an audience and pause their suspension of disbelief otherwise. This is something that everyone who works on a production brings to it; the reason a costume has particular details, why a set has a picture on the wall, why a character bites their nails:

> 'There's a danger in that we think [film] is just like life and it isn't. It's distilled. It's still really not natural to work as we do as film actors; in little bits, in other words that aren't our own and with that big circus around us. I think it's very important for an actor to understand those differences from life: that acting is about very dramatic moments in life, that everything that you do on that screen is going to be really seen. So, if you touch your lapel it's got to be for

> *some reason, either emotional or practical… an audience are going to want to know why, so you have to have a good reason to be doing that, nothing can be wasted on screen.'*
>
> Mel Churcher, Acting and Dialect Coach, UK and USA

Screen acting is more intimate than stage acting which has to be heightened and projected to reach the back of the auditorium. Your performance is only with the actors on set within its confines. The camera takes it all in and then transmits it (through the magic of technology, editing and broadcasting) to the audience – on the sofa, in their lounge or the big screen at the cinema.

> *'When you're working in front of a camera, you're usually only convincing one other person or a few people in front of you. Trying to disengage with the space beyond those people is the number one trick of acting on camera – Never engage further than the person you're acting with.'*
>
> Robert Bierman, Director, UK and USA

RECALLS AND CHEMISTRY READS

If you have been brought back for recalls or chemistry reads(11) in pairs or groups remember the creative team obviously think you *could* play the part. Further investigation and work is needed to see not only your interpretation of your character, along with the other actor(s) you're grouped with, but also the other pairings and how well they work together. Don't let your nerves get the better or you or become complacent, keep your focus.

Always be open and giving to the other actor(s). I'm sure you know why, but some seem to forget:

- Etiquette – because it's good form to be giving, paying it

forward, treating others as you'd like to be treated, etc; it creates a better working environment for us all.
- Also on a self-serving level – if you do get the job and work with these same actors then you'll already be on a good footing with each other. They'll know you're not a selfish actor, you'll know that you gel well together and you can go about doing the good work which is your goal and will increase your chances of further employment. Everyone loves a team player.

When you watch TV and film you'll notice that the camera is not always focusing on the actor who is speaking, sometimes the reaction shot is more important or more interesting. Directors, producers and coaches all tend to give the following advice when it comes to delivering a performance for camera, so bear this in mind at your recalls:

- *Always* be seen to be listening, thinking and reacting in your scenes.
- Don't pause between your cues or lose focus.
- Don't add unnecessary mannerisms in an attempt to add to characterisation, as they tend to distract much more on camera than on stage. Trust your initial instincts on the role.

> *'It's terribly important that an actor, if the camera is on them, is always offering that character and moving their character forward in some way or another because that's why we actually cut to them – because they're actually telling a story – Offer, offer. Don't ever feel there are dead moments because you know you're gonna be on somebody else at that moment, and frankly you want to be on the screen as much as possible don't you? And never forget that the most important shot you're ever going to take is the close-up. So even though that may be the tenth shot*

you take on a scene, it's actually from your point of view as an actor, the most important.'

Peter Cregeen, Director and Producer, UK

DON'T OVERACT OR UNDER FOCUS

Coming straight from a long stint in the theatre to screen work or having limited screen experience can sometimes lead to actors overacting. Not because they are bad or hammy actors, but because they are still performing for a larger audience than the confines of a studio/audition room. It is something many directors comment on and it can happen to very good, experienced actors. They will usually realise mid read and ask to start again – which is fine. If this happens to you, do the same.

'Big number one mistake on camera which is overacting and often in auditions, because today lots of auditions are held with a video camera pointed at you, people give a performance to fill, you know, a theatre. And a performance needs to fill literally the intimacy between you and the director or you and the casting director.'

Robert Bierman, Director, UK and USA

Remain aware of the medium you're auditioning for and keep your scale of performance appropriate. Screen performance is generally much smaller than that for theatrical work, depending on the circumstance, character and genre. For example if you are asked for a larger than life performance, comic book characterisation, certain nationalities are often portrayed this way: Italian and Greek chefs are usually written as verging on hysteria.

Screen auditions require as much focus as theatrical ones, it's the level of performance which must be measured. So whilst being sure to not over play the role, keep focused and maintain your projection, without surpassing the needs of the situation.

CAMERAS CAN SMELL FEAR AND IN-AUTHENTICITY

We mentioned in chapter 6, that directors can smell fear, well cameras can too, so you need to be aware of yourself and your anxieties:

- Work to appear relaxed and confident.

> 'The camera has this kind of ability to smell people's presence and it smells when you're not confident, it smells when you're nervous. It smells when you're giving all the wrong vibes, it smells when you're not sexy, all those things, it knows. So if you go on set feeling those things unfortunately the camera always picks up all the bad stuff, it never goes 'Well actually you're a really nice person and you smell great.'
>
> Robert Bierman, Director, UK and USA

- Keep as true to the text as you can and bring a performance with truth and heart.

> 'The actor who comes in and tries just to act, the camera picks up very very quickly that it is not an absolutely truthful performance. The thing you are looking for more than anything is what's happening behind the eyes and the truthfulness. I would say all television acting actually starts just behind your eyes and everything else comes as a direct result from that afterwards.'
>
> Peter Cregeen, Director and Producer, UK

APPEARING RELAXED ON CAMERA

Screen performances need to appear natural, relaxed and effortless. The circumstance of your character's situation may not be, but the audience stop believing if they see you the actor as uncomfortable.

Relaxation in front of the camera requires concentration, be it on set with an entire crew or in the audition room with perhaps a team of 4 or 5 creatives. Peter Cregeen gives examples of adept actors with fluid performances:

> *'The best television acting is an amazing mix of concentration and relaxation and if you can find a way of really getting relaxed in front of the camera that's when it really starts to work you know. You look at the best American actors, you look at Al Pacino, you look at Dustin Hoffman, Robert De Niro, that's only the fellers. You look at people like Julia Roberts on screen, I mean they're just so relaxed on the screen, that's very difficult to achieve but if you can achieve it, that really is what makes you really watchable.'*
>
> Peter Cregeen, Director and Producer, UK

There is one easy thing that anyone can do to help themselves relax, it's common advice from directors and actors alike: focus on your breathing. Are you taking in shallow breaths because you're pent up with nerves? If so you need to relax your shoulders and go for a longer, deeper intake of breath and hold it for a moment. This will help slow your heart rate down and your breathing should become more regular. This may seem nigh on impossible when your nerves are stretched taut in an audition room, but it will help. Remember some of that apparent relaxation of successful screen actors is because they are aware of all the technical considerations we went through earlier in the chapter and are at ease with them all. They are second nature, those actors are not anxious about whether the camera can see them they *know* it can, so they can afford to relax and just 'be' in front of it.

RECAP ON TIPS FOR CLOSE UPS

There are various technical tips for close ups which are useful on set and in auditions.

- Getting a good eye-line: When you deliver your lines to the actor/casting person with whom you are reading in the audition, look them in the eye. For an extreme close up, look at whichever of their eyes is closest to the camera. This gives the audience a better view into your eyes and the emotion therein.

  > *'The things that Michael Caine says are to some extent true, that it does make a difference if you're in very tight close up and you're looking at your fellow actor who's very close to the lens. And you decide to look at the eye nearest the camera or the eye away, it will focus you more if you chose the eye that's nearer the camera, because the further you go from camera the gaze will appear to be much further away because distances are very different.'*
  >
  > Mel Churcher, Acting and Dialect Coach, UK and USA

- Stay in shot: Don't move your head around too much, or lean in whenever you speak:

  > *'The most important thing is that I can actually see what's happening behind the eyes, that really is the most important thing. It can be quite useful to ask the operator*

how close the close up is, don't move your head around too much. Don't let your eyes go more than, certainly more than 45 degrees in any direction and that's up and down as well, because it looks really strange if you seem to be looking at something that's outside the camera in a long way.'

Peter Cregeen, Director and Producer, UK

- Believe in the role: Feel the truth of what you are conveying because when the camera is looking at you that closely there's no room for a lack of concentration:

'You have to believe that you are thinking and that that camera can see that thought, so you're not sharing with the camera but you're allowing it to scrutinise you.'

Mel Churcher, Acting and Dialect Coach, UK and USA

- Etiquette: If a close up is being taken from over the shoulder angles for both of you, give as much in your delivery on their close-up as you do on your own.

Hopefully you are feeling less intimidated by the camera and more aware of the necessary practicalities. Here are some useful camera terms it is helpful to know if the director and producer are talking technically about what they want to do next in the audition. It will allow you to judge how much you can move around and what the camera will see:

- Mid Shot (from the waist)
- Two Shot (two actors in shot)
- Long Shot (full length)
- ECU (extreme close up – usually just your eyes or mouth)
- Over shoulder (over the shoulder of the foreground actor, facing the other actor)

Don't fear the camera, trust it to capture what you do (as long as you do what you do where the camera can see it). You usually get the chance to read your scenes more than once for screen auditions, some casting sessions however may have a director or producer who is particularly rushed for time or just impatient. So whilst there's generally a second chance to get it perfect, on rare occasions there may not be. If they want to move onto another scene and you genuinely weren't happy with your first read, it is OK to ask if you can read it again, the worst they can say is no. No one will hold it against you for wanting to show yourself at your best, as long as you don't continually ask every time you audition for more and more chances.

SUMMARY

You should take from this chapter a better grasp of technical considerations and practicalities of camera work. We've looked at forming a relationship with the camera, learning to trust it and to see it and to know where it is. We considered how to project your voice so you don't whisper, tips for out of sequence acting and why every action and gesture on camera needs a reason. We went on to the levels to pitch performance so it is not over acted or under energised on camera, but confident and relaxed. We finished with a few tips for close ups for good measure.

CHAPTER 8

TREADING THE BOARDS

In this chapter we will firstly look at the nature of theatre productions, how everyone is part of the production. We will cover the technical side and techniques important for stage work. We'll look at:

Technical aspects:

- Proximity and cheating angles.
- Vocal Projection.
- Auditioning on a stage/in an audition room.

Theatrical considerations:

- Differences for Musical Theatre and plays.
- Being familiar with the script whilst auditioning with script in hand.
- Bringing something new to a role seen many times.
- Working with Shakespearean text.
- Complete emotional journey every night and keeping the performances fresh.
- Stage fright.
- Remaining relaxed on stage.

As with chapter 7 we will look at the technical considerations first.

FOURTH WALL THEATRE

Most theatre takes the form of fourth wall theatre, this allows for suspension of disbelief.

> *'In theatre you are always with an audience so you're always to some extent sharing even if you're in a fourth wall production, there's going to be some part of you that needs to be heard by the people at the back.'*
> Mel Churcher, Acting and Dialect Coach, UK and USA

Not all theatre follows this style; Musical Theatre and verbatim theatre often acknowledges the audience, stage shows where audience participation is essential, as well as improvisational productions such as 'Improbable Theatre' produce.

PROXIMITY AND CHEATING ANGLES ON STAGE

The piece you are enacting on stage has to, of course, be played out to the auditorium, whatever the size of venue. You have to be aware of your performance space in relation to your fellow actors and the intimacy of your audience's view.

Obviously theatre and screen work differ in terms of staging. On camera you are placed closer to the actor in your scene so that you both appear in shot. For theatre your performance has to fill a stage and you have to cheat the blocking and the angles in order to play out to the audience, if you were stood too close that would be apparent so different tricks are employed, Mel Churcher elaborates:

> *'One thing that happens when you're in theatre is that you always have to stand a little further away from your fellow actor. In camera work you always have to stand*

much closer than feels natural... Something that Robert Donat said... is that in theatre the director starts very close to the actors and gradually moves away till they're at the back of the stalls. Whereas on film you tend to start with the master shot, where you're covering the whole thing in a wide shot and then you gradually go in to a two shots and so on until you end up on the close up so the director moves closer and closer and closer.'

Mel Churcher, Acting and Dialect Coach, UK and USA

For audition purposes this means if you're reading a scene with a fellow actor or reader and you will be sat with your chairs at a slight angle so the creatives can see more of your face. You have to cheat the way you are reading. You'll have learned blocking when you were training and when rehearsing a production, but it is a device which often gets forgotten by nervous actors when auditioning. If you deliver everything to your fellow actor – the director, casting director and producer end up missing a lot of your performance, they only get the side of it if you don't cheat your angle.

- Practice. Run some scenes with a couple of actor friends as though auditioning. Put your chairs opposite so you face each other, then at a 45 degree angle to each other (facing out) and at 90 degree so you are just facing the audience not each other at all. These are extremes of course, but the point is if you all take turns watching you can see the difference and how much is lost. Ideally run the scenes with a director friend. You'll find that somewhere a little before 45 degrees to the audience gives you the optimum for acting with your co-actor/reader and giving the performance out to the audience and not just each other.

Actors are sometimes unsure of where to look, where to focus their attention when auditioning for theatre. Here are some simple tips:

- Look towards the creative team. Not above their heads, miles behind them, or at their feet. Give your performance to them as your audience.

If you focus away from the team you lose their attention – and you want to capture it. You have to be instantly responsive to your audience on the stage in a way that you can't be on film. This attentiveness to the nuances in the room, to where the attention is focused and being able to work with it creates a dynamic energy for stage performers:

> *'In the theatre… you want a sort of mercurial quickness, a visibly mercurial sort of quickness of wit and response and that's what's very engaging in the theatre. So there are actors who are astonishing in the theatre, have a terrific presence and energy who just seem much, much too busy on film and vice versa.'*
> Sir Richard Eyre CBE, Director, UK

VOCAL PROJECTION

Vocal projection for stage work and its implications when auditioning, must be considered.

> *'Vocally when you're in a theatre you're sharing across a great distance.'*
> Mel Churcher, Acting and Dialect Coach, UK and USA

Projection and a supported voice are integral to theatrical work. Your voice has to carry across the auditorium, up to the Gods if you're in a huge West End theatre, to the back of the room if it's above a pub. Either way, your voice needs to be supported.

There are breathing exercises you may recall from training, but do you ever practice them? Allocate some time to vocal practice, it will help you project your voice and spare your vocal chords the discomfort and possible damage you can cause by shouting on stage instead of projecting. Every theatregoer will have heard the difference even if they do not know the terminology. Someone whose voice is straining to be heard is causing damage, someone who is projecting can turn away from the audience and still be heard.

Create a quiet space where you can concentrate on some breathing exercises, alone at home.

- Sit on a chair and centre yourself. Put a hand on your stomach and one on your back, so you can feel the regularity of your breathing.
- Inhale deeply through your nose and see how far your hands move from their starting position. Exhale through your mouth.
- Breath in and say 'A' on the exhale, repeat through to 'Z'.
- Imagine you are trying to be heard by someone stood a little further away on each letter.

If you feel light headed at any point stop, you may need to put your head between your legs – another reason you may want to do this at home and not say on the tube.

An exercise you can do to build strength is:

- Recite a few lines of dialogue.
- Jog or jump on the spot for 20 seconds or so then recite the same lines again.
- Repeat a few times and of course, stop if you need to.

One which is helpful for Musical Theatre performers:

- Stand and hum an easy note in your range.
- While concentrating on your breathing, chest and diaphragm, slide into a lower note – you should be aware of the vibration of the humming.
- Try again with a much lower note and feel the difference.
- Repeat with a much higher note, with the higher notes you will feel the vibration in your head as well as your chest.
- Take a deeper breath and repeat this time with your mouth open. You should feel the vibrations now in your mouth too.
- Repeat the lower note and the higher note and concentrate on the difference in how they feel physically.
- Finish by humming the lower note.

When you are auditioning for stage work, be it straight plays or musical theatre, warm up before you go in. We can often hear singers doing vocal warms ups in the loos, this is fine as long as you can't be heard from the audition room itself, check with the casting assistant first for the most appropriate place to warm up.

AUDITIONING ON STAGE OR IN AN AUDITION ROOM

Auditioning for theatrical work on stage or in an audition room is evidently different. Take the time to acquaint yourself with your surroundings and what they will require of you.

Auditioning on the stage:

- Make sure you look to see how far back the creatives are sat in the stalls. You need to be aware so you know how far to project and perform to today. You must be heard easily.
- Remember you need to connect emotionally with the team

you are auditioning for, so your delivery should be directed towards them whilst being aware of the size and acoustics of the venue you are in.
- Are there specific spotlights on a particular area or is the whole of the stage illuminated? Make sure you're stood in the light and your face can be seen. You can always ask.
- Are you auditioning in a scene with another actor reading on stage? If so, try to cheat the angles where possible so you face the creatives more. The reader will know you are doing this and they are there to help *you*.
- Don't wander around needlessly but use the space, take your opportunity to be mobile.

Auditioning in an audition room setting:

- Will you sit or be on your feet for the scenes? Again make sure you are always cheating your angles slightly for the creative team.
- Be aware that the confines of the space of that room will not require the level of vocal projection which acting on a stage will need so you can be more intimate.

Whichever space you audition in, give yourself a moment to connect with it when you walk in, so you can relax.

DIFFERENCES FOR MUSICAL THEATRE AND PLAYS

When auditioning for straight plays the process is quicker than when auditioning for musical theatre. Musicals have rounds upon rounds of auditions and recalls. Each time you come back there will be more or different creatives until the finals, when it seems like everyone and their dog has come in to sit behind the desk.

If you are coming in for a straight play generally you would be asked to prepare from the text of the play, occasionally you will be asked to come in with one or two monologues. If so, it's normally a classical and a modern piece they will want to see.

When choosing monologues in that situation make sure you choose appropriately:

- Don't choose a role which is not within your age range just because it's a lead and great role. Mrs Bracknell from 'The Importance of Being Earnest' is a great role for a more mature woman, not a 20 year old. King Lear is a great role, again not for a new graduate.
- If it's a comedy you are auditioning for or two comedic plays running concurrently then choose a monologue which shows off your comedy bones rather than the tragedy you have already perfected and have up your sleeve. And vice versa if you are auditioning for a drama or tragedy, don't go in with slapstick.
- If they don't send you the full play (as is sometimes the case with well known plays), then be pro-active: find, borrow or buy it and read it *in full* before your audition. Chances are you can find it on the Internet.

'Miscalculating the part in relation to the audition. Oh yes and doing too long a piece thinking "if it lasts for 5 minutes it's good," it isn't! It drives you mad, because generally speaking you know quite soon, whether this is an actor that you're interested in or not and for it to go on and on and on and on is very against the grain.'

Braham Murray OBE, Artistic Director, UK

With musical theatre, auditions usually take the following route for actor-singers:

- 1st round audition; Bring a couple of songs to show off your range in the style of the show. These early auditions are usually with the musical director, casting director or their associate/assistant and the pianist.
  Always bring the sheet music. Only ever sing a cappella if asked to, generally speaking they want to hear your voice accompanied by piano. Research the show.
- 2nd round; Your agent will be sent music and possibly scenes for you to prepare. You will sing the material and possibly your own choice of song again. You are coming back for the same team, possibly with the resident director.
  Prepare all the material they have given you. Bring your own choices of song back just in case. Dress with acknowledgement of the kind of show it is.
- 3rd round; Your agent will be sent scenes if they have not had them already. This round is if the resident director or MD want to do more work with you on the show material, the same creatives will be there. You may be asked to come back for further recalls.
  Dress for the show, bring all material you've had, still bring your own songs.
- Various (semi) finals; You will be asked to attend a singing final, acting final and dance or movement final (depending on the role(s) you are up for and how much dance is required). There are often character workshops prior to the acting finals which you will be advised to attend.
  Always bring all material given and your own songs. Dress for the part. If required to attend a dance/movement call bring dancewear/clothes you can move in and appropriate footware.
- Finals; The whole team will be present, director, resident director, choreographer, dance captain, casting director's team and the producers.
  As with the semi finals, bring everything and dress for the show.

For dancer-singers the auditioning process will often follow this path:

- 1st round; A dance call. This may be invited or open. Sometimes on the day of an open call, a selection of dancers known to the creatives previously will be invited to attend. The resident choreographer and dance captain will be there, the casting director and/or associate/assistant and sometimes the resident director and musical director. They will teach you routines from the show, at various stages people will be let go if they cannot perform the choreography.
  Bring dancewear, any dance shoes required which you will have been advised of by your agent or if it's an 'open', bring whatever was specified in the advert. Bring a couple of songs with sheet music just in case as often the dancers who are liked by the creatives are asked to stay back to sing. Make sure the songs are in the style of the show and really show off what you can do vocally.
- 2nd round; You will be dancing more complicated routines from the show. You will likely be asked to sing, you may have been given songs from the show to prepare.
  Always bring all your dancewear and shoes, any material previously given and your own choice of songs just in case.
- 3rd round; This is quite likely to be just singing and acting with the resident director, musical director and casting director. If they like you, you will be asked to come back to the finals.
  Bring all the material, your dancewear and your own songs again. Dress for the show.
- Finals; As with the actor-singer route, all the creative team will be present.
  Bring your dancewear and shoes, all the material you were given, your own songs and dress for the part.

Auditioning for MT can be exhausting physically and mentally. You will be recalled umpteen times and the odds are often against you.

> *'It's easier auditioning for musicals because it's – 'Can you sing, can you dance?' That's a measurable talent… Whereas with acting it is subjective. I mean of course it's not in the sense that it's a very highly developed talent but you know, there are people whose acting is very highly thought of… it's not to my taste and vice versa.'*
> Sir Richard Eyre CBE, Director, UK

Sir Richard doesn't mean the auditions are easier for the performer, because of course they are not, just that the key skills are quantifiable.

A relatively recent addition to musical theatre auditions is that some productions will tape recalls, so whilst it's never ideal, if you are unable to attend the finals, they will at least have your footage to show the exec producers and creative team again.

If they are taping your recall:

- Don't look into the lens unless asked to.
- Do perform your scenes and/or songs/dance routine to the team unless asked to deliver to camera.
- Think carefully about what they are taping, is it a dance routine, a song or scenes?
- Take into consideration where the camera is, i.e. is it on a tripod at the back of the audition space? Is it hand held by an assistant?
  If they are taping scenes and it's on a tripod at the back of the room, then you need to project your voice enough to reach it, if it's hand held the assistant will no doubt be much closer to you following you so you can be more intimate.

If they are taping your song or dance then sing/dance as normal, they will advise you if they need you to alter your performance.

'CAST CHANGE' COMPLEXITIES

Long running shows be they West End or touring will have a yearly audition process in time for the cast change. This is when the 12 month contracts of the existing cast members may or may not be extended for another year. The creative team have many considerations during this time and there are various reasons why you may not get the role though you are talented enough and did really well at the finals. All the roles and cover (understudy) tracks have to be auditioned for whether they will be available or not.

Which tracks (positions) in the cast will be available depends on: 1) which current cast members have said they want to leave the show and 2) which have indicated they would like to stay, but the creatives (for whatever reason) would rather let go should they find a better option during the auditions.

- Vocal range and dance ability may mean that of the roles you've auditioned for, if your vocal range cannot cover that of the departing cast, then the show would not have the vocal sound it requires. Dance wise, if you're a mover not a dancer but the tracks available are dancer/singer not actor/singer the choreography will be too hard for you.
- You may not quite fit the line up for the ensemble. If you are way too tall or short in comparison with the others on stage you will stick out.
- Sometimes performers are just not ready yet and need to come back a year or so later when they have had more experience which has broadened their performance skills. Everyone in

the cast must be physically, vocally, mentally and emotionally able to cope with what is usually an 8 show week.

Persevere, if you really want to be in the show and the feedback your agent has had for you from the casting office is positive then they will want to see you the following year. We have all seen some of the same actors come back 3 years running, getting down to the last 2 each time and then on year 4 they've got it.

BEING FAMILIAR WITH THE SCRIPT WHILST IT'S IN YOUR HAND

Whereas with auditions for screen work we say it is always best to have learnt your lines, for stage work unless told to be 'off book' you can just be familiar with them. It is general practice to audition with script in hand but for recalls you should be off book.

Being 'familiar' whilst holding the script doesn't mean 'wing it on the day'. You need to feel secure you understand the scenes, you don't want to be reading the whole piece with your eyes glued to the words. You need to be able to move around and play nuances. As John Hubbard explains:

> *'If you've thoroughly prepared yourself and you've looked at the stage directions. I mean good actors read everything, bad actors just read the dialogue, there's just so much information.'*
>
> John Hubbard, Casting Director, UK

I've said it before, if you have been given the entire play, *read it all* so you understand your character and their journey in the wider context of the story and all the sub plots. If you have only been given scenes, then make as much analysis of the character as you can. Even in small excerpts of script the way in which the dialogue is written will give you clues as to the character you are playing:

> 'Very simple textual analysis, I might say: does the character talk a lot or does the character ask questions or does the character respond to questions? I might ask myself about the fixed givens: which are facts which are not open to interpretation.'
>
> Sam Rumbelow, Method Acting Coach, UK and USA

We covered in detail the reasons for knowing the script scene by scene and your character's journey in chapter 7. We'll now look at why it's important for theatre as well. Of course you perform the story in its linear form, but as the actor you still need to know in advance what is happening and why, before the story unfolds. You have to acknowledge and build in the subtext if a great secret is to be revealed in act two or act three. Perhaps there is a build up of tensions, political or personal, which the dialogue alone may not give away. 'Pass the salt please' can have myriad meanings and knowing the script will present you with the appropriate choices in terms of how you may choose to play it.

You need to come in for your meeting ready with your ideas of how you will play the character and scenes. That requires forethought. Make your choices, be brave about them and really go for it as you would do if you were auditioning for screen. There should be no less preparation just because you are not off book. You're still aiming to communicate the essence of the play.

Think about your scenes and ask yourself the same questions as in chapter 7.

> 'In theatre we use: who am I; where am I; what's my relationship; what do I want and how do I get it? And because you're rehearsing for 6 weeks you can go all the way down to the end. You know somebody like Max

> *Stafford-Clark when he's rehearsing in theatre will make people write those down so: "I humiliate", "I plead", it's great you're doing it as a joint exercise.'*
>
> Mel Churcher, Acting and Dialect Coach, UK and USA

There are many directors who like to improvise around the scenes and characters when auditioning. Although it is rare that you would be asked to do this without prior warning, it can happen on the day. Knowing your script and character is essential for this and winging it can be very apparent.

Some directors prefer actors to come to the read-through on the first day of rehearsal not yet quite off book. So there is less danger of an interpretation that may not be in line with the director's vision yet the actor finds hard to let go. Directors are for the main part very open to actors' ideas and input, Braham Murray OBE's thoughts are:

> *'I do like actors to know a great deal about the part and have all kinds of ideas. Therein there is a danger because if they then turn up and they listen to your speech on the first day and it's diametrically opposed to what they've been thinking that can be a problem. But hopefully that problem is not long lasting... I don't think the actors are simply empty vessels that are going to be filled with the director's genius. I much prefer actors who are coming with something and who have gone into stuff and are bringing stuff to the table right from the word go.'*
>
> Braham Murray OBE, Artistic Director, UK

BRINGING SOMETHING NEW TO A ROLE SEEN MANY TIMES

With stage work you may be auditioning for a role in a play that has been produced countless times. This happens in many long running West End shows at cast change. You must bring something new.

- Think very clearly about your choices, if it is a well-known play, how can you carve out this role as your own?
- What can you bring to it others have not?
- Along with the director's vision and staging, what can you (and only you) discover in the role of Hamlet, Othello, Cecily Cardew, Lady Macbeth…
- What truth are you finding and enacting?

> 'As a director I love it when actors come in and they really want to play and they say "Give it to me" and you hand it over gratefully. You think "I don't have to worry about that anymore because I've got this guy and he's gonna be good."'
>
> Phil Davis, Actor and Director, UK

Come in impassioned with inspired, brave ideas, talk intelligently about them, even if they don't fit with their vision, you will have made a connection with the production team. If they don't choose you for this production the team will remember you for future projects. People enjoy working with others whom they feel a creative kinship with, where there is the possibility of trust in each other's abilities and ideas, Braham Murray OBE's take is:

> 'I think theatre's an extraordinary thing, if society could work like theatre we'd all be alright. It's people of different talents coming together in common cause and merging their talents, their different talents in order to create something. And obviously what you want them to do is to have a group of actors who you sense will trust you and that you will trust them and who are there for the

right reasons. And then try to bring about (in what always seems to be too short a rehearsal period) a springboard from which they can finally jump and be themselves in the best possible way.'

Braham Murray OBE, Artistic Director, UK

WORKING WITH SHAKESPEAREAN TEXT

Whether you are working on a stage play which is modern or classical, the aim is undoubtedly to bring the truth of the piece to the audience. With Shakespearean text actors often get nervous or stuck in a creative rut because of the language. People become intimidated, focus too much on the iambic pentameter and forget the meaning. Not that many directors nowadays would ask their cast to stick so closely to the IP. Many respected actors find putting too much emphasis on it a distraction:

> *'There are directors who will put a metronome there and all that rubbish – and it is rubbish, I think.'*
>
> Sir Derek Jacobi CBE, Actor, UK

- When you're learning your lines for audition or performance, try reading them aloud once paying particular attention to the iambic pentameter and then just as dialogue. See which feels more naturalistic and has more resonance.
- Are you losing the meaning when you're concentrating too hard on the rhythm?
- Did you find when you concentrated on the meaning that it had it's own rhythm anyway?

> *'Shakespeare for me it's just to make it – the text – sound a) the way that you express yourself quite naturally, this is the way you express your thoughts and your feelings,*

[b)] to make it accessible to the public, a healthy disrespect for punctuation; not the dah-di-dah-di-dah up at the end of the line, dah-di-dah-di-dah up at the end of the line, sending us all to sleep; to make it sound contemporary. The marvellous thing about Shakespeare is that it has a pattern, a bloom, a veneer of poetry about it, even the prose. Because it is so well written that it is in-destructible, so you can alter the punctuation to make things mean other things.'

Sir Derek Jacobi CBE, Actor, UK

The text within Shakespearean plays requires studied preparation. If you've not read the play previously or studied it when you were at school or training, then you need to read it in full and give yourself time to digest it. The language is difficult. We do not speak in rhyming couplets in present day Britain – apart from budding teenage lyricists at the back of the bus and Far Side greetings cards.

'Shakespeare, yes it's written in the English language, but it's a very very dense verse and a lot of the language and syntax is archaic. So what you want is an actor who has mastered the meaning of what they're saying, so that they're not groping for meaning while they're rehearsing. They understand the words; they understand how each word is working. And it's a tremendous waste of time if you're spending weeks of rehearsal simply translating for actors who should have done the work at home. And particularly as Shakespeare, there are some actors who can speak it fluently and some actors who take a lot of time and you see productions, Shakespeare productions that open and the actors are sort of lurching from line to line.'

Sir Richard Eyre CBE, Director, UK

The classical plays of Shakespeare and his contemporaries are often staged in a different time and place or with a different agenda nowadays. I saw a production of A Comedy of Errors at the Globe a few years back which was played like a Carry On film… and quite hilarious it was too. The staging of a play can change the context and consequently an actor needs to be very familiar with the text in order to almost transcend it and express its varieties of meaning to an audience. I've seen many fantastic productions of Othello over the last decade, my top 3 in date order not preference: a traditionally staged one at the Globe in 2007, Frantic Assembly's frenetically paced violent council estate set one in 2008 and a modern Britain/desert warzone one at the National Theatre in 2013. Each individual Othello, Iago and Desdemona was played very differently, every Emelia, Roderigo, and Cassio brought new truths to their roles. Each production broke my heart.

So when you are preparing for an audition for a classical play:

- Study the text; give yourself longer than you would a contemporary piece because understanding the actual language needs adequate time and attention.
- Whilst you can most likely read at the audition with script in hand, you must be very familiar with the text because you can't adlib Shakespeare and you don't want to get flustered if you momentarily lose your place.
- Find a way to make every line sound not like you are reading poetic verse, but like your character's dialogue. These are the thoughts they are voicing for the first time, just the same as anything that you might say on a typical day. Acting should never look rehearsed and that goes for classical and modern plays, even Greek tragedies.

> '[I find] a lot of actors, when they come to Shakespeare they stop inflecting. They stop using intonation. They recite, they don't know they're doing it... Whereas they would quite naturally in a contemporary play as we are doing talking now, they would inflect, they would intone, they would use their voices, the range of their voices. When they come to Shakespeare all that seems to disappear and they become quite rigid in their delivery... they don't say it as if they just thought of it. They don't say it with what it suddenly means to them to come out with this – in other words they don't inhabit it as they would naturally inhabit a contemporary text... For me the hardest thing is to make it sound as if you've just thought of it and they're the words you're going to choose to express that thought.'
>
> Sir Derek Jacobi CBE, Actor, UK

Enjoy the beauty of the writing without letting it stop your performance, have a spontaneous natural feel to it. Don't lose the truth or story. Richard Briers had a deep love of Shakespeare:

> 'A Shakespeare role will take you into the sky because the way he writes is as we all know monumental but also terribly exciting. The actual rhythms and sound of the speech it's like playing Beethoven on the piano or something... Doing Shakespeare is like pumping iron and you actually develop your personality rather than your biceps. You develop it through the vocal stress you put in your voice. How you develop your voice, the range of your voice, the range of personality, your personality can be developed, it can become bigger, it can be more. And these giants of the theatre were the ones who did so much really hard graft in the classics for very little money.'
>
> Richard Briers CBE, Actor, UK

CREATING A HEIGHTENED PERFORMANCE IN AN AUDITION

After you've read in an audition, the director, producer or sometimes the casting director, will give you notes. Take them on board, give yourself a moment to interpret what they mean so you can read again with what they asked for. Every take in an audition should feel different. They are looking at how you take the directorial notes and shade your performance. The team may want to see a different part of that character brought to the surface for a moment, or may find the performance to hold more truth or impact if played in a slightly different way.

> *'There's an essence of truth going on and for that truth to live, the instrument of the actor has to be very relaxed, flowing, technically astute, able to access many parts of themselves at the same time.'*
>
> Sam Rumbelow, Method Acting Coach, UK and USA

If at any point when being given notes you are not entirely sure what the director means or wants, ask. You can always repeat back to them in your own words just to clarify, so you're on the same page and making the alterations they have asked for.

Not only must you be able to alter your performance in an audition but also, of course once you inhabit a character every night on stage. Reacting to your fellow cast members' personalised performances adds to your own interpretation, as does feeding off the audiences' responses. All the time following your character's journey. Audience members often see a theatrical production more than once; variation enhances their experience. A stage production is not a finished piece, unlike a film, it is an organic evolving experience which not just the actors, but the audience are part of.

You're are always aiming to bring the truth in your performance, but stage acting is slightly larger in comparison to the intimacy of screen acting – in other words it is heightened.

> 'To work on the stage, what you're having to do is to fill an auditorium and the gestures, everything that you do has to transmit to as far back as you can see, which is sometimes dealing with 1500 people, that's an enormous amount of people to convince.'
>
> Robert Bierman, Director, UK and USA

You need to be able to evidence this in an audition, so that the production team can see that potential in you even in the confines of a small room.

> 'Acting on stage, you're always asked to give more than that, even if you're playing a one speech part in a play there are much greater demands put upon you than if you are doing that on television.'
>
> Peter Egan, Actor and Director UK

Looking at keeping a performance fresh for a long theatre stint or indeed for the 4th recall for play or a musical can sometimes be difficult. Kate Maravan gives the Meisner perspective on re-discovering the truth each time and it provides helpful advice for the auditioning actor:

> 'You have your imaginary set of circumstances, which is the context within which you're working. But under those imaginary set of circumstances, it feels like you're experiencing something new, exciting. And I think for actors who work a lot in the theatre and you know and have to do months and months and months and feel very jaded and they can't find the freshness; it certainly helps re-discover each night the moment. So even if you know

> *you have to hit a certain point or you have to express a certain feeling or for the story you have to arrive at a certain place; you can still arrive at those places with a truth found now, not what I found yesterday and three weeks ago and in rehearsal room and when I sat with my script in my bedroom...'*
>
> Kate Maravan, Actor and Meisner Acting Coach, UK

How much to heighten your performance for auditions depends on the material as much as what the team are looking for. Whether you are in a room or on stage should inform your levels. You can however always be in a heightened state even if your voice does not need to carry that far and the creatives are sat very close to you. These considerations are all personal to you as an actor; you need to think about your intentions and intensity of performance. You can give an intimate read without being as small as you would be for a screen audition. Again, you can practise with a director friend and another actor reading with you and taking turns to see how the differences in levels actually affects you when you are the audience. There's no need to have a booming voice in a small room or to emote wildly across a stage.

ALTERNATIVE AND PHYSICAL THEATRE

If you audition for physical theatre or alternative theatre, perhaps a production in which audience participation and/or improvisation are required, there are further considerations.

You may be asked to take part in group workshops, play games, and improvise sketches within your audition. How these are worked, whether you audition on your own first with material or to demonstrate a key skill, or if you are whittled down from a group is reliant on each production.

The skills you will need to present depend on the requirements of the show. They will likely include some if not all of the following:

- Improvisation, dance, acrobatics, Butoh (a Japanese movement form), comedic timing, dealing with hecklers, musical ability, singing, rhyming.
- For some physical theatre companies the first round will be an open dance call/audition so they will need to see dance or movement skills and then go on to work with any text or improvise around the particular story or issue the show will be about.

Make sure you feel confident in your skills and are relaxed before you go in for these auditions, because with work as challenging and inspiring as this can be, you should to be able to enjoy the process as well as performing in the show.

Do be aware that some forms of physical theatre very much border on dance/movement, so you need to be physically fit and limber and have core muscle strength. On-going Pilates or Yoga can help with this; as physical performer and lecturer Natalie Persaud mentioned:

> 'Those pursuing physical theatre need to keep themselves in shape – fitness and flexibility – running, yoga, Pilates, cardio etc. I would say that it wouldn't matter if you were bigger as long as you had the stamina and flexibility.'
>
> Natalie Persaud, Performer and Lecturer, UK

If the auditions are for a new piece which will be devised then you may be asked to bring a monologue and be given ideas to play with on the day. You need to be as open as possible, don't be intimidated by the freedom to create – embrace it.

DIRECTORS' RELATIONSHIP WITH ACTORS

The Guardian critic Michael Billington was one of a select few critics who were asked to direct a play and he said the experience opened his eyes to a different perspective. It made him appreciate the relationship between cast members and directors.

> *'The thing it taught me was something fairly obvious, which is that no outside judge ever knows who contributed what. Because obviously in the rehearsal room, if it's a good rehearsal, everyone is contributing, the actors are contributing as much as the director if not more sometimes.'*
>
> Michael Billington, Guardian Critic, UK

Every director is different and has their own vision for the production they are directing, the staging of a production can change everything. It is therefore vital that at audition stage you know the story, context and your character's journey and when you get to rehearsal that you know the lines inside out:

> *'Different directors work in different ways so you have to go with that, I mean the text is the bible… I just think the number of times you've said a line the chances are when you say it on the first night you'll say it better if you've said it a hundred times as opposed to ten.'*
>
> Tim Pigott-Smith, Actor and Director, UK

Directors each have their own ideal for their working relationships with actors, how open they are in auditions or rehearsals differs for each individual. Whether it's: 12 months in the West End, 6 month tour, 3 weeks at a fringe venue; understanding the director's vision is paramount to a good working relationship with him/her. The audition process is an opportunity for you to work out if you want to work with them not just for them to work out if they want to work with you.

STAGE FRIGHT

Stage fright affects many actors, newcomers and old hands, this sometimes occurs at auditions as well as on opening nights. It's personal in how it affects each individual and how they get over it.

> 'It's essential that actors are vulnerable, essential, because if you're vulnerable you receive. Now if we're talking about fear in the sense of it being overwhelming terror, then of course that's very, very frightening indeed. A little bit of fear, or the right mount of fear is… like the nerves for an athlete, it focuses you, you have to focus.'
> Ann Mitchell, Actor and Director, UK

You need a certain amount of fear in performance so that the nervous energy and adrenalin can be channelled into creating stage magic:

> 'I think adrenalin is useful and maybe some adrenalin comes from fear…You can't avoid it, it's there, you're dealing with tensions, it's just how you do it. It's like my convincing myself that I can get through the audition because they'd want me, I convince myself that I'm not afraid you know [laughs].'
> Tim Pigott-Smith, Actor and Director, UK

Some of our greats have combated that anxiety when it tries to take hold and have some great advice and tips to share.

If feeling anxious Tim takes a moment, centres himself looking at items in the wings, then thinks about the scene:

'If you get really frightened you tend not to focus on things, you think inwards and you don't see what's in front of you. So I... look for things in the dressing room, things in the corridor as I walk down, things in the wings, and then on stage before I go on... if you're thinking out, if you think about the other actor and about the scene, it's much more constructive than thinking what's wrong with you, I don't find that helpful at all.'

Tim Pigott-Smith, Actor and Director, UK

Richard Briers took time to settle into his roles and would feel better after a week or so in front of the audiences:

'I think the trouble with fear; stage fright is that it really does try to destroy your natural talent and it's a shame. Because you know you go on and either you're terrified you might forget something, you're terrified about making a fool of yourself. I've done both those things and you know; it is the fear. Whereas after a week or ten days you're in control of yourself you can probably bring the best out of it and serve the writer better.'

Richard Briers CBE, Actor, UK

Ann Mitchell sought advice from fellow actors, for her relaxation and then concentration were the key factors in keeping fear at bay:

'I realised that this was stage fright, that it could be named. I then set about asking other people and people gave me various tips to do like, I find steaming before I do a show very very relaxing, for me I have to be there a good two hours before curtain up, that's just my ritual. I took things like Rescue Remedy and things like that and I just concentrated and I just did not allow that voice to come in.'

Ann Mitchell, Actor and Director, UK

For the audience to believe in you the actor, be it on stage or in your audition, you have to put your all in. Fear can make you hesitant about immersing yourself in your role. Phil Davis suggests just throwing yourself into it:

> *'Holding your nose and plunging in, don't be afraid to make a fool of yourself... fear is your enemy, that's the thing that's gonna hold you back and another reason why I always think of the character as him and not me, in order to banish fear, you know. We've all got this little imp on our shoulders going "You can't do it, you're not very good" whether you're a writer or a director, or actor, whatever, painter. Whatever you're doing, there's always someone saying "You can't do it, you're not very good" you've got to get rid of that bastard on your shoulder and then you can actually try things out. Fear is the worst thing, it's your enemy.'*
>
> Phil Davis, Actor and Director, UK

Relaxation and then concentration are the two fundamental principals you will need to focus on. Find the way that works for you personally, e.g. 10 minutes quiet contemplation, looking at your props, classical music, a steam bath, a jog round the park or a massage. Follow it up by concentrating on your role, journey and the play text.

REMAINING RELAXED ON STAGE

We looked at state management in chapter 5 and at techniques for appearing confident and relaxed in chapter 6. For stage work or theatrical auditions when you are auditioning on the stage itself, relaxation is essential. Auditioning on a stage can be so much more daunting than auditioning in a more intimate room, even when confronted by the casting team and a camera.

> *'The voice teacher in New York practiced also Alexander relaxation technique and that was part of my lesson with him. He would kind of roll me out like a piece of pastry on the floor and so I was absolutely flat and then he would start working on the voice. And of course the Alexander technique was created in order to make performers relax... I think when you are relaxed you can fly, you can do things and things will occur to you to do. They need only be tiny little things which are immensely satisfying to you as an actor – and only from that state of knowing exactly what you're doing so you can relax a bit – can you. I suppose, inspiration they say it's 90% perspiration and it certainly is but it's that 10% which is pure inspiration can only come when you are relaxed.'*
>
> Sir Derek Jacobi CBE, Actor, UK

Whether you employ the Alexander technique, think about state management or use meditation is down to personal choice. What is important is that you centre yourself and ease the tension in your head, neck, shoulders, upper body and down your spine so that you release any pressures which could affect your concentration and attention. Finding a way to relax will aide you in each aspect of your performance. Remember you're not alone in finding the experience of auditioning on a stage frightening, the important thing is to get through it – as after all you are here because you want to be on the stage.

THE 'CHAT'

Now whilst the chat is equally as important with screen work as it is for stage work, something which you should always bear in mind, is the contractual obligations of the particular stage show you are auditioning for. As I've said, if you don't want to do the job, don't meet for it. Why is this particularly important for theatrical work?

- Are you auditioning for a tour or an ensemble role you'd rather not do? But you thought there's not much else out there at the moment and hey, you can probably get a betterment clause…

Be it a 12 month or 3 month contract, West End or a UK tour, you need to be committed to giving that amount of your life to this production, this role, this company of actors and this creative team. Period.

- You need to have really thought about this beforehand, especially for tours. What are your personal circumstances, are you in a family situation where leaving home for 3 months or a year is just not practical or emotionally possible? Are you and your partner trying for a baby, is one of your parents very ill and one or both of you take on a lot of their day to day care? Is someone close to you getting married and having a rather extravagant wedding, hen/stag do in another country of which you are a key member of the bridal party, if so can your absence be covered in the show?

Tim Pigott-Smith explains why he as a director has chosen not to cast actors in tours before, though they were talented enough:

> 'They didn't have the right make up to cope with a 12 week tour that they would have become depressed half way round. And that would have dragged other people down and it would have become a burden for other people to cope with you don't want that.'
>
> Tim Pigott-Smith, Actor and Director, UK

You must be honest about any other obligations you have. You never know, the dates concerned may not impact the production, or you may need to slightly rearrange things at your end rather than not doing them at all. Do not accept it and try to get days off, there may not be any cover for your part.

You need to be sure you want to be a part of this production, because in the chat, you have your opportunity to tell the creative team how much you love touring/ensemble/West End/TIE or a stint in an English speaking theatre abroad.

SUMMARY

What you can take away from this chapter is a further understanding of the requirements for theatrical auditions. We've looked at fourth wall theatre, proximity and cheating angles on stage and in auditions. We've covered some exercises to help with vocal projection. We looked at the difference between plays and musical theatre auditions, working with Shakespearean text. We then investigated how to break down your scenes so you're familiar with them even if you're not off book and to be able to deal with the possibility of improvisation in the auditions and how you have to bring something new to an iconic role and play. We finished by focusing on directors' and actors' working relationships, finding a way to relax on stage and the considerations for alternative and physical theatre and the all important chat.

CHAPTER 9

GIVING A PERFORMANCE

In this chapter we will cover the various ways in which you can help yourself to bring a better performance to your auditions. How you approach a role before and on the day of your meeting, we'll look at:

- Finding the truth of the role.
- Breaking down the script.
- Set up, build and pay off.
- Situation vs Character.
- Similarities or differences between you and the character.
- Remaining flexible and open about your decisions on the character.
- If you get stuck creatively with the role or scenes.
- Listening and observing.
- Working Outside in.
- Your voice and physicality.
- Comedy – being worse than you are.
- Relaxation.

APPROACHING A ROLE

How you approach a character and deliver your performance is naturally an individual process. Whichever methodology you trained under will have taught you a system for tackling a role and we'll borrow helpful points from each where appropriate. First and foremost, you must start with the script.

> *'The text is the bible, that's all, just work, work, work on the text, read it, read it, read it.'*
> Tim Pigott-Smith, Actor and Director, UK

> *'The first thing is: what I've got to say and the context in which the dramatist has put what I've got to say in; i.e. the situation. I think that's also whether my gut feeling is positive about the character that I'm playing.'*
> Sir Derek Jacobi CBE, Actor, UK

Whether it is the use of language in setting up scene and character, snappy dialogue or a story full of twists and turns; it is the writing that has to grab your attention: as the reader, as the actor, as any of the creative team and eventually as the audience.

> *'If you're a genuine actor you will, you will be inspired by the words and rhythms on the page… The adrenal glands simply start together with the ego and [laughs] you end up hopefully being honest to the writing.'*
> Richard Briers CBE, Actor, UK

FINDING THE TRUTH OF THE ROLE

The truth is in the script, it's all there, your character's life. Some of it is in the dialogue, some in the subtext and some in the stage directions. Upon reading the script you should be able to get a feel for the whole thing and then set about really exploring it.

Richard Briers CBE quoted Harold Finch who directed him when he was a young actor.

'Always be true to the text and be true to yourself.'
Richard Briers CBE, Actor, UK

The full script will give you the truth of the character. Think about:

What can you glean about their personality?

- Are they a good, bad or flawed individual?
- How many layers do you find and what contradictions make them who they are?
- Are they intelligent or not that bright?
- Are they funny, caring, or mean spirited, do they laugh or cry easily, or are they reserved?
- Does their dialogue represent who they are without artifice or do they choose what they say carefully, are they manipulating the situation toward some end?

What research can you do outside of the script?

- Is the character a real person either living or deceased? If so research them, you're not aiming to be a mimic, but you're trying to get to their essence. Spend some time on the Internet; find out as many facts about them, their life, their career, their personal and family life.
- Is it a historical figure best known for their terrible deeds i.e. a war criminal, serial killer, fraudulent politician or a breaker of hearts? Or conversely were they known for their heroism or altruism: a human rights activist, small town lawyer taking on the big guys, good cop in a bent department... Find out some specific details, they will give truth and depth to your performance.
- Are they a fictitious character but representative of an individual in a very particular situation: a victim or survivor

of domestic abuse or indeed the perpetrator; a solider recently returned from a war zone, suffering PTSD (post-traumatic stress disorder); someone fighting a debilitating illness (physical or mental). Again research can be your friend here to look at general behaviour patterns in these specifics groups.

- Does their job define who they are or is it just what they do from 9.00 – 5.00? If they are say: a nurse in an intensive care unit, a newly qualified teacher teaching teenagers in a rough school, a junior doctor doing 80 hour weeks, a sex industry worker, a religious leader, a research scientist dealing with a lack of funding whilst trying to find a cure for cancer, an investigative journalist… These can define a person much more than working in a particular field where you leave your work at your place of employment and do not take it home with you.
- What time is the piece set in, is it current or period drama, or even futuristic? Is it real or a skewed version of reality or Sci-Fi? Knowing that life expectancy for example was much shorter back in the day has a bearing on how age was viewed. Gender roles and rights have changed tremendously. Commonplace institutional racism was just not considered to be an issue until recent years. Sexual orientation could lead to imprisonment in the west the way it still does in some countries today.

These things all have a huge impact on personality and therefore characterisation.

> 'I will always try to find out what the reality is behind the character, the reality of their lives, whether that's historically, emotionally, physically. I find that when you go to the reality of their world (if this is making sense) you can find something quite specific, that will inform what

you do. I'm very interested in the psyche of the characters and I'm very interested in finding the contradictions in a character that I play.'

Ann Mitchell, Actor and Director, UK

'It would be based in truth really, trying to find the truth within the character that I am investigating and then hopefully going to play.'

Peter Egan, Actor and Director, UK

Whilst Meisner, Method and Stanislavsky techniques all approach creating a performance in differing ways, they all look at finding the truth. Meisner uses reaction and impulses, Stanislavsky through understanding objectives, beats and subtext and Method works via internalized characterization.

'The fundamental principal is that acting is living truthfully under an imaginary set of circumstances. Meisner was particularly interested in getting into the truth of the moment and he said acting isn't lying it's telling the deepest truth.'

Kate Maravan, Actor and Meisner Acting Coach, UK

With Method there is often a misconception about just how in character you as an actor have to be, how much you *live* the role. It is still the truth which is being sought. There are renowned actors famed for how earnestly they research and immerse themselves into a role. Diligent analysis is always good, it will enhance a performance and make characterization rounder, fuller, more layered, but you will never actually 'be' that character. Sam Rumbelow explains:

'The biggest misconception is that you have to live the role… one of his [Marlon Brando] early roles where he

> *played a veteran in a hospital suffering from stress from the war, went to a special medical unit and was there for two weeks. Now some people think that he's going there to develop his character. Well he is going there to develop his character, but he is using his intellect, he's looking around the environment, he's saying: what kind of environment it is; how do these people respond; what are their backgrounds? He's absorbing information, but that won't allow him to play the role any more, it assists him to understand the role better.'*
>
> Sam Rumbelow, Method Acting Coach, UK and USA

BREAKING DOWN THE SCRIPT, CHARACTER AND PLOT POINTS

We looked at making decisions on character and notes on your script in chapters 5 and 7. This aids you no end because knowing what has happened to your character prior to your audition scenes adds depth to your portrayal. This goes for both stage and screen work, for auditioning and rehearsing.

For the scenes you will be auditioning with, then rehearsing and playing, you need to know your character's emotional state of being. To inform you of that state, know the answers to the questions you should ask yourself when reading the script, the 'where, why, what, when and how's.

> *'Ask what is the character's essential need or want. So it's not a scenic one in the sense of "I want to get a hundred quid off him" or "I want to leave my wife" or whatever. It's what lies slightly beneath and the idea of this is that you then attach to it what's called an "As if" in a way that you can personally identify with. Not that you've necessarily had the literal experience, but that in some way you*

> can go "Oh yes, that reminds me of when I..." or "Umm that relationship" or "The time when..." or whatever, so you've got the material in you in your guts. Obviously you can't play an essential need and essential want, it's just to inform you, all of this information is to inform when you next approach the scene. The context within which your impulses are going to flow, so that clearly it's not just you the actor's impulses, it's the impulses filtered through the imaginary set of circumstances.'
>
> Kate Maravan, Actor and Meisner Acting Coach, UK

In screen work you may be in a situation with many different camera setups for the same scenes so you may not get to play the entire scenes from any one angle. Any of those takes may end up being used in the final edit so you have to know all the answers to those questions at any point.

> 'Even when you shoot a scene quite often you're not necessarily ever gonna get a chance to play that whole scene through from beginning to end because it could be broke down into a lot of different shots... Scenes will be cut out altogether, so as a director if it's a 50 minute episode of a series, I always want to shoot at least 55 minutes of material so that I can edit the show and not just join it all up. This makes it quite difficult for the actor because they don't necessarily know what's gonna end up on the screen, never mind within the course of a scene which shots are gonna be used that they know were taken of them and what the emphasis is going to be on their performance.'
>
> Peter Cregeen, Director and Producer, UK

In auditions the scenes will at be read through as a whole and it's not likely you'll have to deal with many different camera setups. You may be asked to do another take of just part of the scene.

The casting director and their team also edit around line fluffs or if the beginning of one take was great but the end lost its magic, we will always show you the actor at your best.

SET UP, BUILD UP AND PAY OFF

Most stories follow a three-act pattern. They have a beginning, a middle and an end. They also have set up, build up and pay offs. By this we mean: the setting up of the scenes, the story, the characters in their situations; the build up of the themes, relationships or tensions which are being explored and finally the pay off; where the resolution is found, the culmination of everything coming together, or a big reveal. This can happen within particular scenes as well as the script as a whole. If you've been given 2 or 3 scenes to prepare, the chances are there will be some dramatic content.

There will usually be an early scene to show your characterisation before a dramatic event occurs. A scene where there is something brewing for the characters involved, possibly an argument, a declaration of emotion. And you will likely have a scene with the climax of the event or where all is resolved.

John Wright, stage director and author explains his theory on these component parts to scripts/scenes:

> *'The anticipation of something; the release of something and the pay off of something. Now all action can be broken down into all these different things. For example, if you're about to sneeze: you're about to sneeze – that's the anticipation, something's about to happen; then you sneeze – that's the release, you've actually sneezed. When that's finished you feel different, so the change of feeling becomes the pay off. Now you don't always have to have those things, you might in the course of a scene*

> *not want to go to the pay off, you might want to leave us suspended. The important thing is to know where you are in the action and I find this really useful even the most simple bit of action if you don't find a pay off it can be very unsatisfying, if you get stuck in the anticipation and don't get to the release.'*
>
> John Wright, Physical Comedy Director and Author

So when reading the script and looking at scenes to prepare you need to consider the dramatic content and when you are going to choose to give the pay offs. Stage shows will often do this before the interval, a lot of TV drama will keep you waiting for the next episode for the pay off, those cliffhanger endings we all love to hate. They work. We come back as an audience so this gives you the actor an opportunity to really enjoy the anticipation and the release you give to us as much as to yourself.

SITUATION VS CHARACTER

> *'I think character is sometimes a dangerous word, I think because character is very often moulded by situation rather than who you are, but what situation you find yourself in. Like either of us in a given set of circumstances could probably kill somebody, in a given set of circumstances, but we're not killers, we don't have that instinct. So it's situation that moulds and Hamlet's a prime example of that.'*
>
> Sir Derek Jacobi CBE, Actor, UK

Break down the script, scene by scene and in terms of your character as a whole:

- What facts about your character's situation have you been

given, e.g. their job if they have one, their home life, are they involved or single, are they financially secure?
- What are you told about their past, if anything, where are they from, did they have a traumatic or happy childhood, what have they been doing for the past 10 years say, has their career or their family always been the most important thing in their life?
- What are their likes and dislikes, their political ideology, etc? What are their relationships with the other characters?
- What is the main factor creating the dialogue/action of the scenes you are looking at? Is it character driven or situation driven? How much thought have you put in to how you're going to play the scenes in terms of the situation, it's something to consider.
- What is your character reacting to?

> 'The emotions in a sense are a by-product of what you're experiencing by responding to someone's behaviour opposite you... Meisner would say that instincts are more honest than words... To produce honest emotional responses to what was happening in front of them not pre-determined, already decided upon. "This is what my character would do/this is the kind of thing I think they might do because they're generally a sort of angry person." It was about an honest instinctive impulsive response in the moment.'
>
> Kate Maravan, Actor and Meisner Acting Coach, UK

Playing against the text for levels can make for a more interesting read, tipping the script on it's head so to speak. A calm anger rather than shouting, an intelligent calculating baddie rather than a thug. A reserved declaration of emotion can be more interesting and have more poignancy than a read that is too 'on the nose'.

> 'As an actor (and this is what Method is really about) you develop the ability to become heightened and experiential and in that heightened experiential given state become creative with it. If I'm playing Othello, I should be able to actually create genuine truthful desires to kill, whether it's a gnat, my Mummy, my Daddy, my puppy, wherever the motivation comes from; and then I have to be able to look at an actress.'
>
> Sam Rumbelow, Method Acting Coach, UK and USA

If the scene has crying are you going to sob or hold back? If you are going to have tears running down your cheeks, from where are they originating? And I don't mean your eyes, obviously. Are you going to use an emotional memory to bring this about or will it just be your connection with the script and your empathy for the character?

> 'Christopher Walken talks about when he was working on a scene in "The Deer Hunter" and he has to put a gun to his head and he said (there's this amazing look of sadness and look of loss) he's working on when he was a kid and he had to go to summer camp. He's never shot anyone, he's never been in the Vietnam war, he's accessing something of the same value to him, different from his fixed givens.'
>
> Sam Rumbelow, Method Acting Coach, UK and USA

Scenes chosen for audition purposes will as a rule, have an emotional content, we need to see that you the actors coming in have connected with the script and can deliver that emotive quality. You may have to make us laugh, think, or move us. I'm not the only one who's been near tears when taping an actor's tender read before. How you play the level of that emotion whichever it is, is important and individual, Mel Churcher talks about a way to get though heavy emotionally laden scenes:

'Generally speaking emotion happens of it's own volition and we continue to pursue the need we want and we drive through that emotion and it kind of gets in our way. And what we find moving I think as an audience, is somebody that pursues what they want and the tears are happening, but they are trying to get rid of them to carry on to what they want... If you're telling some terrible thing that happened to you – this awful attack on you when you were twenty – the character has lived through that. The character is flashing pictures up and the reason they're putting [it] into words is they want you to see it with them and they will flash between seeing the pictures and checking that you're still listening. They'll often laugh at the most awful parts in order perhaps to protect you from the pain they felt. What I suggest they rarely do is this strange traumatised slow delivery where the person thinks it through, they don't have to think it through, they've done it, they're telling you... Think all the pictures through, so that when you come to tell it the thoughts are just rising fast, the pictures are coming, the emotion is maybe happening through the pictures but you're driving through to tell the story.'

Mel Churcher, Acting and Dialect Coach, UK and USA

SIMILARITIES OR DIFFERENCES BETWEEN YOU AND THE CHARACTER

'If my job as an actor is to reveal the life of another human being, whether it's Hamlet, whether it's Ian Beale, whoever it may well be, the character. Before I can start to enter into a relationship with the character, first I must be willing to enter into a relationship with myself, because the character doesn't exist. It's a figment of the imagination of

> *the writer and if you played Ian Beale and I played Ian Beale they would be different Ian Beales because you're a different person and I'm a different person.'*
>
> Sam Rumbelow, Method Acting Coach, UK and USA

Do you see the character as an extension of yourself, using your imagination to get there, or as a completely separate entity that you use your inventiveness and imagination to reach? What you are creating in performance is a physical reality for the dialogue and story, two actors will always shape that dialogue and therefore the story with different form, even if the confines are restricted and/or the director's vision rigid. Look at 'I'm Not There' a handful of actors all playing Bob Dylan in the same film, they're all different expressions of that role.

> *'I start off by finding out how similar I am to the character I am about to play, how different the character is to me. And when I rationalise the differences I then try and concentrate on the things that I can identify with of myself, that I can use for that character. And then what I have to stretch to in order to bring myself to the character rather than adapting it all to me… There's always a kind of misnomer in acting which is when my instinct says "That doesn't work" or "I'm trying to find the character's truth" and the misnomer is that you're always dealing with your own truth actually, you know. It's finding out how differently you relate to that truth which makes the difference between you and another character… Then reaching out towards the aims and the tasks the writer is giving me within the play through my character and using my own energy, my own emotions. I don't think you can create emotions, you can only use the emotions that you have, you can extend them and make them bigger and make them more powerful.'*
>
> Peter Egan, Actor and Director, UK

Ask yourself what similarities and differences you have to the character, even if they are apparently a polar opposite to you in terms of job and home life, do you have similar personality traits? Does your joy in performance come from leaping into a character that is nothing like you and making their truth appear?

> *'Always think of the character as somebody else, it's always him and not me... Think of him as having characteristics I don't necessarily have and so there's a space, a space you have to jump across to go into character and out of character. It's crucial for me, you know when we're shooting... If the director doesn't say cut I just keep going and if there's nothing in the script I just make something up, or maybe there's just a silence. But that thing of just keeping going, keeping the concentration on and then turning it off at the end, is something you can only do if you're not playing yourself.'*
>
> Phil Davis, Actor and Director, UK

In portraying a character truthfully you have to play them from their own perspective, by that I mean: no one ever thinks they're not a well liked person – unless they are quite embittered or on their way to becoming a sociopath/serial killer. Playing a selfish character, or someone completely manipulative, if you play their perspective, rather than seeing them through your own values or moral compass, gives them a layered richness. Richard Briers CBE, who was one of our most beloved actors often played characters whom we liked, but when you think about it, are actually incredibly selfish:

> *'One of the writers very sweetly said to me about Martin in "Ever Decreasing Circles", he said "Well we thought we saw this little man on a football pitch being an umpire, very officious and we thought we'd write somebody like*

that that everybody hated and couldn't stand." And he said "We thought of you" and I said "That's very kind of you" and he said "Well you're the only actor we know that can maybe get away with playing a really awful man and yet either you pity him a bit or you almost like him, you understand his problems." In other words what they were saying was they needed a very sympathetic actor to play an unsympathetic guy which is roughly what happened.'

Richard Briers CBE, Actor, UK

'I like to inhabit what I'm doing, I like to, to believe and to, to discover the reason and the spirit behind the person I'm trying to convey.'

Sir Derek Jacobi CBE, Actor, UK

Look at the contractions within the character, what can you bring to that mix, which side of their nature will you play most to? If you play a bad guy/girl who hides a heart of gold will you choose to lift the curtain on their inner softness often but only very slightly or rarely but with depth?

'When I played "Mary Queen of Scots" at the Citizens, which Philip Prouse directed, first of all I asked Philip for his permission to play the part French because historically of course she was brought up in France and it occurred to me that she would speak with English with a French accent... So that was very interesting to me, also I wanted to look at the ways in which a woman of power and (although there were grave difficulties for her) her position if you like, her status. I was very interested in ways in which she would have been submissive and quite possibly masochistic, I was quite interested in that. I pursued that and looked at

that, and romantic, I was interested in the romantic notion. When I played Mrs Malaprop I was very interested in what I took to be the innocence of the character and I thought a lot about Marilyn Monroe, I felt it was someone wanting to please, that there was a slight desperation of wanting to please.'

Ann Mitchell, Actor and Director, UK

Finding the balance of those character traits and choosing how and when you play them is what makes your characterisation different to another actor's reading for the same part in the auditions.

REMAINING FLEXIBLE AND OPEN ABOUT YOUR DECISIONS ON THE CHARACTER

Directors like to see actors auditioning with a clear interpretation of the role. No hedging of bets in terms of the characterisation. Once you've read the script and made notes, what do your instincts tell you about how to play the character and the scenes you've been asked to prepare?

> 'Start making some decisions about what your character wants, because even if they're wrong decisions they're going to see you're thinking. They're going to see you giving them something that they understand and then they can say "Well, maybe she's not so angry why don't you try to get her to console him" but they'll give you another chance.'
>
> Mel Churcher, Acting and Dialect Coach, UK and USA

More often than not there's more than one read per scene, usually a couple at least and the director, producer or casting director will give notes. When you get the opportunity to read the scene again, you need to listen to the creatives and be open to adjusting your performance as per the notes. This can be difficult on the day, so always:

- Breathe, focus, listen what they are saying and implement the notes.

As I mentioned in chapter 6, directors will sometimes give notes to get you to change your portrayal just to see how well you take them and how flexible you are on your view of the character and how you play him/her. The end result of brilliant characterisation and a great show, stage or screen is a working relationship between you and the creative team. There has to be co-operative dialogue between you all for it to be successful.

> *'With the pace of particularly TV drama these days a director is looking as much for flexibility of approach as they are for, you know, your created input which is a given, but that's what you're there for. But for instance if you read with me, once you're on set with the regular or your fellow cast members the whole scene might be in a different tone or tenor and of course we all know that scripts change over night these days and therefore they need to see that you can think on your feet.'*
> Alison Chard, Casting Director, UK

Some directors will give a lot of notes so you have to be open to altering your interpretation at audition stage as well as rehearsal.

> *'I do work the kind of Stanislavsky system which is to analyse the script in to beats and movements, objectives i.e. take the play bit by bit, read it, give them the*

movements and beats that I've written down on the strict understanding that it's just a guide and a beginning, that any of it can change, that it may be quite erroneous but it starts them thinking.'

Braham Murray CBE, Director, UK

IF YOU GET STUCK CREATIVELY WITH YOUR ROLE OR SCENES

All actors get stuck from time to time with a scene or a character they're looking at. It can happen at any time during the production, whilst in a theatre run, guest appearing on an episode of a TV show, as a regular or semi-regular character or crucially for you when first looking at an audition script. If you get stumped liked this, it's more than a little perplexing and can eat away at your confidence.

Ask yourself why are you stuck? Is it that:

- You can't feel the character?
  Is there enough in the writing to give you what you need as an actor? Is the script too cryptic? Is too much left up for interpretation and you're not sure where it's going?
- The situation is too unreal for you, you have no experience of anything similar and cannot empathize?
  Is it out of the realm of your imagination? Are you stopping yourself from getting to the character's journey? Is it just too fantastical, can you not find the truth in it?
- The vision of the director seems at odds with the script and you can't bridge the gap?
  Is it that his/her vision is too rigid or are you not being open to something daring and exciting out of fear?

If you don't feel there is enough in the script to find the character, you have two choices: 1) make the decisions as you would normally, but in the knowledge that you will have to be braver with your choices because you won't feel they are backed up by the text as you would have done otherwise; 2) talk to your director about it, during the early stages of rehearsals.

Ideally you should be able to do a combination of 1 and 2.

If it's before your audition and you really don't feel there is enough for you to make something out of, talk to your agent. Ask if you can call the casting team, there may be more information on that role which is not in that particular script. If for example, you are auditioning for a part in a serial he/she may come back in a later episode when all is revealed. As long as you don't tie someone up on the phone for half an hour there is no harm in asking questions at an appropriate time. You can ask the assistant on the day when you're in the waiting room if there wasn't time to before, if say you only got the script the previous night. Everyone wants you to get the part so they will help if they can.

> *'Just do what you do, you make do… you can sit at home and you can decide "Oh I'm gonna play it like this" or "I'm gonna play it like that" then you stand up and your feet won't do it… It's very interesting working with Mike Leigh, you know you do all this research and all this talk about the character. But concurrently alongside that you're doing the thing of being the character and you have to find a way of doing the things that are necessary to make the character work in a way that you're comfortable with, and that can take some time you know. You're putting your body into a different shape, that's a metaphorical image, but you are.'*
>
> Phil Davis, Actor and Director, UK

Sometimes just taking some time away from that script will help everything work itself out in your mind. This often happens when you let your mind focus on something else. If it's when you're preparing at home, go and do something else for an hour or so. Take a break from concentrating and working too hard; read something unrelated, watch something on the telly, make your supper, go to the gym, have a cuppa and do a crossword, something to take yourself out of it and let your brain percolate in the background. If you're already contracted on a show, sometimes this 'time out' can come in the form of a few days work on another production.

> '... During the middle of this period of filming which is a long period. I was offered a short independent film to play a woman who's completely opposite to the woman I'm playing in the television series and that was amazingly liberating... To go away from this character, play this other woman who if you like was the antithesis of this woman and then come back to Lillian, I found that that was liberating.'
>
> Ann Mitchell, Actor and Director, UK

Many actors suggest if stuck; turning the role on its head. Ask yourself could you play this character with a completely different approach? Whilst this might not be how you end up playing the role, it may open you up to an idea you've not had because of feeling blocked. I suggested playing against the text earlier when looking at your levels, this is really worth investigating if you're stuck. If the role is a murderer, exploring him/her to contrast the 'normal' interpretation might allow you to bring out a more disturbing or even likable side to the role.

If a creative block happens – almost like stage fright – that anxiety once you're stuck or disconnected from the character can take over. Don't over compensate or the audience, camera and/or creative team will become aware of it. Take some time to relax, just think about it all in your usual process, don't labour or panic over getting the audience there, they will be watching your interpretation of the character's journey so have some faith in yourself, your communicative powers and ability to give a great performance.

> *'I think you learn sort of not to panic really because if you do too much to compensate it just draws attention to what's wrong. It's like a big sign post, he's panicking, he's working too hard you know... That's the only good thing about experience, sort of seven o'clock on a first night you think "Well half past eleven tonight we'll be in the bar having a drink, it will be over, I will have survived." So the less panic I can let myself get into, the better I'll be.'*
>
> Tim Pigott-Smith, Actor and Director, UK

Work through it. Sometimes the process (when you have felt confounded by finding the characterisation of the role) can be much more rewarding than a simpler experience. Even great actors such as Sir Derek Jacobi CBE, take time to properly inhabit a character:

> *'[It takes] about 40 performances before I can start really sailing, you know and you never really stop finding and twitching and tweaking in the course of a run. But It's after about 40 performances that I'm beginning to ease up, it's beginning to be part of me, my head, my heart, my mouth are all working on the same thing. But I find acting very difficult. I mean I don't find it easy at all. I love it but nothing really comes easily to me and I sometimes do get blocks about things... It's much more interesting, the job satisfaction is greater I think if you struggle to find something. And many different things are clues along the*

> way and all the clues are not necessarily from yourself, from what you take from the other actors and what the director puts in. I mean there is so much from a first read through, the process to that first performance, the changes that you go through, the internal and work that you do and the external pressures that are on you, that are moulding you, which is what makes it all so exciting.'
>
> Sir Derek Jacobi CBE, Actor, UK

LISTENING AND OBSERVING

One of the most important ingredients to a convincing performance is simple: *listening*.

Nerves all too often counteract this and performers at the audition stage will have concentrated on knowing their lines and their cues, but in practice are not thinking about the lines of the other character, therefore not actually reacting to them.

> 'In Meisner you're encouraged to work in the moment so that perhaps exciting discoveries can be made that you wouldn't have rationally have predetermined doing your homework at home.'
>
> Kate Maravan, Actor and Meisner Acting Coach, UK

How can you know what to say in a conversation if you are not listening to the other person and observing what they do? In real life we all rehearse those important exchanges we are going to have in our own head in advance: a break up, a proposal, a resignation, an argument... How often do they actually turn out how we imagined? We can't always second guess how another individual will react, what they will say or do. So even though you have a script and you know what lines are coming you have to listen to the delivery and watch the body language of the other actor.

> 'You find a way of saying a line perhaps in the bath and you take it into rehearsal and somebody says something else in a completely different way to what you were expecting, so your line you can't say the lovely inflection you had on your line because it doesn't fit with their line anymore.'
>
> Sir Derek Jacobi CBE, Actor, UK

Everything can change depending on interpretation of the same lines of dialogue, subtext you'd not considered maybe, or just another way of seeing the scene.

- Listen to the reader's delivery – be that a reader, an actor or the casting director.
- At recall stages when you may be paired up with another actor for particular scenes or even in a group listening becomes even more imperative.

   This is when the creatives get to see how you interact with other actors, therefore how open you are on stage/set. When you're at your first audition and it's usually the casting director or their assistant reading in with you, that individual is facilitating you, they are not giving a full performance which could detract from yours. Reading at auditions is a particular skill in itself, giving enough for the auditioning actor to work with without distracting attention.

Kate Maravan sums up the Meisner philosophy on listening:

> 'The Meisner technique helps you primarily to listen, to fully listen and I saw a quote which was "Listen, observe, listen, really look, listen, concentrate, listen." And I think you know that most people would say that one of the most basic principals of acting is to listen but it's amazing how easily we forget.'
>
> Kate Maravan, Actor and Meisner Acting Coach, UK

Keep your eyes, ears and mind open, as Phil Davis advises:

> 'I had no training, I had nothing, I had no idea how people worked, so I just tried to keep my ears and eyes open and catch on... stands you in good stead, you know. Because people work in wildly different ways... It taught me that kind of pragmatism, that there was more than one way of doing things. There's not a right, a correct approach, it's just finding what's appropriate. I mean obviously things change as you get older and you do more telly and films and everything and you're left more on your own. But the lessons I learnt from Joan [Littlewood] stayed with me forever you know, it was about listening and it was about actually engaging in what was going on. You know if a piece of the set fell over you couldn't ignore it, you'd get a kick up the arse from Joan if you ignored it, you had to incorporate it into the play.'
>
> Phil Davis, Actor and Director, UK

WORKING OUTSIDE IN

Most acting methodologies teach you to work from the inside of the character outward, getting to the inner truth before you think about their mannerisms or physicalities. When John Wright directs and creates physical comedy, he works from the outside in, a far less common approach. It may at times be worth thinking about his approach as well so that you explore your character from different angles, especially if you have been stuck.

> 'It's not to say I don't value the internal approach if you like, the outside-in or inside-out argument, but I tend to work very much from the outside in. I tend to work from impulses what are called memo-dynamic, which really

means you try to find a physical movement, an attitude, an image which you find inspiring which takes you to a level of play which you wouldn't normally go to yourself without this impulse. So a lot of my work is about working from the outside in, but fundamentally these are very much false distinctions because once you've actually got from the outside in, it ends up being from the inside out.'

John Wright, Physical Comedy Director and Author

On occasion at auditions for both theatrical and screen work you may be required to do some improvising around a character. Starting from a different viewpoint gives you the opportunity to think and create with distinctly diverse results.

'When Stanislavsky started his work at the turn of the last century, he was largely concerned with interpretation. And all the techniques that he came up with: the idea of the "Magic if", the idea of breaking things down to beats and these are really wonderful analytical tools, but they're tools of interpretation. They are not tools of creation, in other words they are not tools which help you devise or to make things up right from scratch and this is where working from the outside in becomes really vital, because when you work that way you're working at a point where you are generating material. You're writing basically, you're making things up, you're finding things, but you do need to be able to repeat it and then you need to work from the inside out.'

John Wright, Physical Comedy Director and Author

YOUR VOICE AND PHYSICALITY

Your voice and physicality are two of your attributes and tools which you should always be working on. On the day of your audition you need to be warmed up. This is where not taking those vocal exercises you learned at college for granted pays off. They were taught for a reason. All to often we see actors rush in late, unconcerned and apparently 'ready' to come straight in for their meeting, even though they are flustered from having run from the tube. Give yourself a short but sufficient time to relax and limber up as you would were you to be doing a dance call, I don't mean start stretching and 'do-re-mi-fa-so-la-ti-do'-ing all over the casting office, but you may not have spoken aloud yet today if it's an early meeting. Find somewhere quiet that will not affect the venue in which you are auditioning and take a moment to centre yourself and relax vocally. We covered some exercises in chapter 8.

Think about your vocal register:

- What part will you use?
- Do you feel this character lives in a specific part of your voice?
  If so why and, how does that make you feel emotionally, physically and practically?
- If you're going to be re-creating that feel and vocal intensity again and again you need to know where it lives.

> 'I try to use all that I've got as an acting instrument, vocally, emotionally, spiritually and particularly in a classical role, if you're doing a Hamlet or a MacBeth. What is very important of course is your voice and if they're going to be listening to your voice a great deal in the course of the evening, you've got to play more than one instrument. So you've got to have a well-honed orchestra in your throat and it's gotta be strong and resonant. And I think voice is terribly terribly important, speech, the vocalising of the pieces is very important and your ease with the text.'
>
> Sir Derek Jacobi CBE, Actor, UK

In terms of your physicality, how do you approach the role?

- Does the character move the way you do? Are they a completely different being to you?
- Think about how you will create some kind of physical presence in your audition if you will be sat down for most or the entirety of it. Your physicality is still important, sitting down does not change that. A reigning king or queen is still regal when sat in a throne or a chair. A Politician is always statesperson like whether stood or sat. A cowboy or farmer – probably less so.

With physicality, as I mentioned in chapter 7, remember to think about how you prepare/rehearse your audition scenes at home. If you always rehearse your lines pacing up and down your house, lying in the bath or sat in the lotus position, your body will feel very differently when you are sat in the audition room chair opposite a reader and camera or perhaps on a stage.

COMEDY – BEING WORSE THAN YOU ARE

One of the keys to comedy (unfortunately lost sometimes) is that you have to take it seriously. There are some actors who are great in serious roles, absolutely believable and yet in a comedy they seem unable to suspend their own disbelief. They seem to be laughing along with the audience when the forth wall has not been taken down, smirking to themselves rather than being deadpan. It's very difficult to suspend *our* disbelief as an audience if an actor is apparently finding it all immensely funny themselves, unless the production is using the device of comedy asides intentionally like Michaela Coel did in 'Chewing Gum' recently.

> *'It's difficult to describe comedy, I mean it's very tricky, you simply play it as sincerely as you can with a cunning that you know how to put an edge on a line like perhaps hitting a ball in cricket you know.'*
>
> Richard Briers CBE, Actor, UK

One of the ways to devise and look at comedy which John Wright explains is to be better or worse than you are. To exaggerate:

> 'Being worse than you are is quite literally that. Capitalising on the things that you think "Oh I mustn't do that because I'll look really stupid" or "I mustn't do that because that would be really awful." It's acknowledging what these things are and capitalising on what they are. So in other words it takes us towards the grotesque. So you get to know yourself and find out these things that we often suppress, that we often put away, the fact of "I must be better, I must get this right, I must play this like this." We're often hiding something of the raw humanity that makes an individual really fascinating.'
>
> John Wright, Physical Comedy Director and Author

If you're feeling out your character and performance at home whilst preparing for your audition, this is an area that may be worth having a play with. In terms of performance levels and also the questions you ask yourself as an actor when exploring the role and discovering the truth within it. This can apply to drama as well as comedy as often the more colourful performance is one which hints at the other parts of a character. It can play a big part in what informs the choice between two or three equally talented actors all up for the same role.

RELAXATION

Relaxation, both in terms of you as an actor and you as yourself a person are very important for your performance.

> 'Harold Finch was a director... I was very young and he used to say you know "Don't press". When you say "Don't press" you mean "don't over act, don't push the line too much, don't get desperate", or "don't get nervous or frightened". That's what he was trying to say, "be yourself" he'd say "Always be true to the text and be true to yourself."'
>
> Richard Briers CBE, Actor, UK

In terms of the Method approach, the need for relaxation exercises is imperative as Sam Rumbelow explains:

> 'Something that defines Method from any other technique, it's the exercise "Basic Relaxation" that Lee Stasberg developed... Lee used to say that "Without relaxation there is only result." And of course when we walk into an audition we want the job, when we walk on stage we want to be brilliant, we want to be inspiring... But it's such a complex journey, that I have to really slow down and take time and the first place to start is relaxation. Because how I perceive myself, how I see myself, how I experience myself will be based upon my tensions and my agendas.'

Sam goes on to say:

> 'If I could really relax I might get to experience myself differently, which means that I can transcend from my civilian agenda which is to be nice and respectable and loved in the world, to someone who's prepared to deal with the whole array of my humanity. You know my deeper

darker subconscious urges, needs, impulses as a human being... It's no different from having to do voice work or having to work your body and if you don't, it's a muscle, it atrophies, it gets weak.'

Sam Rumbelow, Method Acting Coach, UK and USA

Here's a 'Basic Relaxation' exercise to release any physical tensions, this is one to do prior to your audition, *not* in the waiting room:

- Sit in a straight-backed chair and allow your body to relax and become limp, rest your neck against the chair back. Gently and slowly let your head fall back. Raise one of your arms up and be aware of any tensions or pains throughout the muscles of your arms starting at your fingers, then your wrists, focusing on each individual muscle as you go. Lower the arm so it is limp again. Repeat for the other arm, then each leg right the way down to your toes. Focus on your back and shoulders, neck, face and the back of your head. For your neck you can gently roll your head from side to side. If you have difficulties in relaxing your facial muscles, you may want to pull expressions in order to feel them working. Relax your throat, mouth and tongue, stick out your jaw, your tongue in every direction, raise your eyebrows and work your cheeks. Sometimes all this relaxation can have an emotional reaction, if this occurs, take a deep breath and make a long 'Ahh' sound you can also try a short 'Hah' sound. Always be careful not to do any movements too quickly so as to avoid unnecessary injuries. This exercise usually takes between 15 to 30 minutes.

You need to find a way to relax, be it the Method's 'Basic Relaxation' exercise or something that strikes a more personal resonance with you. As an actor you have to have all your emotions ready, under the surface, which can at times be difficult to deal with as a person and as a performer. Relaxation can protect you from the emotional onslaught that a particular character may be.

> 'I think acting keeps you young because I think actors have to have a kind of foot in the cradle, you know they have to remember what it was like to be a child and to have your emotions absolutely there. If you hurt, you scream; if you're hungry, you cry for food; your emotions are absolutely raw like a child's and you've got to remember what it was like before maturity blanketed you.'
>
> Sir Derek Jacobi CBE, Actor, UK

Finding a way to relax mentally, physically and emotionally is essential for performers. It is key to being in a resourceful and relaxed state when preparing to deliver your performance both prior to auditioning and before going on stage or set.

SUMMARY

What you can take away from this chapter are ways to think about the performance you want to give at your auditions. We considered how you can explore the script to find its truth, looking at the similarities and difference between the character and yourself and how much is dictated by the situation. We went on to remaining flexible about your interpretation of the piece and how to look from different perspectives if you have become stuck creatively with a role. Finally and very importantly we covered remembering to listen and observe when in the audition room, thinking about your voice and physicality before auditioning and, relaxing mentally and physically and emotionally.

CHAPTER 10

COLLABORATIVE WORK

In this chapter we will look at what happens on the occasions when you didn't get cast in the role you auditioned for. We will approach this in two ways:

1) Everyone can't get the part they audition for and with this in mind you need to look at:

- Reasons you didn't get the role.
- Remaining positive after a disappointment.
- Luck – that elusive component… Practical things you can do.

2) Positive steps you can take to continue working:

- Acting work you can collaborate on to keep working and be seen by the industry.
- Considerations for that work, be it fringe theatre or films, short or feature.

WHAT TO DO WHEN "YOU DIDN'T GET IT"

Many times in an actor's career, the call from your agent will be to say 'You didn't get it'. After picking yourself up of the floor and trying to chalk it down to experience and other old clichés, there are a few things to think about.

There are plenty of reasons why you may not have been chosen for that role. Some are to do with you, your performance, professionalism, your manner. Some are not to do with you personally but down to other considerations. You need to reflect on the experience and the best way is to start by asking yourself some honest questions.

Was it down to you?

- Were you unprepared? Had you learnt your lines and prepared your scenes well enough? Had you really thought about the role and the piece as a whole?
- Had you researched the show and the creatives? Were you able to talk through your ideas and their vision?
- Were you in any way dismissive or rude to anyone on the day of your meeting? Were you late and is that a habit of yours? How did you present yourself?
- Did you get on with the creatives?
- Did you give a good reading?
- Did you take the director's notes well and amend your performance accordingly or just ignore them through nerves?
- Did you come back for a chemistry read and the chemistry wasn't there? You cannot manufacture chemistry with other actors, you may not like them as individuals off set but that creative spark where you can bounce off each other as actors is all important and it either happens or it doesn't regardless of interpersonal relationships.

'Be really, really rigorously honest with yourself after an audition – "Was there something that I didn't do?" or "Oh, I shouldn't have said that" or "Why did I read it like that?" or "The director said this and of course I just thought no that's wrong I'll do it this way." Is there something you

could do to put it right? It's kind of what I call "Bathroom mirror moment." Really, it's when you're on your own and you're just being really quite ruthless with yourself. Was it something that I could have done or could not have done or was it really something that was just, you know up the chain of producers. And therefore I'm perfectly happy with what I did and I seemed to be going along the right lines and it's gonna work eventually.'

Alison Chard, Casting Director, UK

We explored the considerations of each of the key audition room creatives in chapter 4, in some depth. If you can honestly say you were prepared, gave a good reading and were your nice charming self, then quite possibly it was nothing to do with you, so approach your reflection from the other perspective.

Was it them?

- Is the vision of that role and piece something that on the day you didn't really fit, through no fault of your own. Perhaps the creatives wanted a different feel to that role than you give. Who did the role go to? Are they a very different 'type' than you?
- Is that role paired with another character, a married couple or two best friends/work partners who are always on screen together? These have physical considerations, height for one which is often forgotten by actors. In real life the height of your friends, romantic choices and colleagues is not generally an issue. On screen it can be difficult to film two individuals with a great difference in height. Do you look too alike to an actor already cast? If you look too similar producers can worry the audience won't remember which character you are.
- Was there a clash of artistic viewpoint or personality that whilst not aggressive, would not have been conducive to an easy working relationship? Was someone cold to you?

- Did the role description change, i.e. age or gender, size of the role?
- Did the role get cut?
- Did the network/exec producers apply some pressure for a more 'namey' actor to be hired for that role?
- Were you down to the last 2 or 3 choices for the role and it went to someone else? – In these situations it often comes down to personal preferences and discussions within the creative team. Some of it will be down to how well you clicked with the team creatively and personally and you can't fabricate a genuine human response to anyone either.

You may not have been quite right for their vision of this role, which does not mean your audition was pointless. Casting directors, directors and producers all remember good actors they've met and would have liked to work with, but couldn't cast in a particular role at that time.

> *'If you're a good actor, there's no such thing as a wasted audition. The biggest gap between me seeing an actor and casting an actor is 28 years I think. And sometimes I see and actor and I think he's absolutely brilliant and nothing for a year or two comes up for which I can suggest that actor and then something will come up and I'll say "Oh, that actor that I saw in Salisbury in 1995 is absolutely perfect for this."'*
> Joyce Nettles, Casting Director, UK

TAKING FEEDBACK

Richard Briers CBE had some great advice about reviews that I think is applicable to audition feedback. After all one person giving their opinion may be just that, a subjective opinion, but if a handful of reviewers or the auditioning panel all say a similar thing then there is something you need to be aware of. Listen to the feedback your agent gives you and apply it, they have listened to and distilled the comments given by those that 'reviewed' you.

> 'If you read say eight notices through as one notice, you will get what's wrong with the second act, they will have spotted it, that there's a weakness in the second act. Because the repetition here and there (not every paper will say it) but there'll be a line through and you think "Yeah that's right." Or in a performance "Yes I'm being to insisting, I'm too, overacting that a bit too heavy, it's too heavy" or "I could do more" you know. It comes through if you read eight notices treating it as written by one person, you get an idea of what is wrong... if you don't read the writer who says "Richard Briers last night was a pain in the arse" if you don't read it and you go in and you get some funny looks or people can't quite meet your eye, you know [laughs].'
>
> Richard Briers CBE, Actor, UK

You might not like the feedback you are given but if you want to progress in the industry you need to take it on the chin. If everyone in the audition room thought you needed to tone your performance down, or lift it up a notch, they may be on to something. Equally if feedback was only negative from one person, e.g. the producer didn't feel you were emotive enough you still have to listen, but perhaps not alter your acting. Unfortunately we can't please everyone all of the time.

REMAINING POSITIVE AFTER A DISAPPOINTMENT

The feedback and lack of job offer is what it is, how you deal with it and grow from it is part of what will mark you out as a professional, capable individual in this industry. There are many variables as to why you might not get a role. How you choose to look at that will have an impact, it is personal to you as an individual. Was it luck? Were you not meant to get that role because there's something better out there for you or, was the opportunity meant for someone-else? You must find a way to remain positive if your performance was good but it just didn't work out.

> '... As an actor you've got to be prepared for all comers, all types of directors, all types of casting directors... if you don't think they like you, just don't get personal, don't take it personally. You know you're there to do a job, you're a skilled person.'
>
> Robert Bierman, Director, UK and USA

Highs and lows come with the territory and it seems most individuals working in the arts are sensitive souls, what a combination! Positive thinking – a terrible buzzword from yesteryear that always makes me (at least) envisage people in oversized tie-died clothing – could be applied here. Jeff Turner gave us some tips on State Management and getting into resourceful states of mind for auditions, he also has some pearls of wisdom for mood enhancement. This is particularly useful after a disappointment, as hearing your Gran's voice in your head saying 'Dust yourself off and start all over again' may no longer be working.

> 'Your mental focus, what you're thinking about is one of the things that helps contribute to your mental and emotional state. So if you're thinking good things, if you're thinking about winning, if you're thinking about how well you're going to do in any given area, that's gonna enhance that performance... Your mind is locked away,

> *it's hidden in a bone box in your skull, it has no access to the outside world apart from through your senses.'*
>
> Jeff Turner, Life Management and Performance Coach, UK

He goes on to mention music and dance, so instead of crooning and crying uncontrollably to 'All By Myself' put on some upbeat music when you've had bad news. Once you're in a lighter emotional state, a better frame of mind, try to talking yourself round to the idea it's not the only role for you, there will be others. It may help put things into perspective.

> *'Movement by the way is a very quick and effective way to change your state, most of us familiar with dancing, the reason we like it is because it changes our state. Try putting some music on and bopping around the flat, that'll change your state instantly... How we talk to ourselves, by the way you can change the quality of your inner dialogue if you're aware of talking to yourself... You may notice that when you're not feeling that great, you talk to yourself in perhaps rather a critical voice, it may not even be your voice, it may be the voice of a teacher from the past or perhaps a parent. Try being a bit more supportive.'*
>
> Jeff Turner, Life Management and Performance Coach, UK

HOW MUCH IS DOWN TO LUCK

Of course there is another element that we haven't looked at yet, a very elusive element in the job equation... Serendipity. Right place, right time, right voice, right face and right human interaction; the list goes on.

Luck shouldn't be underestimated and you can't change the chance role of the dice. Sometimes it will be a deciding factor, the fates will be on your side, or not. However, people often misinterpret situations and personal characteristics which may lead to more opportunities arising. Don't assume another actor is a jammy so-and-so and getting your dream job because he/she is just more 'lucky' than you. Perhaps they are more driven and ambitious, or simply more prepared.

Sir Derek Jacobi CBE rather positively sums up which personality traits form what might be viewed as luck:

> *'I think obviously you have to have talent or flair, you have to have an enormous almost Olympian stamina, health yes, and a sort of spiritual generosity about what you do.'*
> Sir Derek Jacobi CBE, Actor, UK

Braham Murray OBE adds his perspective to the notion that 'luck' is an external factor that some people just 'have':

> *'I don't believe in luck, I believe that you give off a kind of magnetic force that people recognise and respond to… The people I'm talking about are actually quite happy… working for a company where they know they're gonna be loved and respected and the work is going to be valuable. I think generally speaking in the theatre you find kind of what you need, if you merit it.'*
> Braham Murray OBE, Artistic Director, UK

We can all do a number of things to improve upon what appears to be how lucky we are in finding work, most of which we've covered in the previous chapters. In practical terms you have to make the best of what you have:

- You must be proactive.
- You need to market yourself and network well.
- You always have to present yourself well at auditions, on time and prepared.

- You need to love what you do.
- You must take your craft seriously, put the time and effort in.
- Always remain humble about your successes, because a failure can be just around the corner and you want to be able to chalk it down to an experience and carry on.
- Keep your skills up-to-date; keep learning.
- If there is an area of the industry that you'd like more experience of what can *you* do about it? If you've not worked in a particular medium before, can you do a course or be involved in a small production where you can learn?
- Importantly but sometimes forgotten – make some time to enjoy other interests so your whole existence is not solely about your career.

Those who are proactive and positive seem to enjoy their career and life in general a lot more than those with a pessimistic outlook.

How ambitious are you? What are your ambitions? What are you doing to try to achieve them? Are you pursuing the kind of work you want to do which will make you happy? And remember ambitious doesn't have to equate to a ruthless determination to win at all costs and walking over your friends, it generally means acknowledging what you want and striving to achieve it. Phil Davis remembers his ambitions when he was young:

> 'What I wanted to be was an actor, you know, I loved it. I loved doing the Am Drams and I loved doing the National Youth Theatre and for me I thought "If I could do this for a living and make a living out of it" then that would do it for me. So I wasn't ambitious in the sense that I wanted to be Lawrence Olivier or I wanted to be a big movie star, but I just wanted to do this thing that I enjoyed so much for a living. And that was it for me really, so I didn't think of myself as ambitious, although

you know I was ambitious to do the work properly and to do it as well as I could and to do interesting contemporary stuff.'

Phil Davis, Actor and Director, UK

There's a lot of superstition that comes with the arts, I would honestly say if you don't get the role, or something goes wrong, it's very unlikely to be down to those clichés. If someone wishes you luck rather than hoping you 'break a leg' or you refer to Shakespeare's 'Macbeth' by its name rather than as 'The Scottish Play' are these the most important factors, really?

TYPECASTING CAN LEAD TO MORE WORK, BUT CAN LIMIT AN ACTOR

Typecasting – that horrible word. It is difficult if you are always going up for the same type of roles not to get typecast as such, as your audience (industry and non-industry) only ever see you playing those characters. Generally speaking actors want a varied career. Don't we all – everyone loves a challenge. Typecasting is something that both casting directors and agents try to avoid. Agents, whilst instinctively knowing the types of roles particular clients will get seen for, will also suggest them as leftfield choices. They will take casting directors, directors and producers to see those clients in roles outside their usual casting bracket and comfort zone. Casting directors love to see actors stretched and in roles which an audience is not used to seeing them. Actors like to explore characters and use their full range and imagination. None of us actually want to take the seemingly easy option.

You may feel that you are being too typecast and a lack of progression and job offers is down to this. However Phil Davis and Tim Pigott-Smith both speak in positive generous terms about typecasting, which at the time is very frustrating for actors.

'For me typecasting was something of a problem, I was a working class kid, cockney and all that, so I played a lot of bad guys in episodes of this and that and it kept me ticking over. But every so often you get a role and it kind of sets the trend for the next couple of years and then hopefully after that the next couple of years you'll get another role and that will veer you off into another direction. And I always, even from the very beginning thought of myself as a character actor and so fitting myself into the shoes of other people was the job and I was just lucky really that roles came along that were in quite a wide spectrum of types... I've been very lucky and typecasting, you know I have turned roles down because it was very much like the thing I did last time, but that's a luxury that not everyone can afford.'

Phil Davis, Actor and Director, UK

'I said to Tony Quale once, "I'm really sick of it, all I play is these evil parts." It's actually something to do with the way I look on screen; you know something that happens to my eyes. I don't know what it is, I don't do it, it happens, it's just there, and it's not what I'm like, it's what I look like. And I said to Tony "I'm sick of it" and "Oh don't worry" he said "One day you'll be very good as a fairy in a pantomime and you'll have ten years of that, count your lucky stars" you know [laughs]...'

Tim Pigott-Smith, Actor and Director, UK

STEPPING-STONES AND LEARNING

Often, when actors aren't in paid work or at least in something in a recognised venue they will choose to take on low budget or no-budget productions and I will speak about these in more depth later in this chapter. This allows the actor to be in fairly regular work, build up their C.V, get to know a wider group of people and develop new skills.

Each production you take on when building up your career can be seen on some levels as a stepping-stone to something greater. This can however, be a dangerous and/or deceiving outlook. If being in a fringe show or short film meant you were seen by industry professionals who then actively chose to seek you out to work with, then yes, it has led onto something. But you should always treat every production you are in with the respect it deserves; this unfortunately is not always the case.

> *'You have to take satisfaction from each part of your evolution really of your development. I think too often it's regarded as a stepping-stone to something round the corner, quite what is round the corner I don't really know. You know, you want to get your first telly, then when you've got your first telly you get all sorts of little telly jobs. And then you think "Well I don't want to do that anymore" or "I don't want to do a soap" or "I only want to do this kind of thing." And I think well that's fine, except of course people may stop offering it and unless you have put in the work then you're gonna flounder somewhere along this grand plan.'*
>
> Alison Chard, Casting Director, UK

The rules you would apply to being in a West End stage play or a prime time TV programme should apply to your working experience of pub theatre, short films or micro-budget feature films.

- Remember the 3 P's of professionalism: be Polite, Punctual and Prepared at rehearsals and at your call times.

- Enjoy the production for what it is and who you're working with, not for who may or may not see it.
- Choose work that challenges you.
- Learn from your fellow cast and crew.

You should also expect to be treated with the same respect from everyone-else working on those productions.

> *'If you audition for unpaid work, you're auditioning them as much as they're auditioning you. If the script is good, then that's a good start, so if possible always ask for and make time to read the whole script, which can be easily sent to you on email. It will also make you more prepared and give you a better understanding of both the project and the role. Once at the audition, have questions – not too many just a couple of key things. But a well organised low budget production should be able to answer any question you have, if they know what they're doing.'*
>
> Lance Nielsen, Writer and Director, UK

Develop all the skills you have and maybe take some time to learn some new ones – as long as these are ones you will enjoy. This will always help in your next role, or the one after that and if not for practical application within your acting work just for enjoyment. Due to the vast numbers of performers today, you have to bring more to the table than before.

- Look at the list of skills you ticked on your Spotlight CV, are they still current? Should you be brushing up on them? Could you be going to a higher level with them?
- Of the physical skills nowadays, weapons training for TV and film is very handy as are combat skills. Stage and screen fighting is much more realistic and less dangerous if you know what you are doing. This is *not* just for the guys.

- Do you take vocal lessons, singing, period dance, can you play a musical instrument?
- Take another look at the template in chapter 1. What have you been putting in your career and talent columns?

> *'I do think this is important and would say this to any young actor now, you have to develop every single skill you have now much more so than you did 30 years ago. If you can sing a bit – develop it, if you can dance a bit – develop it and of course if you can act – develop it as much as you can. You still needed to kind of present your energies and your talent in a kind of very specific way, but there was more opportunity and more work in those days. So now the pressure on young actors now coming into the profession now is extraordinary and it's very demanding.'*
> Peter Egan, Actor and Director, UK

Michael Billington sums up very positively how modern actors are, by definition, more versatile in so many ways. But this is not just a compliment it's an observation of skills borne out of necessity.

> *'... Physicality: it seems to me there's a new generation of actors who can do anything that directors ask of them. They can stand on their heads, they can turn cartwheels, they can use their bodies to express not just themselves but ideas, images in a way that wouldn't have been tolerated I suspect, or expected in the 50's or even the 60's. There's this loose limbed physical sort of pliability that has come into theatre, I mean some companies as we know, Frantic Assembly and groups like that specialise that is their territory, they are physical theatre pure and simple. But my point is that even in more conventional classic theatre we now expect actors to have sort of versatile ability.'*
> Michael Billington, Guardian Critic, UK

There has been something creeping in to the UK, the way many things stealthily commando crawl in from the States, this one is a good thing – continuing acting classes when working as an actor. The British actor's standpoint in the past tended to be 'Why would you need to take a class when you're already an actor?' American actors always seem to keep on training and Brits historically had a kind of secret smugness that they didn't need to. Perhaps when work was more frequent, when there were less actors and they had for the large part spent years in the theatre honing their craft… but nowadays, there really is no shame in continuing classes.

Sam Rumbelow puts gives the example as though actors were sportsmen:

> '… It would be like me being a sports agent and you saying "Yeah, I never practise and I never train" the sports agent will look at you like you're insane. "You don't have a sports coach, you don't work on your technique, you don't have fitness conditioning coach?" "No, I'm just very talented" and they'd say "Well you're talented but in a really strange way." But we still have this problem in this country that we think it's about talent and it's not about application and technique. That's why the USA is still the number one leader in the arts and entertainment field because they understand that they must address the given circumstances, which means they have to be prepared to go to the umpteenth degree.'
>
> Sam Rumbelow, Method Acting Coach, UK and USA

Challenge yourself in terms of performance styles, medium and genre. Keep flexing your acting muscles. Every time you work on a piece of text be it for stage or screen you are sharpening your skills. This continues the development of your potential:

> 'I think you need to perpetually keep challenging yourself, rediscovering yourself, making sure that when you

have periods that are out of work you can actually still workshop and find out what you can do perhaps. And maybe you've never even thought of doing [that] before, you know as an actor. So I think, I think it's invaluable that there are organisations like the Actors Centre in Covent Garden that you can belong to and you can go to television workshops on an ongoing basis. Working with a whole load of different directors in an environment where the end result of it is not going to be broadcast.'

Peter Cregeen, Director and Producer, UK

SHOWCASES AND CASTING DIRECTOR LED AUDITION WORKSHOPS

There are many organisations nowadays offering actors the chance to take place in a showcase or casting director led audition technique workshops.

These can lead to you being seen by industry professionals who might not have seen you otherwise as well as gaining a valuable insight into the process you may not have already.

There are generally speaking fees associated to taking part. This is where you need to be a little savvy and selective, don't go for a scattergun approach and apply to all of them, because it will cost you a fortune and may not lead to anything. Legitimate casting director led audition technique workshops have a statement on their websites, (some read it before the sessions start) stating they will not necessarily lead to auditions in the future with those casting professionals.

Research – there's that word again.

- How long has the showcase/audition workshop organisation been active? What can you find out about them on the

Internet? Have any of your friends or peers taken part with this one?
- If it's an audition technique workshop you're thinking of applying for; who is the casting professional, what can you find out about their work past and present?
Check imdb.com and google.com if they have a history of good work you can usually safely assume there will be more.
- If it's a showcase, have they got testimonials on their website from which you can glean that industry professionals do go to their events?
- Where is the showcase held, is it easy to get to for busy casting directors and agents? If the showcase organisation chooses an inconvenient location it is unlikely to garner the industry support and attendance that a better situated venue could.

Casting directors often work on more than one project at a time and so do not have the time to run workshops when busy. Many only lead workshops once we become available, as they are a valuable experience for the actors as we can dispel some myths, teach good habits and techniques and as a bonus because we may spot someone not on our radar.

N.B. asking the casting director what we are currently casting, can you be seen for it and looking forlorn when the answers are 'Nothing currently' or 'No' does not do you any favours.

There are some fantastic showcase and audition technique workshop companies out there, you need to research them and see which is right for you. Do remember, however as mentioned in the CDG guidelines for the workshops, they do not equate to getting auditions with those casting directors.

One last point on these – don't take part in one for the same casting director more than once. These are audition technique workshops, we are there to impart some wisdom, tips, dos and don'ts. Seeing the same actor repeatedly means they have missed the point of the workshop and are a bit desperate.

CO-OPERATIVE WORK – OR, ME, MYSELF AND I?

The development of skills is of course entirely contingent on continued work and practice. At the end of the day you don't want to be a Barista that fences, you want to be an actor with skills in fencing (sword play not stolen goods). There is no point in having developed a range of convincing ways to cry if the only one to see it is your cat. Sometimes in order to develop your talents you have to generate work or opportunities to be seen, not wait for them to appear. This may be hard to hear when you undoubtedly spend a lot of time going to auditions, searching for auditions or performing in very low budget productions. The problem can be however, that those all require industry professionals to be present and sometimes those individuals are busy with other people and other projects. This leaves you with one real positive choice – working with others collaboratively in order to generate work.

There are many reasons why you may want to work on your own projects:

- Do you have an idea for a production, which no one has done before, you can't get this idea out of your head, a passion project?
- Are you tired of being typecast; is no one seeing beyond the work currently on your CV if it is mainly of one medium?
- Do you want to try writing or directing on a small scale to begin with, as it may be another part of the process that you love?
- Have you worked with someone before and loved the journey from the initial idea stage all the way through to the finished product and want to try being at the helm?

Many well-known industry professionals worked on small-scale collaborations early in their careers before they were able to get the funds for larger productions. We all have to start somewhere.

You need to be relatively entrepreneurial to get these ventures off the ground, we'll look at things to consider. Are you going to be involved in a co-operative group where you are all aiming to put on your own ideas with the help of each other on a continuing basis? Or, do you want to do your own production, but have your friends and peers help you out, a favour that you'll return when they need you down the line?

These are very different set ups. Don't join a co-operative if you do not mean to *fully* co-operate. This may sound odd, but think it through logically. If it's a co-operative and you won't get your turn for your idea for say 6 to 9 months; but you need to do your idea at a particular time of year, i.e. open air theatre or a film which is set in a specific season; how will this work if you've got to wait? Will you really put your best efforts in for 2 other people's projects before your own? There is nothing wrong with just wanting to focus on your own project and asking for help if it is more appropriate for you, just be honest with yourself and everyone-else.

Co-operatives are great things when everyone is co-operating. Director Phil Willmott describes how he first started working collaboratively:

> "'The Steam Industry" came about and I would recommend this to anyone really, I'd written a play which I sent to "The Man In The Moon Theatre" and then I got to know the administrator there... he had a number of friends who also wanted to start a theatre company and had no money. So what we did is we all put in £200 quid into a pot and then we, I think there was 5 of us so that was enough money to get going and we all took turns to put on the shows, so you were allowed to take the money

you put on a show, you weren't supposed to f*ck up, so you'd make the £1000 back, put it back in the pot and then someone else would have a turn and then someone else would have a turn and it kind of sort of went round and round like that really. And that's how we all got started and pretty much all of us now are making a good living as stage professionals, as directors and writers, but that's how we started out.'

Phil Willmott, Director, UK

So if you want to work in a filmmaking or theatrical co-operative think on Phil's advice. They all put in £200 of their own money. Unfortunately that wouldn't go far enough nowadays so you might all need to create a realistic small budget together and then divide that figure by the number of key people involved. Remember the Director of Photography or Director might be prepared to put money in but the person helping out by making lunch is less likely to.

- Could you all stretch your finances just a little bit more?
- Do you each have equipment as well as the skills that you are bringing to the table?
- Do you each have enough time to give for each other's projects and your own?
- Very VERY importantly, do you share an artistic vision and passion? I don't mean your ideas are all the same, but that your goals and outlooks are. Are you all genuinely supportive of each other?
- Make a list of all the positives each member has, personally, skill set wise and equipment. Be pragmatic: what are the strengths of this group of people; what are the weaknesses, practically and interpersonally. If someone is a very talented writer but has a brusque manner with people, probably best that he/she is not a key speaker at events.

Do you just want to do your own production, something you've written and want to see come to fruition? Can you pull it off either on your own as writer/director/producer/editor or to borrow from the Beatles 'With a little help from your friends'?

Phil Davis was frustrated at the parts he was getting back in the day, so he put a play on and was pretty much a one-man production team:

> *'I'd written a play called "Skulduggery" which I put on myself at the Old Red Lion, I did everything, I raised the money, designed it, cast it and put it on. And we did alright really, we made our money back for our investors and we had a good four-week run and packed the place out. And I always felt there was a film in it, that my way of writing was more naturally angled towards film. I mean there's lots of short scenes and it was out on the streets and so eventually I sat down and wrote a screenplay and I sent it to a producer... I didn't hear anything for 6 months and then suddenly I got a call out the blue saying that the BBC wanted to do it. They were planning to do another film and they had a legal problem with it and mine was kind of first on the pile of possibles, and they decided to do it. Because it happened so quickly I was able to go in and say "Look, um, how about me directing it?" and they were a bit resistant at first, but I said "Let me give you 15 minutes to tell you why I should do it."'*
>
> Phil Davis, Actor and Director, UK

If you're going to take the bull by the horns, then you need to be very driven and proactive. Find out the practicalities and just get on with it, whether that's on your own or collaboratively. Don't be put off by what may seem the enormity of putting together a show or a film, if you have a great concept and the where-with-all to do it, you can.

> 'It's not rocket science you know, you get a play, you get the money, you get the theatres, you get the cast, you have four weeks rehearsal and you stick it on… There's a great myth about it, which I think directors like. They like to extend that myth and keep it alive because it makes their job seem a little more mystical. It's absolute tosh, I mean it's a craft, it's a job and there are certain steps, if you've got three weeks rehearsal you've got to do it slightly differently than if you've got four, you know – you've got to do it quicker [laughs].'
>
> Tim Pigott-Smith, Actor and Director, UK

> 'It's an awful thing to sit around at home waiting for your agent to call thinking "Nobody wants me" you know, get off your arse. Get together with your friends, invent something, of course its gotta be good. But that's how companies like "Theatre de Complicite" started, you know they wanted to do something different and so they experimented and they worked together.'
>
> Phil Davis, Actor and Director, UK

Something which you must be aware of though in all this talk of putting on a show or making a film, sometimes the writing is just not good enough. Make sure if it is someone-else's work, that you have read it before you say yes to being involved. You can always say no to work at any level if you feel it is not the right choice for you. And similarly, if it is your project, ask peers to read it – those whom you know will give honest feedback and not just fluff your ego.

> 'You can afford never to do rubbish. You can afford to turn down rubbish, 'cause there's never any shortage of rubbish.'
>
> Richard Briers CBE, Actor, UK

And whichever choices you make always:

> *'Work with good people.'*
> Tim Pigott-Smith, Actor and Director, UK

Collaborative working shouldn't mean throwing money away because someone wants to use their girlfriend/boyfriend as producer or lead actor. At this stage in an actor's career, collaborative work is about enhancing and showcasing their skills and it should not be taking the place of A levels/BTEC/degree in Performing Arts for large parts of the cast and crew. Remember while you may all be great friends at the start, or at least acknowledge being a mutually beneficial group, that any work has its stresses. Stress will only multiply on an unworkable project. It is hugely important that the writing is good, that you have open and honest communication and that participants are actually able to do what they say they can do: I may want to be an astronaut but unfortunately that doesn't mean I actually possess any relevant technical knowledge or that I defy gravity.

ACTORS DIRECTING ACTORS

You may not have any experience as a director but really want to direct a piece of work. Perhaps you're about to embark on a collaborative project where the director is another actor, maybe one you know.

It can be an advantage when directing actors if you yourself are an actor. You will have been directed before, so hopefully will have seen a certain amount of what works in bringing out a great performance and also what to avoid.

> *'The real advantage of being an actor directing is that*

you've had the experience of working with a lot of directors, directors don't, they work with themselves. So you can look at a play or a situation and you can think: "I'm not quite sure how to solve this challenge that I've come across, this problem. What would Peter Hall do, what would Michael Blakemore do, what would Howard Davis do, what would Ian Brown do, what would Michael Joyce my old friend Mike do?"'

Tim Pigott-Smith, Actor and Director, UK

Having directed other actors you may find you have more empathy for directors and their trials and tribulations in attempting to bring out the best performance they can from someone. You should also *in theory* be a more empathetic director in terms of the actors' needs.

'All it helps me do is sympathise because I know the trouble they're going through and sometimes that makes you too caring a parent if you like. I've worked with directors who have no understanding of actors but get very good performances out of you, because they don't know how difficult it is, they say "But you can do that, go on gently or go further, no, no that isn't right go further" and they force you through their indifference... Whereas sometimes I might be being too kind of coercive and careful and caring and might limit what the actor can offer because I understand how difficult it is for them... I don't think it's essential to be an actor to be a director, but I think it's good for all of us to have done all those things, I learnt to trust directors more after I directed.'

Peter Egan, Actor and Director, UK

FRINGE THEATRE CONSIDERATIONS

There are considerations: financial, artistic and personal; which you must pay the necessary attention to when embarking on these low-budget collaborative works. Bear in mind in recent years Equity has been negotiating with Fringe theatre producers to try for an agreement to pay minimum wage. This has an implication as now some actors and their agents will refuse profit share work.

Financially:

- How are you going to pay the cost of the venue hire?
- Is the production going to be profit share? How can you make this work with the minimum wage restrictions if they come into law at any point?
  You do not have to pay Equity rates. However this ongoing issue is something to be aware of. Will you pay minimum wage plus a share or just minimum wage, how will your cast and crew feel about the decision? You will need to look into the legal definitions of co-operative work or employment if you are going to work on a purely profit share basis.
- Is there going to be a box office split with the venue?
- How are you going to market the show, what is your budget for publicity?

Artistically:

- Have you got a clear vision of what you are trying to achieve?
- Do you have people on board with *relevant* experience in each creative department? If you are all inexperienced in production, how can you be sure that all your bases are covered adequately and to a professional standard?
- Are there any ego issues that are affecting the strength of the work in any area?

- Do you all feel proud of what you're aiming to achieve?
- Have you considered the audience? You have to be as objective as possible, some fringe work can be quite masturbatory (figuratively speaking) – and no one wants to watch that. If you're thinking of doing a one-man show or a two-hander, do the audience want to see this work as much as you want to show it?

Personally:

- Are you all as committed to the project as each other?
- You need to look after yourself physically and emotionally when working on low budget and shoestring productions, because there just aren't the resources for everyone not to be giving 100% and how can you if you're exhausted.
- Is anyone (including yourself) involved just for a credit for the CV? That is not the reason to work on something.
- Don't become despondent if not many industry members come to see the show. Casting directors and their teams try to see as much theatre as they can. Assistants are often spotted at fringe venues nowhere near where they live, (often a real pain to get home from) in the hopes of seeing something different and finding good actors, new to them. Sometimes however, they cannot make it to your show.

If you're all having a great time and you can see the artistic merit in what you're doing then you've succeeded. It is all ongoing work that you can put on your CV. Sometimes an actor's CV can look like a bit of a desert. Although you have gone for many auditions you may not have got a part for almost a year. This collaborative venture has you working during that time, honing your skills, extending your range and hopefully not getting depressed over roles that went to other actors. This is all good.

FRINGE FINANCE

You need to approach the financial side to any theatrical venture with your eyes wide open. It is very expensive to hire the well-known fringe venues and actually theatre spaces above pubs are pricier than you may assume. The likelihood of you making money or breaking even is slim. Taking a show to the Edinburgh Fringe Festival is much more expensive than many imagine. Bear that in mind.

You may be able to strike a deal with the venue:

- Can you get a reduced rate with a box office split? This will mean that the venue has a vested interest in making sure the show does well and they will help with the marketing of the show.
- Can you hold out and see if any venues have a dark slot with nothing booked or where another production had to cancel?

Ticket sales and marketing:

- Ask all your cast and crew to try to secure at least 10 people to come to see the show as fully paying customers not complimentary tickets. Keep the comps for industry invites.
- Make sure you have fliers for the show, electronic and physical.
- Can your cast and crew hand out flyers for the show at the neighbouring tube/train stations to the venue, local pubs and bars, colleges, libraries, etc?
- Ask everyone to email out the electronic fliers to everyone they know.
- Create a social media invite and a Facebook page. Tweet about the show. Instagram photos of the set and actors in rehearsal.
- If you get good reviews in your previews, make sure you spread that word of mouth in every way possible as quickly

as you can, email them out and through the social media you're already making use of.

Phil Willmott has a nice idea for drumming up an audience:

> 'You can print up a postcard and you put a big box of postcards in the corner of the rehearsal room. And you say to the actors whenever you're not rehearsing a scene "Go through your address book and write a postcard out to absolutely everyone in your address book, the girl you once met in Ibiza and didn't stay in contact with, your aunty Jean who you haven't seen for 5 years." And then we put all those postcards in a box and then the company pay for the stamps and we send out a load of those so that reaches loads of people.'
>
> Phil Willmott, Director, UK

Remember that part of your marketing is to draw industry attention, but please remember any invites to casting offices, directors, producers or agents should always be comps. We looked at mail outs in chapter 3. Always present everything professionally in the aim of getting their attendance.

And on this point – how much fringe theatre are you going to see? You have to support other people's creative endeavours in the industry if you want the industry to support yours, the same goes for independent film and short film screenings.

SHORT FILM AND MICRO-BUDGET FEATURE FILM CONSIDERATIONS

Many of the considerations for filming on a shoestring budget are the same as fringe theatre. Additional things you need to think about are:

Practically and financially:

- Are you going to pay equity minimum for your cast? The Equity minimum daily rate for micro and low budget feature films (and short films) is £132 or £528 per week (April 2016 rates), they'll go up again in 2017. There are various buyout percentages to be added if you are aiming for a cinema release.
- Are you going to work on deferred payment or offer a back end deal? If so you need a producer on board who understands how to contract this appropriately.
- Is it going to be expenses only? If so see the below industry standard.
- Where are your locations? Can you limit them in terms of numbers and also to places you can get for free or very reduced rates?
- Equipment hire, do any of the crew you're working with have cameras/lights/sound recording equipment/make up/props, etc, of their own?
- What about transport? Are people driving to get to and from locations? Car-pooling as much as possible keeps costs down.
- Are any of the cast/crew not based locally, can anyone within the production put them up for the duration of the shoot?
- How are you going to get a distribution deal? This is really important and you need to do your research.
- Have you considered your final Dolby sound mix? It will not get a cinema release without one.
- Are you going to make a teaser trailer in the hopes of securing funding?

Something to point out here is that the industry standard for working for free on short films/low budget features is that *all* cast and crew *must be:*

- Credited appropriately on the production.
- Fed on set and have travel costs refunded.
- Given a copy of the finished film once edited.
- Recompensed for any expenses incurred for the production.

People would also expect to be invited to the first screenings of the film.

When everyone is working unpaid/deferred payment for film, or below equity/profit share for theatre (so unpaid, as there's rarely any profit after production costs) you all have to feel respected, valued, an integral part of it and you must all enjoy it.

> 'If you're trying to make something out of nothing with no money you have to really get the people that you're working with to feel that they have a stake in it. To get everyone to kind of share your vision of it, to believe in what you want to achieve… When I'm auditioning, just before I cast, if there's someone I want to cast I'll ring up directors they've worked with in the past and say "What are they like to work with?" And if someone's brilliant but I hear that they're a bit of an arsehole to work with then I just won't cast them because it it's not worth it. It's better to have a group of people together who have a really good laugh, who are very creative, who are very supportive of each other and then you produce the best work.'
>
> Phil Willmott, Director, UK

Again, you have to market this work, you want it to be seen. You will need to do a mail out asking industry folk to attend a theatre production or screening, or ask that they watch a film on a link. This inevitably has some small expense attached and arguing over whether you will pay a share of that £50 to get everything printed up, in the big scheme of things, where you all might have invested £250 in real cash and many thousands of pounds in unpaid time, seems short-sighted and foolish. I say this in the full knowledge that £15 may feel like a lot of money to someone who is not in full time *paid* acting work. These conversations of financial considerations have to be had before rehearsal and/or production starts; it looks dubious if you wait even if it was just poorly timed.

APPLYING FOR FUNDING

If you are going to apply for funding for a micro-budget feature, short film or stage show, you really should have a producer on board who has had some experience of this already. Funding applications read like complicated instruction manuals, they are for most people headache and tear inducing. Be aware that many people call themselves producers on low-budget projects who are not *really* producers, they may be someone's friend or good at organising large groups of people. This does not make them a producer – a producer has to source all the finance for a project as well as bringing the group together. You may find that you will all have to take on producer responsibilities on this type of project and consequently you should all get credited as producers. A bit of work in this area gives you a whole lot more appreciation for the work producers actually do on large scale productions.

There are many funding bodies for both theatrical and screen productions, the most well known are Arts Council England (ACE) and The National Lotto who work in partnership. You can find their page for funding applications at:

www.artscouncil.org.uk/funding

You can look on the cabinet office's own website for funding at: www.fundingcentral.org.uk once you have registered you can then use their search facility to find appropriate matches in the multitude of funding organisations available.

The Prince's Trust is always a popular thought for grants, be aware there are age restrictions (16 –25) and it cannot give huge amounts of money so it would need to be in conjunction with other funding initiatives:
www.princes-trust.org.uk/need_help/grants.aspx

The BBC has a Performing Arts Fund and offer grants:
www.bbc.co.uk/performingartsfund/grants

There is also Crowd Funding – a popular modern concept where individuals give what they can to support a project they like the sound of. I have listed a few in the Resources section.

Microwave Film has a very helpful website full of helpful information:
http://microwave.filmlondon.org.uk

> *'In the digital era there is no excuse for not getting out there and making and creating your own work. Yes you always need a good script, so network, find a writer who has something and get a digital camera, get a small crew and shoot it. So many people have DSLR cameras now that you can shoot something over a weekend for £500 and make it look like it was shot for £50,000. There are a number of courses that are good at instructing you on how is the best way to go about doing this, along with a number of good books as well. The one I would recommend is The Guerrilla Film Makers handbook, which is invaluable on the sharp end of low budget film making and it will also give you a very good idea on*

> *what a production has to endure to get made and will make you appreciate what it takes to get something done. What it takes is teamwork. Be prepared to help others on their projects too and it will come back to you.'*
>
> Lance Nielsen, Writer and Director, UK

So if you do want to make your own work there are plenty of organisations ready and able to help you, if you apply. In terms of funding for short films, if this is your first personal project you may want to keep your costs down by limiting the number of locations, cast and crew.

Also ask yourself if you should *really* be asking other people to fund your first venture? Just something to think about – many of us in the industry have self funded our projects especially the early ones and we might think you have to show that *you* have invested in your own ideas before asking anyone else to. To some extent, if you are that invested emotionally and financially there is more riding on the success of the work and this may encourage you to really pull out all the stops.

On the flip side of this have you actively helped crowd fund someone else's project, be it word of mouth or actual cash? Make your own breakfast/lunch for a week and use the money you saved by not buying it to donate to a crowdfunded project. Pay it forward and support our industry.

MAKE THE MOST OF HOSTING SITES LIKE YOU TUBE

If you want to gain more screen work and are finding it hard to be seen by screen casting directors you can always set up your own YouTube channel to share some of your own work. Many actors do this if they are aiming to get in to comedy. YouTube is a great facility for hosting short clips of work and sketches. There are also web-based serials, if you're after more dramatic work there are opportunities on the net. These webisodes are often shorter than a TV show would be so it takes up less viewer time. You may get hits on the site if the work is punchy and original.

> *'There is no point in having the talent and being in your room. Who's going to know you, who knows you?'*
> Ann Mitchell, Actor and Director, UK

Practical points to think about:

- Film and edit a piece of work good enough to send out; copy the link to the clips.
- Check to see that your clips are being viewed, that the numbers are going up and the comments are positive. Ask your friends and peers to watch and like.
- Email out the link to the clips with a good cover letter email to relevant casting directors, directors, producers and agents. Always make sure you have done your research first. Some comedians and comic actors have been offered their own shows on TV from the strength of the work they put out personally on YouTube.

SUMMARY

What you can take away from this chapter is hopefully a more positive way of viewing the situation when you do not get the role you auditioned for. We have also covered ways in which to create opportunities for yourself and other like-minded individuals who may want to work on your project or collaboratively in a co-operative style environment. We've looked at the artistic, financial and personal considerations for both fringe theatre and low/no budget filmmaking. Not getting a role in the audition room doesn't have to be the end of it, it is just part of the process.

A CONCLUDING FINAL WORD

Having read this book you should feel better acquainted with the practicalities of the industry you are a part of. Sir Derek Jacobi CBE believes all actors should ask themselves a key question:

> '"Do I want to be an actor or do I need to be an actor?" Wanting isn't enough, you have to need it.'
>
> Sir Derek Jacobi CBE, Actor, UK

That's a difficult question to ask yourself if deep down you know your answer is not an immediate and emphatic 'Need, of course!' from your very core... However, if you merely want and enjoy acting, is this really the career for you? Be honest with yourself because it's such a fantastic career, the possibilities are endless, but the realities of a jobbing actor's life are also often full of hardships.

The audition is often seen as the stumbling block where an actor may go wrong and then not get the job. I've written this book to show that the audition is just one part of the process; that as an actor you must apply yourself diligently to the whole process in order to be invited to audition for a production.

I have tried to demystify some of the working practices to give you an insight into why particular decisions may be made in terms of casting. We've also tackled the often-ignored necessity of marketing and all that it entails: CV, headshot, showreels, voicereels, cover letters, Internet presence and face-to-face networking. We've broken down the process of casting and auditioning, what you should work on prior to your meetings, how to be as prepared as you can be and the sort of research you should be doing before the audition. The very specific nature and variances between auditioning for screen and theatrical work. Ways in which to bring out a performance for your audition.

And, lastly making your own work, be that individually or as part of a collective.

You have to take the reigns of your career and steer it in the direction you want it to take.

> *'I think you have to organise things you know, and I also think it helps to have an ambition.'*
>
> Tim Pigott-Smith, Actor and Director, UK

It has all been practical steps, which you can take to better your chances of being seen and then making the most of your time when you are. Applying business strategies to your career should not come at the expense of artistic choices or fulfilment. They should just help to ensure time well spent and a more proactive and pragmatic view of the entertainment industry and your place within it.

I covered the three 'P's, there's also a 'T' of vital importance: Tenacity. You have to be tenacious not just to last in this industry, but also to get in and through your allotted time in the audition room. Put the time into your preparation, be truthful and – having put into practise the advice offered – focus your attention to the requirements of your audition.

I sincerely hope you will take on board the ways in which to relax in the audition environment so you show your potential and enjoy your meetings.

I wish you good luck and broken legs.

RESOURCES

THE TAXMAN

Her Majesty's Revenue and Customs
www.hmrc.gov.uk
Self Assessment helpline 0300 200 3310

ENTERTAINMENT INDUSTRY ACCOUNTANTS

Alexander & Co
www.alexander.co.uk

Bambridge Accountants
www.bambridgeaccountants.co.uk

Raymond Benn & Co
www.raymondbenn/co.uk

Bowker Orford
www.bowkerorford.com

Breckmman & Company
www.breckmanandcompany.co.uk

Dan Brown
www.actorstax.com

Centre Stage
www.centrestage-accountants.com

Mark Carr & Co
www.markcarr.co.uk

Easy Accountacy
www.easyaccountancy.co.uk

David Evans Chartered Accountants
www.evansaccountants.com

HW Fisher
www.hwfisher.co.uk

Jonathan Ford & Co
www.jonathanford.co.uk

Goldwins
www.goldwins.co.uk

MGR Weston Kay
www.mgrwk.co.uk

Indigo
www.indigotax.com

Lachman Smith
www.lachmansmith.co.uk

Mazuma
www.mazumamoney.co.uk

MGO Midgley Snelling
www.midsnell.co.uk

PL Accountants
www.pl-accountants.co.uk

Saffrey Champness
www.saffrey.com

Sloane & Co
www.sloane.co.uk

Taylorcocks
www.theaccountants.co.uk

Theataccounts
www.theataccounts.co.uk

Theatrical Accountancy Services Ltd
www.theatricalaccountants.co.uk

TWD Accountants
www.twdaccounts.co.uk

USEFUL WEBSITES

The Audition Room
www.auditionroom.co.uk

Contacts
www.contactshandbook.com

Spotlight
www.spotlight.com

Equity
www.equity.org.uk

IMDB
www.imdb.com

CDG (Casting Directors Guild)
www.thecdg.co.uk

PMA
www.thepma.com

The Stage
www.thestage.co.uk

Youtube
www.youtube.com

Vimeo
www.vimeo.com

GRANTS AND FUNDING BODIES

Arts Council England (ACE)
www.artscoucil.org.uk

The Cabinet Office
www.fundingcentral.org.uk

BBC funding programme
www.bbc.co.uk/performingartsfund/grants

CROWDFUNDING WEBSITES

Kickstarter
www.kickstarter.com

Sponsume
www.sponsume.com

Crowdfunder.co.uk
www.crowdfunder.co.uk

Peoplefund
www.peoplefund.it/arts

Indiegogo
www.indiegogo.com

PleaseFund.Us offer crowd funding/some grants:
www.pleasefund.us

Microwave Film has advice
http://microwave.filmlondon.org.uk

GLOSSARY

1) GDP: (Gross Domestic Product) this is the total market value of all recognised goods and services produced within a country at a given time.

2) NESTA: (National Endowment for Science, Technology and the Arts) An independent charity working towards increasing innovation in the UK.

3) Personal pension plan: A defined contribution scheme. Provides retirement benefits based on the build up of a 'pot' of money, accumulated through the investment of contributions.

4) Stakeholder Pension Scheme: A type of personal pension plan, offering a low-cost and flexible alternative and which must comply with requirements laid down in legislation.

5) Corporates: A filmed piece which is generally solely for internal use within the company who is hiring the actors to perform their material. Often medical and financial companies use corporate videos for internal training and conventions

6) General Meetings: A meeting with a casting director that is really just a chat, for them to meet you in person quickly and get a sense of you. Sometimes you will be given a short piece to read.

7) Contacts: An indispensible directory listing Agents, Casting Directors, Production Companies, Theatres, Drama Schools, etc. Published by Spotlight.

8) Gsm: grams per square metre. It's a measure of paper weight.

9) Self-tape: A self-tape is when the actor has someone else film them reading the scene, ideally learnt

10) CANS: Casting Advice Notes or Deal Memos are a short form industry standard document of the main points which will be in the contract e.g. fee, billing, credit, travel arrangements, dressing room facilities, etc.

11) Chemistry reads: A recall either in pairs or groups where the director and producer want to explore the chemistry of potential lead actors together. This is often used for television comedy shows and for feature films with romantic leads or a pair/group of best friends.

AUTHOR'S BIOGRAPHY

Sharon brings well over a decade of professional experience in the field of casting and 20 years of involvement in independent and fringe productions to 'The Audition Room.' Her knowledge and experiences, along with those of the interviewees, is intertwined to give the reader help and advice in a practical fashion. Originally a Midlands lass, she moved to the big smoke in 2000 and is now very much a confirmed Londoner. This book marks Sharon's first non-fiction work; though she has written creatively over the years, mainly short films some features and one play. She is very proud to present the Audition Room book so she can share the knowledge she has acquired. She is confident it can help jobbing actors and new graduates alike in raising their chances for gaining auditions and improving their success rate thereon in. Her imdb profile can be viewed at: http://www.imdb.com/name/nm3231759

ACKNOWLEDGEMENTS

I would like to thank Moray Watson for originally commissioning me to write the series of kindle single volumes which evolved into this book. It was a great opportunity and an interesting and scrupulous process. Taking my personal and general industry experience and knowledge, distilling the sincere advice given by the renowned industry professionals interviewed by Creative Edge Audio into bite sized relevant quotes and interweaving them into this form of advice and tips. The full length unabridged interviews whilst lengthy are an informative and enjoyable package.

Jeremy Thompson and The Book Guild for taking on this 2nd edition of the book.

My industry peers and friends who reviewed the chapters as part of the refining process, offering their own pearls of wisdom:

Damian Winter-Higgins
Miriam Sorrentino
T'Nia Miller
Claire Stangroom
Ivan Sorrentino
Andrea Ware
Jane Anderson CDG
Graham Kirkman
Annika Magnberg
Amelia Hashemi
Kim Wright
Lance Nielsen
Dan Styles

Natalie Persaud
Lorna Gayle
Janine Snape CDG
Sophie Hallett at the CDG for her positive nature and encouragement.

My sister Miriam Sorrentino for her ongoing help, guidance and belief in me. My Mum and Dad for their continuing support, great food and anecdotal horror stories generally at my expense. My brother Ivan Sorrentino for his help and support and for always reminding me that full stops are not in fact my enemy. And lastly my friends for their constant support in my endeavours, trials and tribulations – you know who you are.

For the use of the following additional quotes:

> 'By 2013, NESTA*2 expects there to be around 180,000 creative businesses in the UK, contributing as much as £85bn of added value to the economy – and 150,000 new jobs.'
>
> Dame Helen Alexander CBE, Chair of the Port of London Authority and Incisive Media, UK

> 'Marketing is the magic fairy dust you apply to a business to get your delicious offerings found by the people who want them, who in turn reward you handsomely with money.'
>
> Ameena Falchetto, Marketing Consultant, UK, France and UAE

> 'What does marketing do to help make money for a business? That's simple – it exposes people to your product and your brand. How many songs do you know just because you heard them on a Mac commercial?... We need marketing to be seen, to be found, to create an interaction that will lead to the ultimate desired goal.'
>
> Duran Inci, Internet Marketing Expert, USA

> '*From 1998 to 2010 the value of the worldwide entertainment industry grew from $449 billion (£285bn) to $745 billion (£474bn).*'
>
> Mike Masnick, CEO of Floor64, USA

> '*A brand is simply an organization, or a product, or a service with a personality. So why all the fuss?*'
>
> From Wally Olins. On B°and. by Wally Olins. © 2003 Wally Olins. Reprinted by kind permission of Thames & Hudson Ltd., London, UK

> '*Those pursuing physical theatre need to keep themselves in shape – fitness and flexibility – running, yoga, Pilates, cardio etc. I would say that it wouldn't matter if you were bigger as long as you had the stamina and flexibility.*'
>
> Natalie Persaud, Performer and Lecturer, UK

> '*If you audition for unpaid work, you're auditioning them as much as they're auditioning you. If the script is good, then that's a good start, so if possible always ask for and make time to read the whole script, which can be easily sent to you on email. It will also make you more prepared and give you a better understanding of both the project and the role. Once at the audition, have questions – not too many just a couple of key things. But a well organised low budget production should be able to answer any question you have if they know what their doing.*'

And

> '*In the digital era there is no excuse for not getting out there and making and creating your own work. Yes you always need a good script, so network, find a writer who has something, and get a digital camera, get a small crew*

and shoot it. So many people have DSLR cameras now that you can shoot something over a weekend for £500 and make it look like it was shot for £50,000. There are a number of courses that are good at instructing you on how is the best way to go about doing this. The one I would recommend The Guerrilla Film Makers handbook, which is invaluable on the sharp end of low budget film making and it will also give you a very good idea on what a production has to endure to get made and will make you appreciate what it takes to get something done. What it takes is teamwork. Be prepared to help others on their projects too and it will come back to you.'

Lance Nielsen, Writer and Director, UK

ORIGINAL ACKNOWLEDGEMENTS

Moray Watson and Calm Publishing who originally bought the rights to the initial interviews would like to thank Paul Albertson, Abi Coyle and John Alastair at Creative Edge Audio for the original audio interviews and in particular the contributing interviewees, these are listed alphabetically:

Robert Bierman – Director
Michael Billington – Guardian Critic
Mark Bowden – Marketing Author
Richard Briers CBE – Actor
Marina Calderone – Radio Director and Producer
Alison Chard CDG – Casting Director
Mel Churcher – Screen acting coach
Peter Cregeen – Director and Producer
Phil Davis – Actor and Director
Simon Dunmore – Director and Author
Peter Egan – Actor and Director
Sir Richard Eyre CBE – Director
John Hubbard CDG – Casting Director
Sir Derek Jacobi CBE – Actor
Kate Maravan – Meisner acting coach
Ann Mitchell – Actor and Director
Braham Murray OBE – Director
Joyce Nettles – Casting Director
Tim Pigott-Smith – Actor and Director
Sam Rumbelow – Method acting coach
Bernard Shaw – Voice Actor

David Thorpe – Voice Actor
Jeff Turner – Performance and life management coach
Phil Willmott – Director
John Wright – Comedy Director